Understanding Yourself and Others® Series

CREATIVITY AND PERSONALITY TYPE

Tools for
Understanding and Inspiring
THE MANY VOICES OF CREATIVITY

Marci Segal

Telos
PUBLICATIONS
Huntington Beach
CALIFORNIA

CREATIVITY AND PERSONALITY TYPE
Tools for Understanding and Inspiring the Many Voices of Creativity

"Marci Segal's pioneer work integrating creativity, psychological type, and temperament provides a valuable tool for organizational development and the counseling/education world. *Creativity and Personality Type* includes the understanding, methodology and exercises that enable the reader to free the creative potential unique to each person be they client, team member, student, or child."

Kathy Myers
Co-Guardian of the Myers-Briggs Type Indicator® and Coauthor of *Introduction to Type® Dynamics and Development*

"Reading this book can be an involving adventure! Although the subject is to be taken seriously, it is written in an informal, light-hearted manner. Notwithstanding the reader's experience with creativity and/or personality type, this work offers a refreshing look at these specific areas and challenges the reader in a variety of introspective exercises."

Ruth B. Noller, Ph.D.
Distinguished Service Professor Emeritus, Center for Studies in Creativity, State University College at Buffalo (NY)
and Coauthor of *Leading Creative Change*

"Marci Segal's new work brings excitingly different insights to the field of creativity. She has tied temperament patterns in personality and Jung's theory of psychological type together with a wide range of creative problem solving processes and tools and techniques in a wonderfully readable, understandable, and immediately useable way. This is not a bookshelf book. It is a powerful handbook that advanced facilitators and leaders will carry with them wherever they go."

Rolf Smith, Colonel, USAF (Retired)
Managing Director, The School for Innovators and Author of *The 7 Levels of Change*

"For people who may not have had, or may not have the opportunity of meeting Marci Segal personally, this work of hers may be the next best thing. Practical, thorough, entertaining, logical, and thoughtful—page after page after page. Beyond its value to the practitioner, *Creativity and Personality Type* is an intriguing source of personal discovery and self-understanding for any individual. It's impossible to just browse through this book; it will touch the personal curiosity of anyone who picks it up."

Peter Noble
Principal, Peter Noble and Associates

"My office shelves are packed with books on the creative process and innovative tools and techniques. But putting these to use—with authentic results—requires really understanding how people will use the tools. Segal explores, thoroughly, how different kinds of people with different thinking and different behaviors express their creativity. This is great for building teams. It's great for helping people to be more creative, to work at their maximum creative potential. It's useful simply to understand yourself and the people close to you. After reading *Creativity and Personality Type* I feel like I have a much stronger foundation to use everything else I've learned about creativity a lot more effectively."

Maggie Dugan
Author of *Brainstorm Alone: An Audio Cassette Guide to Using the Osborn-Parnes Creative Problem Solving Process*

CREATIVITY AND PERSONALITY TYPE
Tools for Understanding and Inspiring the Many Voices of Creativity

"*Creativity and Personality Type* provides the reader with practical tools for enhancing creativity. [Segal's] personal passion for psychological type provides new insights into personalized creativity. In what ways can you be more creative?"

Stanley S. Gryskiewicz

Author of *Positive Turbulence: Developing Climates for Creativity, Innovation, and Renewal*
Vice President and Senior Fellow, Creativity and Innovation, Center for Creative Leadership

"Marci has given us a rare gift—the recognition that creativity is in all of us, it can be nurtured and developed and it can be both a continuous and sustaining part of an enterprise. When recognized and celebrated, it brings to the individual a heightened sense of self worth as our realized creativity is a window to our core, our very spirit. For the enterprise it unleashes enormous energy and competitive edge. For the executive interested in making creativity a fundamental value and operationalizing it within his/her enterprise, it provides a framework and a language. If you are an individual interested in understanding and developing your creative potential, or someone of influence in extending the boundaries of creativity in your enterprise, this is a must read. Once begun, it will not be your last."

Richard Hossack

Partner Leader of Strategic Change practice in Canada, PricewaterhouseCoopers LLP

"*Creativity and Personality Type* is clearly determined to help people understand people and the consequences of their behaviors. Very illustrative and friendly reading, even for people who are not deeply familiar with psychology, human temperament, and holistic views. Gone is the time when business management was based on information and intuition only. In today's business environment, The Knowledge Era is the course for success. You need to be creative more and faster, and Marci [*Creativity and Personality Type*] is helping to conquer this knowledge."

Rodrigo do Vale

Director, Corporate Services and Finance, TETRA PAK Canada

"Marci Segal has provided a thorough guide to matching individuals and their Creative Voice to tools and techniques for generating ideas in their lives and workplaces. This book provides the foundation for understanding each individual's Creative Voice in order to maximize our creative thinking abilities and skills."

Robert Alan Black

Author of *Broken Crayons: Break Your Crayons and Draw Outside the Lines*

"In this inspiring work, Marci Segal integrates and simplifies concepts and principles, and offers practical "how-to" tools and techniques to stir the creativity within ourselves and others. An invaluable resource for any learning and development practitioner who values diversity and creativity in the workplace."

Sandy Schwartz

Former Corporate Education Manager Warner-Lambert, Canada Inc.

"Marci is a wonderful teacher. Her unique skills in the area of creativity will bring future thinking to many organizations that currently don't know how to unleash it from their people."

Dave Blair

President, Brantas Performance Inc.

PRINTED IN THE UNITED STATES OF AMERICA

Published By:
Telos Publications
Publishing Division of Temperament Research Institute
P.O. Box 4457, Huntington Beach, California 92605-4457
714.841.0041 or 800.700.4874 / fax 714.841.0312
www.telospublications.com / www.tri-network.com

International Standard Book Number: 0–9664624–0–8

04 03 02 01 00 10 9 8 7 6 5 4 3 2 1

Cover Photo: Carr Clifton/Minden Pictures
Cover/Layout Design/Illustrations: Kristoffer R. Kiler
Illustrations: Chris Berens of Thumbnail Productions

ORDERING INFORMATION
http://www.telospublications.com/orderinfo/
Individual Sales U.S.: This publication can be purchased directly from the Telos Publications Web site or at the address above.
Individual Sales International: A list of international distributors can be obtained directly from the Telos Publications Web site or at the address above.
Quantity Sales: Special discounts are available on quantity purchases by corporations, associations, and others. Details can be obtained from the Telos Publications Web site or at the address above.
Orders for College Textbook/Course Adoption Use: Information can be obtained directly from the Telos Publications Web site or at the address above.
Orders by U.S./International Trade Bookstores and Wholesalers: Information can be obtained directly from the Telos Publications Web site or at the address above.

TRAINING AND CONSULTING INFORMATION
http://www.tri-network.com
Individual Training: Training is available for further exploration of the information provided in this book. Please contact Temperament Research Institute at the address or telephone number above for a list of TRI-Certified providers.
Organizational Consulting/In-House Training: Temperament Research Institute provides organizational consulting and in-house training for communication, team building, leadership development, coaching, and organizational development.
Facilitator Training: Temperament Research Institute is an approved provider of the Myers-Briggs Type Indicator® (MBTI®) Qualifying Programs. TRI also provides train-the-trainer workshops for The TRI Methodology™ and The Self-Discovery Process™.

This book is dedicated to the memory of my late father, Albert J. Segal, my mother and step-father Jackie and Irwin Wyston, my sister Karyn Segal, and to creativity and type practitioners, researchers, and students who question, guide, learn, and inspire.

Acknowledgments
Thanks go to:
- Linda V. Berens, for taking the risk and throwing down the gauntlet.
- Kris Kiler, for guidance through the pathways of the labyrinth.
- Paulo Benetti, for steadfast encouragement and enduring support.
- Peter Noble, for opening so many doors.
- Rosemary Gaymer, Carol Bobb, Ruth Noller, Sid Parnes, Angelo Biondi, John Moffat, June O'Reilly, and the Center for Studies in Creativity, State University College of New York at Buffalo, each a guide by the side who supports the notion that the impossible can be done—it just takes a little longer.
- John Sedgwick, Gretchen Bingham, Brigitte Webb, and Gus Jacacci, and all my CPSI friends and colleagues whose collective spirit, impactful learnings, and selfless sharing floats throughout this work.
- Margaret Hartzler, Gary Hartzler, Bob McAlpine, Kathy Myers, and other contributors to the type community who encouraged the birthing.
- Paul Hewitt, for his attentive questions and cyclical wisdom.
- The busy people who took time to review the book whose invaluable comments helped this to read better.
- Participants and co-leaders of all the programs I've led over the past 20 years for helping me feel the light
- My clients all who continue to stimulate, cajole, and challenge.
- Vicky Jo Varner for persevering for perfection.

About the Author

Marci Segal

Marci Segal is principal of Creative ProblemSolving, an international innovation and creativity consulting network, founded in 1984 in Toronto, Canada. She uses the principles of creative studies and personality type to help individuals and communities within organizations develop a "best work" environment. Her education includes undergraduate and graduate work at the Center for Studies in Creativity at the State University of New York College at Buffalo. Marci is also an MBTI® qualifying instructor and a former president of the Ontario Association for the Application of Personality Type. She is an active member of the Association for Psychological Type and the Creative Education Foundation and is a senior faculty member at the Creative Problem Solving Institute in Buffalo, New York, and San Diego, California. Marci is recognized worldwide for her contributions to the fields of creativity and psychological type by integrating the frameworks for targeted and successful applications. In 2000 she was given the Distinguished Leader Award for exemplary leadership in the field of creativity by the Creative Education Foundation, Buffalo, New York.

A Message from Linda V. Berens...

In times like these, tapping our own creativity will provide solutions to seemingly insurmountable problems—on an individual level as well as an organizational level. Marci Segal has had a tremendous influence on helping me tap into my own creativity, and I am so glad she has chosen to share her wonderful wisdom in this book. Marci holds the distinction of being an expert in both creativity and psychological type. She has made a powerful contribution to both fields through her breakthrough thinking about the links between psychological type, temperament, and the creative process. This book is truly a gift to us all as we seek ways to be more productive and more satisfied in all areas of our lives.

TRI has made a policy of lending our widely researched descriptions of the temperament patterns and the cognitive processes to authors such as Marci Segal to use in works as worthy as this one. In the appendices you will find descriptions of the models we use as well as resources where to read more. In the meantime, enjoy the material presented here as you come to understand even more about your own creativity.

Linda V. Berens
CEO and Founder, TRI

Contents

A Word from the Author

The fears that emerged while writing this book were at times overwhelming. Haunting images about the Pandora's box I may be opening loomed. It's so much safer to keep one's thoughts to oneself, I thought, rather than to put them forward for the scrutiny of others. What drove me through these blocks was my vision of the future. Creativity by its nature challenges the conventional and promotes acting on the ideals of a possible future. I imagine a future in which all people acknowledge and affirm their own creating capabilities and use the knowledge about different kinds of creativity to inspire others to be at their best.

Creativity often begins with a stirring or restlessness. The stirring for this book came in 1988 when I was preparing to take my MBTI® Qualifying Program. I read research on creativity in the MBTI Manual that suggested some personality types, rather than all personality types, have creativity. I was motivated to act because I felt this was a wrong that needed to be addressed. After twelve years of probing, adventuring, questioning, and research this book appears.

The story really begins thirteen years earlier.

In 1975–76 I was a student in the Art Fundamentals Program at Sheridan College in Brampton, Ontario. The curriculum included a course in creative problem solving for the visual arts taught by printmaker Carol Schiffleger Bobb. Years later she would again become a pivotal person for my creative growth.

In class one day Carol told us about the Creative Problem Solving Institute (CPSI) hosted by the Creative Education Foundation in Buffalo. CPSI is a five-day gathering of people from around the world who teach, consult, facilitate, lead, and conduct research in creativity and creative problem solving; people who want to network, and people who want to know more about creativity and related topics. Its environment supports creative learning, tools, application and personal growth. Through lectures, workshops, seminars, and other activities, CPSI leaders and participants challenge themselves to explore the nurture and nature of creativity in business, lifestyle, education, and social action. I wanted to go to CPSI in 1976 and wasn't able to until the next year.

In the interim, after college, I worked as a clerk in the Canadian federal civil service. The experience was an awakening. The people in the office didn't get along. They complained so much about each other. I didn't understand why this was so. I wanted to effect a change in the office because the gloomy mood was contagious and affecting my productivity, outlook, and self-esteem.

After six months I accrued enough time to take a week off to attend my first CPSI. There I learned tools to use to shift perspective and ways to apply creativity to problem solving. I learned how to get fresh ideas and how to build on them to actualize and sustain fulfilling change. I returned to work inspired and ready to act. In less than ten days the prevailing office mood reintegrated into my freshly rewired thinking and motivation. I felt blocked and hopeless once again.

Re-enter Carol. We met serendipitously on Toronto's Bloor Street later that summer. I told her my tale of woe over a cup of tea. I was a high-school dropout with no special skills. My job was empty and meaningless. I believed my options for a better life was nonexistent.

After listening very closely Carol said, "Marci, you seem to really like creativity. Why don't you go to Buffalo [the Center for Studies in Creativity at the State University College of New York at Buffalo] to study it?" When she said these words, the angels sang and Thor threw down his thunderbolts! It was an energy-shifting Eureka moment for me because Carol spoke a truth outside my normal way of thinking.

Two weeks later I was enrolled in Buffalo as an undergraduate student with a focus in creativity (that later transformed into my being the first minor of the program). My intent was to study creativity at the graduate level and then come back to Canada and help the civil service to become a better place to work. When I shared my intention with others, many scoffed,"You don't even have a bachelor's degree!" or "You'll never change the civil service!" or "You are going where to do what?" or "Can't you study something real?" or "You'll never find a job with that!" I thanked them all for their helpful comments and persevered.

What I learned in five years at the Center for Studies in Creativity can be summarized in global statements; the particulars are too numerous to list. I learned that creativity is teachable and transferable and that it can be applied to any discipline and in any context. I learned methods, attitudes and tools to access to inspire fulfilling change in others and myself. I learned how to use and critique creativity research. And I learned how to facilitate creativity and creative problem solving from one of the greats, Dr. Ruth B. Noller.

In 1983 I came back to Toronto. When I applied for jobs using my education I was greeted with this great Canadianism, "They'll give you a degree for anything in the States, won't they?" In the early '80s creativity was like a four-letter word. Eventually I found work in marketing as a qualitative researcher and later worked in advertising in strategic planning.

In 1989 our local association of psychological type agreed to let me present a workshop exploring creativity through using type—the first of many I would later be invited to give around the world. My scope broadened. I became aware of creativity practitioners who are limited in their capabilities because they have yet to learn about the different energies and voices of creativity. I began to put the message out in the creativity community as well. This led to my becoming the "type" person in the creativity community and the "creativity" person in the type community. An ambassador emerged as a result of the stirring as I continued to actualize my vision.

Through the years my knowledge and experience of type and creativity has continued to develop and I am confident integrating the two frameworks for greater appreciation and application. As a creativity specialist my work focuses primarily upon helping people in companies arrive at new ideas and in helping those individuals get along to reap the rewards—in other words, by promoting ways each individual can do his or her "best (i.e. creative) work."

This book represents, in a product form, the current state of my searching, matching, experimenting, and discovering success in marrying the discipline of creativity with psychological type.

One stanza in a poem by Mother Teresa helped me persevere through the fears and doubts that occasionally surfaced while writing this book. The poem is called "Anyway." Here's the stanza:

> Give the world the best you have
> and it may not be enough;
> Give the world the best you've got
> anyway.

May your experience with this book inspire and support you to give the world the best you've got.

Marci Segal, December 2000

Introduction

This book was written with two goals in mind: first, so you can recognize your own creative capacities from a style perspective and give allowances and "leg ups" to others whose creative styles are different; second, to partially demystify the notion of creativity. The hope is that in the future, you will be able to articulate an answer to the question, "What do you mean by creative?" from your own perspective and experience.

Section 1 introduces you to the different components that educated practitioners use—culled from research in creativity—for working with others (and themselves) to facilitate growth, innovation, creativity, and change. Read this section for insights into some of the energies involved in creating and to find out more about your own creative spark. Some helpful how-tos are also provided to trigger your thinking and begin moving you from where you are to where you want to be.

The following two sections reveal complimentary psychological energy systems.

Section 2 shows you the temperament framework and conducts you through various exercises to select the temperament that best matches your experiences. Here you will see four unique and complementary approaches to actualizing and sustaining fulfilling change—and how each interprets creativity through a different set of values. Information regarding the relationship of the temperament patterns to creative activities is shared to help you deliberately acknowledge, work with, and shift your energy and the energy of those around you. Detailed information about each temperament pattern is included.

Section 3 reveals the cognitive-process energies of psychologist Carl Jung's theory of psychological type and discusses them from a creating perspective. Insightful, thorough, and enlightening, this section shows what happens in the minds of people when new ideas are sought and selected. Key to this section are the eight cognitive processes and how the interplay of these patterns of energy can be tapped and welcomed.

Section 4 shows how to set up an idea-generating session. It provides a practical approach based on twenty years of experience of observing, participating in, designing, and leading idea-generating and creativity sessions in business, marketing, advertising, academic, and association environments.

And Section 5 is about tools for inspiring the many voices of creativity. It provides deliberately different tools to honor the temperament patterns and cognitive processes to provoke the creative spark in meaningful ways for people with whom you work.

You will, of course, approach all this material in your own way. Please do your best to read the sections in sequence. Each builds from the information of the preceding section.

And please make notes as you go along. Record your reactions, insights, and questions. Capture your ideas rather than letting them evaporate into thin air.

Welcome to CreativityLand.

Notes

1

Exploring Creativity

Exploring Creativity

What Is Creativity?

Creativity is the spark of life, the vitality that stirs desires to improve and change the status quo—meaningfully, responsibly, wisely, and with impact.

This spark is inherent; we are born with it. Using its light, we shift from the past, imprint the present, imagine the future, and connect to forever. We gauge our actions according to how success will be measured, how others will respond, our clarity of purpose, and our personal needs.

Why Do We Create?

Creativity is a condition of our species. We invent procedures, alter behaviors, develop new systems, and create new knowledge to increase our likelihood of survival and fulfillment. Human creativity is an extension or another expression of our biological imperative to procreate.

When Do We Create?

As a species, we continue to develop new social, belief, and subsistence systems as our perceptions, knowledge, resources, population, and environments change. We act to create when we experience a restlessness or a dissatisfaction. And when we do, we feel like life is opening up.

Do We All Create the Same Way?

Like love, the expression of creativity varies from person to person and from culture to culture (Benetti 1997). Ways to access creativity must therefore be tailored to suit the individual, group, culture, and purpose.

How Does It Feel to Create?

Creativity yields a sense of freedom, choice, and personal power. The emotions involved span the spectrum from fear and depression to elation and joy.

Here's what participants in my workshops tend to report about their emotional shifts during creative experiences. They mention panic, curiosity, pressure to perform, anxiety, excitement, doubt, trust, faith, satisfaction,

and glee. What keeps them going, they usually say, is their desire to persevere and their ability to find resources to help them. Here are two examples of comments made:

> *Once the new implementation plan was accepted, I felt a great sense of relief and accomplishment.*

> *To get into the creative swing, I forced myself to step outside my day-to-day pattern in response to a "trumpet call to adventure." This was totally unlike me. So, I jumped in cautiously. The rewards for taking action were far greater than I ever expected. Now I am ready and more able to do it again.*

Emotions are part of the creating cycle. They can signal that a transformation is either waiting to happen or in the midst of going on. Opportunities for creating can be inspired by paying attention to their messages. With perseverance, the radiant light of optimism, clarity and renewed trust can emerge from the darkness of dissatisfaction and boredom.

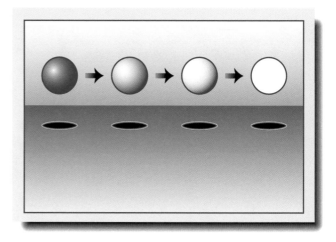

Being more creative involves shifting your energies, like rearranging furniture, cleaning out a drawer, or moving to music.

Emotions are energy patterns related to our sense of health and well-being. How we interact with the world, understand it, and make decisions are also energy frequencies, though of a different sort.

We interpret experiences and make decisions based on how our energy pattern is configured. For example, some people tend to see an item, say, a red ball, as it is while others are inclined to infer what it may lead to—bouncing, throwing, bruises. Some people are drawn to join activities while others prefer to work alone performing a task. Our different energy patterns attract us to some things and not to others. What if we could choose to shift our energy to include others we don't normally use? Personally, that's what I think creativity is all about.

Creativity: **Shifting energies to actualize and sustain fulfilling change.**

What Are Some Ways I Can Shift My Energy?

You can choose to perceive a little differently, such as seeing events with a fresh pair of eyes. You can also make decisions using a set of criteria other than the one you usually use.

Other ways to shift your energy include paying attention to and acting positively on your inner stirrings, attending to people and events you might normally ignore, and/or surfacing buried feelings and thoughts. You might also challenge well-accepted assumptions, ask new questions, and request help from others whose lives are different from and complementary to yours.

Here are other simple energy shifting suggestions:

1. Get out of your way.

2. Take a new approach.

3. Thank all those who impose their standards of perfection on you and move on.

4. Give yourself some "downtime" away from distractions.

5. Do something different: read a different magazine or newspaper, visit a new Web site, eat at a different restaurant, visit a gallery or museum, go electronic-free for a few days.

6. Make a list of all those projects you wanted to do and just never got around to. Then tackle each one, step by step, and celebrate your successes—even the little ones.

7. Clean out a drawer, a closet, the attic, the basement.

8. Invite someone new home for dinner.

How Can I Be More Creative?

To be more creative, choose to be more creative. It's as easy as that. Thoughts and wishes tend to manifest themselves to form our reality.

It helps, too, to relax every now and then. Do it now. Inhale deeply into your belly to the count of three. Exhale slowly. Now, breathe in again. At your next exhalation, feel the tensions leave. Do this again and again until all the vestiges of tension are gone—for the moment. Relax, even for this short time, as best you can.

Often we take our creativity for granted. I've seen this time and time again. One person compliments another on his or her creativity and the receiver says, "Oh no it's not creative, it's just what I do." By bringing to consciousness the talents we have that others remark about helps us to become aware of our natural gifts.

Knowledge about creativity cycles, attendant emotions, motivations, cultural expectations, cognitive processes, and unconscious factors can give you a greater spectrum of choice from which you make selections to actualize your creativity and shift your energies at will. When you remain unaware of these aspects, choosing to be more creative is like deciding you want to travel to Italy for a holiday—without first seeing the map.

Initially, without the information available, you decide to explore the cities of Rome, Venice, and Florence. Then you see the map. Other cities and towns come to your awareness. You have greater choice. Now you can decide to travel to Naples, Palermo or the island of Sicily.

The remainder of this section provides a general map of creativity so you can make the best choice for how to become more creative. Creativity is a systems thing—all components are interconnected. Your entry point to the system is your choice. Welcome.

> *To everything there is a season,*
> *a time for every purpose under the heaven:*
>
> *a time to be born, and a time to die;*
> *a time to plant, and a time to pluck what is planted;*
>
> *a time to kill, and a time to heal;*
> *a time to break down, and a time to build up;*
>
> *a time to weep, and a time to laugh;*
> *a time to mourn, and a time to dance;*
>
> *a time to cast away stones, and a time to gather stones;*
> *a time to embrace, and a time to refrain from embracing;*
>
> *a time to gain, and a time to lose;*
> *a time to keep, and a time to throw away;*
>
> *a time to tear, and a time to sew;*
> *a time to keep silence, and a time to speak;*
>
> *a time to love, and a time to hate;*
> *a time of war, and a time of peace.*
>
> *—Ecclesiastes 3: 1–8, The New King James Version*

Cycles of Creating

Some people believe that creating is a process that starts somewhere and ends somewhere else. Graham Wallas, author of *The Art of Thought* (1926) wrote about the creative process in a linear fashion. He identified four stages in the process: preparation, incubation, illumination, and verification. The Osborn-Parnes Creative Problem Solving Process (Parnes, Noller, and Biondi 1976) is similarly presented in a linear format: Mess Finding, Fact-Finding, Problem Finding, Idea Finding, Solution Finding, and Acceptance Finding. There are others who follow suit. Rather than continue thinking in lines, let's consider that the creating process is cyclical.

As in agriculture and other living systems, creating has seasons—seasons of fertility, barrenness, and transformation—signaling the natural order of birth, death, and rebirth.

Seasonal growth patterns have influenced cyclical thinking for many years. Jungian analyst Clarissa Pinkola Estes (1991) has used the Greek myth of Persephone and the Underworld, a myth thought to explain the phenomenon of seasonal growth cycles, to make this point.

Persephone, daughter of Earth Mother Demeter, was abducted by Hades, the lord of the underworld. He offered her a pomegranate, the fruit of the underworld, and she willingly ate it, thus becoming forever connected to the realm.

Years passed. Demeter went in search of her daughter. She became angry upon discovering what happened to Persephone and reacted by allowing the earth to fall barren. Later, she acknowledged that the world's people may perish due to lack of food, so she compromised with Hades. For nine months of the year, Persephone would live with her mother. During the other three months, she would stay with her dark husband. Every year, on Persephone's return from the underworld, the earth would again return to the fecundity of spring.

Moon phases also show cyclic energies. Used for millennia as guides to planting and harvesting crops, meanings have been attached to each of the four phases:

- At the new moon, seeds are planted. It is time for new beginnings, new ideas.

- At the first-quarter moon, great energy is required for the seed to form into a plant. It must develop roots and push them into the soil, and it must grow shoots and extend them upward. The new idea takes hold and takes shape with effort and perseverance.

- During the full moon phase, the plant bears fruit. Illumination of the idea, including its gifts and consequences, occurs.

- The third-quarter moon brings a crisis of usefulness. The plant, having bloomed and procreated, dies. Its seeds are ready for planting at the next new moon. The cycle repeats. The original idea transforms into newer and more relevant derivatives.

If creativity is the spark of life, then using a life-cycle metaphor to understand its energies and workings helps show the truth.

The stirring of a new idea is birth. Making something happen with that stirring is childhood. Adulthood is marked when feedback is given concerning the actions taken. Like transforming from childhood to adulthood, the initial puberty stage can be a confusing time. When the original idea is no longer useful, it dies or transforms into new stirrings.

You can shift your energy at will by paying attention to your stirrings, acting on them, learning from the feedback, and letting go to allow new stirrings room to emerge.

Keeping the Energy Moving

Many people emotionally stop themselves from creating. Rather than persevering through the discomfort of growth, they remain stuck in one place in the cycle.

As a result, they learn never to do that again. Feelings of resentment, grief, guilt, inadequacy, loss, and anger attach themselves to the memory of acting on the stirring. When a new one occurs, the weight of these emotions denies the creative energies the opportunity to actualize in life-giving ways.

To keep the energy moving, use this deliberate rebirthing strategy: When you are stuck somewhere in the cycle, ask yourself, "What might I do differently next time?" in place of "I'll never do that again." By doing this, you arouse curiosity and promote positive emotions such as acceptance, interest, enthusiasm, and self-worth. The next stirring then is welcomed, not denied.

> **TIP**
>
> Introduce the question, "What might I do differently next time?" into your patterned responses to what may seem like defeat. Doing so moves you from using your strength to avoid the call to adventure in favor of self-preservation toward realizing your potential to actualize a meaningful change.

Many are nervous about deliberately creating because they fear a death or end of some kind. Thinking about creativity as cyclical, rather than linear, encourages expectations of growth.

To be more creative, honor your place in the cycle:
• Where are you now?
• What new ideas are you looking for?
• What new ideas are you in the midst of bringing to life?
• If you're at a crisis point, how is your idea working differently than you thought it would?
• What appropriate and positive learnings are you gaining from your efforts?
• What new idea is emerging?

Making More of Your Creative Energies

Here are guidelines for focusing your energy and attention throughout the creating cycle.

Birth—The Stirring Occurs

Gather personal strength and focus your attention to prepare for an energy shift.

Childhood—Committing to the Stirring

First decide to commit effort to a project that will yield something of form and substance. Then survey the skills, talents, and knowledge required for you to complete it. Shift energies by targeting some learning and self-development to support its successful completion. Interact with others' thoughts, experiences and opinions through project-related courses, books, and workshops.

Adulthood—Acting on the Stirring and the Reactions to Your Act

Shift energies away from the targeted learning. Take deliberate action to execute your project. In this phase you discover what can be changed and what cannot. Here is where you bear the impact of your actions. Others give you feedback, invited or not.

How you respond to feedback is key to a successful adulthood. You may choose to adopt an "I make things happen" attitude and grow from your learning. You may also choose to approach the feedback with the opinion of "Things happen to me."

Remember, thoughts are things. What we think and wish for manifests to create our reality. Maximize the flow of your creating energy by using knowledge, imagination, and evaluation to build on what you've learned. Do your best to embrace an "I make things happen" outlook.

Do this exercise for practice: Recall a recent disappointment in relation to a project you were working on. What do you understand now about that situation? How might you change so a similar project turns out better the next time?

Death—Preparing for a New Stirring

Your project is complete or up and running. Now what? Pay attention to people and things in your environment to source new ideas. Interpret your dreams as metaphors of occurrences in your day-to-day life. See clues for new ideas in serendipitous meetings with old friends or in television programs or movies. Insights and connections from these and other seemingly unrelated sources often hold seeds for new ideas.

Many people report multistreaming through these stages. That is, they may be at different spots in the cycle for different projects. See if this is true for you. In the table below, list a few projects you have underway as well as some you are considering. These can be personal and/or professional. Now, mark the table in regard to which aspect of the cycle is most prevalent for each project. Did you list projects as suggested on page 5, item 6? If so, use those here.

CYCLE STAGES ▶	The Stirring	Committing to the Stirring	Acting on the Stirring	Preparing for a New Stirring
PROJECTS ▼	BIRTH	CHILDHOOD	ADULTHOOD	DEATH

Getting to Specifics

Following are suggestions to help you build strengths for shifting your energy in each of the four stages of the creating cycle. It is important to begin to assimilate information in new ways, both widening and deepening your knowledge and awarenesses.

Look over the following lists and place a check mark next to the suggestions that attract you. These are stirrings. Next, plan a date to act, and then, on a separate sheet, sketch out some ways to do that. The right-hand column of each table provides a place to check off after you have written your plan of action. Set a maximum limit of three activities and dedicate an hour each week, for the next six weeks, toward implementing your initiative. After each session, congratulate yourself. You deserve it.

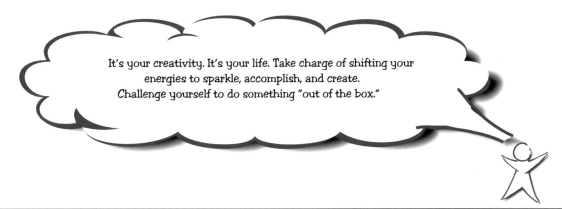

It's your creativity. It's your life. Take charge of shifting your
energies to sparkle, accomplish, and create.
Challenge yourself to do something "out of the box."

Birth

Build personal strength.	INTERESTED?	WHEN WILL YOU DO IT?	HOW?
1. Learn who you are; take an inventory of your strengths and weaknesses.			
2. Find out about your general health and begin to improve or enhance it.			
3. Discover what you like and dislike about yourself and begin to minimize the dislikes.			
4. Take an inventory of what you value by looking through your personal possessions and eliminate items that no longer serve you.			
5. Enjoy pure self-centered creature comforts.			
6. Show someone how you see the world.			
7. Ask questions about subjects you are curious about; learn something new.			
8. Communicate your thoughts and feelings in a journal using words or symbols.			
9. Change something in your day-to-day environment.			

Childhood

Choose a direction and then develop skills, talents, and knowledge to transform your ideas into action and substance.	INTERESTED?	WHEN WILL YOU DO IT?	HOW?
1. Find out the criteria used by others in authority for evaluating your contributions—then responsibly integrate those criteria into your next project.			
2. Engage in an activity that heightens your career development and feeds your professional ambitions.			
3. Discover the nurturing message your father or mother has/had for you.			
4. Be open to love from others; forgive.			
5. Participate in a group or cultural activity.			
6. Do something new and different with friends who share your values.			
7. Withdraw from activities for reflection and dreaming.			
8. Selflessly give an anonymous donation—in deed or dollars.			
9. Enjoy a good fantasy.			

Adulthood

Develop an understanding of ways to assimilate experiences of crisis; sense these as opportunities to learn.	INTERESTED?	WHEN WILL YOU DO IT?	HOW?
1. Examine your relationships with others. What can you learn from them?			
2. Learn how to negotiate, compromise, and cooperate.			
3. Make a deliberate commitment to someone else—then honor it.			
4. Learn how to share power and trust in your partnerships.			
5. Appreciate the process of losing, knowing that the loss signals the beginning of rebirth.			
6. Survey the wisdom of your colleagues and friends for what they might share with you.			
7. Broaden yourself through taking a new course.			
8. Study your culture and then the culture of another land. Travel.			
9. Use a generalizable framework for understanding the larger social environment.			

Death

Be open to the inspirations brought forth from the external world. Pay attention.	INTERESTED?	WHEN WILL YOU DO IT?	HOW?
1. Recognize that all your experiences stem from you, that you are the divine source of all meaning.			
2. Journey into the past. What lessons did your family teach you? Which do you need to pay more attention to?			
3. Learn about your emotions, honor them, and release those that interfere with your success.			
4. Make love with your partner only for his/her pleasure.			
5. Express yourself artistically.			
6. Challenge yourself to be your personal best.			
7. Make a change in your personal presentation through clothing, stance, and exercise.			
8. Discipline yourself to eat well.			
9. Practice humility.			

"Creativity is the process of recombining known elements to produce more valuable ideas than previously existed in the mind of the thinking."
—Sidney J. Parnes

Basic Human Urges: What Compels You to Want to Know about Your Creativity?

Fifteen psychological drives* or energies stir us to create and to seek out different events and experiences. According to the ancient wisdom of astrology, we are motivated to some degree by each of them, with varied levels of pull or intensity. Each energy's attraction varies from person to person and also varies over time. Swiss psychologist Carl Jung wrote that the symbolism of astrology contained the whole of human experience (Malsin 1991, 19).

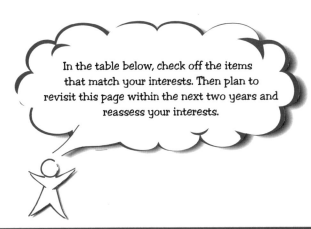

In the table below, check off the items that match your interests. Then plan to revisit this page within the next two years and reassess your interests.

MY CURRENT DESIRES, DRIVES, AND MOTIVATIONS FOR LEARNING ABOUT CREATIVITY	NOW	LATER
To vitalize my basic identity and conscious purpose.		
To receive comfort and emotional nurturing.		
To link conscious and unconscious awarenesses to how I think, speak, learn, and reason.		
To harmonize and attract people and things I value.		
To assert myself and prove my worth.		
To expand my search for meaning, truth, and ethical values.		
To bring order, form, and discipline to my life.		
To develop my uniqueness, break barriers, and make unequaled changes.		
To transcend my finite self through idealizing a greater whole.		
To transform and renew myself.		
To realize my capacity for holistic knowledge and healing.		
To nurture myself and others unconditionally.		
To express my wisdom through original perceptions.		
To integrate and focus my energies.		
To foster and form meaningful intimate relationships.		

(Note: This is also a good exercise for teams, groups, and families to explore individual and shared creative motivations.)

Now that you have some self-knowledge as a base for your learning more about creativity, it's time to shift focus.

"Why do we have dreams and hopes if not to make something of them?"
—Shirley Valentine

* For those who are interested, the urges or desires listed in the table correspond to the names of certain planets and asteroids. In the order listed here, the names are Sun, Moon, Mercury, Venus, Mars, Jupiter, Saturn, Uranus, Neptune, Pluto, Chiron, Ceres, Pallas, Vesta, and Juno.

Understanding Creativity

A Beginning

Creativity is a global umbrella-like notion describing a concept elusive to many. Its scope is limited here for an easy grasp.

Cultural Definitions of Creativity

Beliefs, attitudes, values, and behaviors associated with creativity vary from culture to culture. In Canada and the United States, creativity is within the realm of what is humanly possible. In Greece, creativity lies in the realm of the Supreme Being. More research and dialogue on this topic in multicultural settings would provide important contributions to a fuller understanding and appreciation of creativity on a global scale.*

In Canada and the United States, we primarily associate creativity with the arts—personal expression through drama, music, painting, and sculpture. Some also associate creativity with science because of new theories, inventions, and procedures in the fields of physics, medicine, and technology.

> **In business, creativity is thought of as a condition, a characteristic, and a process that result in a novel product or service that is both unique and appropriate to meet current and future challenges.**

Components of Creativity

Back in the 60s, researcher Mel Rhodes (1961) was pursuing the elusive definition of creativity. He decided to search the available literature to find it. Instead of finding only one definition, he found something remarkable. Four basic themes of research in creativity emerged. As a result, many students, researchers, and practitioners in the field use his model of creativity components today. The components are product, person, process, and the environment.

> ***Creative* describes characteristics of a product that is new and useful in some way.**

An example of a creative product is a clock radio. Years ago, a clock was a clock and a radio, a radio. They were separate from each other. When the combination of the two occurred, the product was hailed as a creative innovation. Its invention and placement in the market spurred other technological combinations—for example, the clock/radio/telephone/answering machine/tape and CD player. A new "product" can also be a new family activity, a new way to get to work, or a new business. Each is an outcome that is useful and new in some way.

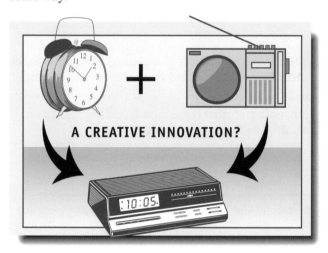

A CREATIVE INNOVATION?

> ***Creative* also describes individuals whose output or lifestyles are uniquely different from our own.**

When we call people creative, it is because they do something different from what we do. Or they do something we would not, or they think of solutions to situations outside of our habitual ways of responding. Reflect on the inventor Thomas Edison. He is considered creative because he did what others did not. In an incremental way, he tinkered with his inventions until they worked. (Do you know the fable surrounding his attitude toward learning from mistakes? When asked if he was disappointed at his needing 1,000 tries to develop a working lightbulb, Edison replied, "Not at all. Now I know 999 ways it doesn't work!" What a great model of adulthood!)

* Mary Evans's audiotape from the TRI Conference 2000 may be helpful in understanding the effect and influence of culture. It can be accessed through the TRI Web site at http://www.tri-network.com.

"How is it, Maecenas, that no one lives contented with his lot, whether he has planned it for himself or fate has flung him into it, but yet he praises those who follow different paths?"
—Horace

Curiosity surrounding the creative product and the creative person led people to theorize that a certain method of thinking and acting must be being used by people to achieve new and useful outcomes.

Creative **has also come to signify the process used, including various tools and techniques, to motivate, encourage, and facilitate the emergence of meaningful new ideas and fulfilling solutions.**

Alex Osborn, one of the founding partners of BBDO advertising, is responsible for coining the term "brainstorming." In his groundbreaking 1953 book, *Applied Imagination*, Osborn outlined the rationale and rules for promoting the generation of creative ideas. Together with Dr. Sid Parnes he developed the Osborn-Parnes Creative Problem Solving Process, modeled after the ways creative people naturally arrive at meaningful new solutions.

Their process, introduced in 1955, has become the basis of creative education at the Center for Studies in Creativity in Buffalo, New York, and is also the foundation for the international Creative Problem Solving Institute hosted annually for the last fifty years by the Creative Education Foundation.*

The Osborn-Parnes Creative Problem Solving Process (CPS) is used in businesses around the world for issues relating to innovation processes, customer retention, global collaboration, cost reduction for new idea development, job performance evaluations, mission statement development, new product development and launches, greater efficiencies, management practices, and leadership and team development, to cite some examples. A cyclical adaptation of the CPS model appears on page 97.

Creative **has also been attributed to the environment in which the creative process occurs.**

The impact of the environment—for example, the characteristics of the day-to-day *interactions* among people, the *attitudes* they maintain, and the availability of resources including time, people, and money, has an influence on creativity.

Which comes first? All components are interconnected—person, process, product, and environment. Choose your own starting point remembering that each affects the conditions of the others.

Creativity researchers have disparate perspectives on the subject (Mayer 1999; Parnes 1992). Their various schools of thinking represent a variety of other lenses through which to view this multifaceted phenomenon:

Psychometric—Creativity as a mental trait that can be measured using instruments.

Psychological—Creativity as the cognitive processes involved in solving problems creatively.

Biographical—Creativity as a life story. The case histories of unquestionable creative individuals are analyzed.

Biological—Creativity as a measurable trait evidenced through physiological changes that occur during creative problem solving.

Computational—Creativity as computation in that it can be formalized, like a computer program.

Contextual—Creativity as context based—socially, culturally, or evolutionarily.

Physical—Creativity as physical environment.**

This book has its foundation in the psychological school, considering the mental processes and motivations for actualizing and sustaining fulfilling change.

---

* For contact information on the Center for Studies in Creativity and the Creative Education Foundation, see Appendix D: Additional Resources.

** Still to come in the field of creativity, which will likely borrow from the fields of architecture, ergonomics, and interior design, is research on what physical attributes are necessary to support creative work.

Components of Creativity

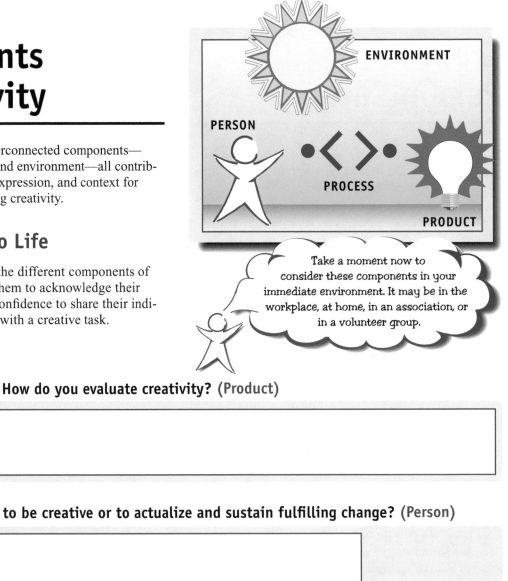

These four unique and interconnected components—product, person, process, and environment—all contribute to the understanding, expression, and context for understanding and inspiring creativity.

Bringing Them to Life

When people understand the different components of creativity, it is easier for them to acknowledge their unique gifts and to have confidence to share their individual voices when faced with a creative task.

Take a moment now to consider these components in your immediate environment. It may be in the workplace, at home, in an association, or in a volunteer group.

How do you evaluate creativity? (Product)

What motivates you to be creative or to actualize and sustain fulfilling change? (Person)

What process or processes do you use to get new ideas?
Where do your ideas come from and how do you actualize them? (Process)

What environmental factors support your creative efforts?
And what gets in the way? (Environment)

(Note: This is a good set of discussion questions for teams, groups, and families to discover both their universal and unique characteristics.)

Creative Person Survey

Dr. Teresa Amabile (1983), a researcher at Harvard University, developed the Intrinsic Motivation Theory of Creativity. She found that a creative person

1. Possesses knowledge about a subject, or in Amabile's words, has "domain competence."
2. Has skills associated with creativity, such as flexibility, independence of thought, orientation to risking.
3. Likes or is interested in the activities and requirements of the task at hand.

Creativity is the spark of life, the vitality that stirs desires to improve and to change the status quo—meaningfully, responsibly, wisely, and with impact.

Do you have these qualities? Here's a survey to help you find out.

CREATIVE PERSON SURVEY

1. Do you know something about a specific area, let's say gardening? In what areas do you have "domain competence"?

2. How do you deal with that subject area? For example, do you garden using different methods or try different watering and feeding techniques? Are you open to considering new ways of weeding and pest control? In your area of "domain competence," do you act in a risking, flexible, independent way? How so?

3. Why are you interested in accomplishing a task related to your area of "domain competence"? Are you personally motivated to see what might happen if you plant new bulbs? Do you nurture your garden for the sheer joy of it? You have heard Joseph Campbell's counseling phrase "follow your bliss"? That's the meaning some derive from this aspect of the survey.

(Note: Consider using this set of questions for a group, team, or family discussion.)

Bottom Line #1

If you are able to respond to the three questions from the Creative Person Survey, congratulations! Using Amabile's theory as a standard you can safely consider yourself a creative person.

Still Not Convinced?

Another researcher, Dr. Michael Kirton of the United Kingdom, developed a theory and an instrument that measures a person's style of creativity. Kirton's Adaption Innovation Theory (1999, 1989, 1976) asserts that creativity is the capacity to initiate change. His instrument, the Kirton Adaptor Innovator Inventory (KAI) measures the style in which individuals approach initiating change, problem solving, and decision making.

As a result of Kirton's research, we now know that when researchers were measuring for creativity in the past, they were testing for style rather than creative ability. Here's an example.

Name as many uses as you can for a brick.

The subjects' ideas were evaluated for creativity using four criteria: quantity, variety of different kinds, elaborations on themes, and originality. Based on these criteria, rankings of more creative and less creative test subjects were produced. The researchers were not measuring if a person could generate ideas or make new decisions. What they were looking for was the quality and quantity of ideas alone. In the old days we used to ask people how creative they were. Now we ask, how are you creative?

Kirton's work was pivotal in showing how some approaches to creativity testing examined creative style and not capability. Thanks to his contribution, we now know that the level at which one creates is unrelated to the style used to do it.

"It is not how smart you are, but how you are smart."
—Howard Gardner

Kirton outlined two general styles of creating. One is called Adaptive Creativity. Adaptive creative people initiate change in step-by-step increments to improve and maintain the status quo. Their ideas and solutions tend to be evolutionary, safe, and sound.

The other style is called Innovative Creative. Kirton's intent is to show a style that initiates revolutionary change and challenges the status quo. Albert Einstein provides an example of the Innovative Creative style. When asked how he developed his theory of relatively, he said he imagined himself riding on a light beam.

Innovation, however, is a socially desired quality these days and people have a tendency to think that the Innovative style is better than the Adaptive one, which is not the case. Both are creative approaches that may be advantageous in some situations and disadvantageous in others.

Is your style more adaptive, more innovative, or a little of both?

Whatever your style, you do initiate change. It may be on a personal level rather than on a level that impacts the culture as a whole. And when you initiate change, you do it in a way that is comfortable for you.

Bottom Line #2

By two definitions, then—Amabile's Intrinsic Motivation Theory and the Kirton Adaption Innovation Theory—you are a creative person. There's one more: You're creative by virtue of being a member of the human race because creativity is another expression of energy based on our biological imperative to procreate.

Enough said. Or is it?

Time after time in workshops I ask people to describe a creative person. How do they typically respond? First, you do it. Then let's compare the results.

It's amazing how the old stereotypes prevail, even after talking about styles of creating. Welcome to the New World! The trouble with the old way of thinking is that many do not identify with the stereotypes about creative people. As a result, they do not consider themselves creative or ever having the potential to be creative.

See if you can shift your thinking enough to recognize that the stereotypes are dying. Do your best to remember that creativity, according to Kirton, is the capacity to initiate change and that we all do that in our own way.

Consider that most everyone you interact with is a creative person. Each likely has his or her way of initiating change.

"A hunch is creativity trying to tell you something."
—Frank Capra

A creative person is someone who is...

Before proceeding, a few words about the creative environment might be helpful for you to fully appreciate what else is required, besides interest and genetics, for creativity to emerge.

Here are some of the usual responses:
1. Off the wall
2. Unusual
3. Imaginative
4. Unpredictable
5. Exciting
6. A loner
7. High energy

Creative Environments

Where are you when you get your best and most interesting ideas? What process do you use? Are you aware of it? Does it just happen?

Many people report getting new ideas when they are away from the workplace—on the golf course, in the shower, in the car—yet employers are increasingly asking their people to "get creative" at work, whatever that means.

To help your colleagues "get creative" at work, set up a climate where everyone feels involved and valued for their contributions. Define what you mean by creative and then reward people for their efforts. It's that easy—sort of. This simple statement represents inherent complexities much as the tip of an iceberg represents what's beneath it.

Dr. Goren Ekvall (1995, 1991, 1987, 1983) of Sweden did some wonderful research about twenty years ago to find out what it was like, on a day-to-day basis, in Swedish organizations that were known for their ability to place and maintain new products and services in the marketplace. In the course of his research he also found what it was like on a day-to-day basis in organizations that failed to sustain their new products and services in the marketplace.

Ten environmental factors occurred in high proportion in the successful organizations and occurred less often in the unsuccessful ones. When the research was brought to the United States and validation studies were conducted, nine factors were found to be most significant (Isaksen, Lauer, et al. 1995). (Yes, there are cultural differences in attitudes, behaviors, values, and beliefs about creativity.)

Before you read the descriptions of Ekvall's findings, engage in this revealing exercise.

"How many of you do your best thinking and get your most creative ideas at work?
When we ask people in our groups this question, no one ever raises their hand."
—Robert Kriegel and David Brandt (from *Sacred Cows Make the Best Burgers*)

Think of a time when you were in an environment that supported your creativity—it may have been in the workplace or related to volunteer activities. It may even have been at home with your family. If an example escapes you, imagine what that environment would be like.

In the column "Best Creative Environment," describe the attitudes of those around you, the way people interacted with each other, the physical surroundings, and the resources available.

Now bring to mind a memory or an impression in which you were in an environment that is totally opposite—one that suppressed creativity. In the column "Worst Creative Environment," describe the attitudes of those around you, the way people interacted, the physical surroundings, and the resources available.

Notice differences in the two environments?

Now, read the research findings and see how well they match your experience.

	Best Creative Environment	Worst Creative Environment
Attitudes of the People		
Interactions among People		
Physical Surroundings		
Resources		

(Note: You may wish to use this exercise and discuss the results in teams to compare creative experiences.)

"Climate" Factors of Creative Environments

Each factor description has three parts: what the environment is like when the factor is in place, what it's like when the factor is not in place, and suggestions for leaders looking to positively influence and encourage that factor. Have fun.

"Climate" here refers to the day-to-day interactions among people who work together. Rather than approach the culture of an organization (beliefs, traditions, and values), Ekvall asserts that a more effective approach is to affect the climate—the way people behave on a daily basis.

Challenge and Involvement

People are personally committed to doing their best work and feel challenged to use their skills in solving meaningful work-related problems. They feel rewarded and motivated to use their natural talents for logistics, tactics, diplomacy, and strategies to meet current and future demands. Intrinsic task motivation is high.

When people are not challenged and involved, they basically punch the time clock and wait for the end of the day to come. They feel that their natural energies are stifled rather than encouraged.

What's a leader to do?

Find out what motivates your team members. Assign challenges rather than tasks. Demonstrate how each successfully met challenge contributes to the success of the organization as a whole and to your area of responsibility in particular.

Trust and Openness

Sharing ideas, thoughts, opinions, and experiences is an optimal condition in which people can do their best work. The key to openness is trust. Trust is demonstrated by respecting and honorably treating people with due regard. Imagine what it's like when there is no trust. People are skeptical and reserved. They hold back their best thinking and suggestions, fearing others might use them to their personal advantage. Where trust and openness exist, people feel welcome to contribute.

When there is little openness among people who work together, important bits of information do not get shared, and often this results in rework. Time and energy are spent correcting mistakes and redeveloping plans. The result is inefficiency and lower productivity.

What's a leader to do?

Find out what each team member considers "fair" in decision making. Have an open dialogue about fairness and listen as if each team member were an ambassador from another country. Then, find a way to honor and set standards for fairness that each can respect. With fairness in place, trust and openness are supported.

Freedom

Freedom may be synonymous with choice. People want the freedom to choose what needs to be done to meet the situation at hand—whether it is planning how a project will be executed, asking questions, generating ideas, or implementing a plan.

When people working together have freedom, they have the opportunity to use their time in ways that are relevant to them in meeting challenges. Rather than rely on procedural how-tos, they are free to invent their best approach. With freedom also comes the choice of the best use of time. If all their time is scheduled and accounted for, then the opportunity for freedom is diminished.

Intrinsic motivation levels drop dangerously low when the opportunity for choice is missing. People lose concentration and motivation to do their best work. It's like knowing you have the ability to fly and someone is keeping your wings tied behind your back.

What's a leader to do?

Pay attention to your team members' time and tasks. Allocate discretionary time for your people to follow their curiosity for learning and experimenting. Sponsor regular meetings for revamping ways tasks are carried out—and, rather than you announcing them, have the team develop them together. You will be amazed at the results.

Idea Support

When you have a new idea or want to "bounce" an idea off someone else, what kind of response are you likely to get? Human nature being what it is, your new idea may be met with reasons why it can't be done. In words, gestures, facial expressions, or intonations, you sometimes learn the value of your new idea in less than supportive ways. This is typical of the adulthood phase of the creative cycle.

Ekvall found that ideas met with affirmative judging promote a climate for creativity. Why do you think this is so?

New ideas are often closely associated with the individual who offers them. When a new idea is criticized, so is the person who offers it up. After we've been criticized a number of times for new offerings, our survival mechanism clicks into gear. Rather than face the hurt, embarrassment, and potential threat of losing our position, we keep our new ideas to ourselves. We resist offering them.

What's a leader to do?

As a tool to start you off, consider using the Angel's Advocate to promote idea support. The Angel's Advocate is exactly the opposite of the Devil's Advocate, a character and archetype we all know so well.

Introducing the Angel's Advocate*

When given a new idea, the Devil's Advocate speaks of how it is redundant or unrealistic or how it doesn't meet his or her personal needs or the needs of the organization. What does the Angel's Advocate do?

The Angel's Advocate finds things that are good about the idea. In a way, the Angel's Advocate affirms the individual's motivation, interest, and problem-solving qualities by mentioning three things that are good about the idea. Then the Angel's Advocate says, "and I have some concerns." It is at this point the individual is made aware of some important criteria that must be met in order for the new idea to work.

Here's an example:

You: I think it would be a great idea if on Fridays we all left the office at 3:30. Not just in the summer, all year round. It would be a boon to the staff, and we could get an early start on the weekend.

Devil's Advocate: You know we can't do that. Our clients wouldn't like it. They rely on us being around for them until the close of business. What

are you really saying? That you want to get paid for work not being done? What planet are you from? Get back to work.

Angel's Advocate: Interesting idea. What you are suggesting to me is a way to reward the staff for all the extra effort they put in. I'm pleased that you brought this to my attention. It shows that you are thinking about the welfare of the staff—and mine too. I do have some concerns about it. It really pushes the envelope regarding what is acceptable around here. Then there's the consideration of compensation and response to client needs, and Pat, our director, might not appreciate this proposal at all.

Here's an idea: What if you were to outline your idea in a proposal and include the reasons behind it, as well as some benefits and obstacles if we implemented it? Make sure to appeal to the objections you think Pat might have. Then, let's take a look at it again with real attention. There may be a nugget in there we can act on.

The Angel's Advocate acknowledges the contribution with supportive feedback. He or she motivates the idea giver to use success criteria to modify the idea for a greater chance of acceptance.

In a climate that promotes idea support, new ideas are more likely to emerge and to be used, either as presented or as derivatives.

Humor and Playfulness

Laughter, spontaneity, jokes—all are welcome as promoters of a climate that supports creative thinking and action. Let's face it, life at work can get a little tiresome. To help people get fresh outlooks for new ideas as well as to relieve some stress, humor can go a long way.

Have you ever noticed how happy a person is when she solves a puzzling situation or gets a new insight? Yes, she has a smile on her face. It's the same smile that comes when she hears and understands a joke.

To achieve the "aha" (the new connection or idea), the "ha-ha" (the humor factor) is often required. Humor also acts as a healthy psychic balancing tool for stress and anxiety and to heighten morale. Humor helps shift energies.

Where there is little humor and playfulness there is little evidence of the vitality of life. People are serious and levels of camaraderie are low.

---

* The Angel's Advocate was introduced to me at the Creative Problem Solving Institute, 1978, by Sid Shore.

What's a leader to do?

Ever think about hiring a clown for a day? Or taking your team to see a movie for an afternoon? Plan something fun or something funny on a regular basis. And be careful that the humor you use has a positive spin rather than an attacking one.

Idea Time

Many people need some time to generate and consider different ideas before going into action. Environments that support high quality work provide regular occasions to do this. The value placed on using creative thinking for new ideas is made overt through this practice.

Imagine the implicit message about the value of creative thinking in an office where new ideas are welcome only during one three-hour idea-generating session. Or new ideas offered up out of context or off the agenda are lost to the atmosphere instead of being recorded for later consideration.

The pressure to perform in idea-generating sessions sometimes overwhelms the individuals involved. While some may favor this form of idea collection, others are less at ease with this and other traditional approaches.

What's a leader to do?

To honor idea time at your workplace, consider using ten percent of your regular meeting for new idea collection, generation, and conversation. If your regular meeting is an hour long, that's six minutes. As idea time becomes routine, people expect it, are prepared for it, and contribute to it. What happens to the new ideas? They are recorded for an idea review meeting that takes place quarterly. Instead of feeling pushed to generate "breakthrough ideas" in one three-hour meeting, your team, group, or committee reviews all ideas that have been contributed to date and selects those that seem most promising. It's a much better use of ideational time and supports your notion of welcoming new ideas.

(Here's the math: Six minutes for idea time at each weekly meeting for one quarter—6 minutes x 12 weeks—72 minutes. That's a meaningful 72-minute head start on getting that big new idea.)

> *"Write down the thoughts of the moment. Those that come unsought for are commonly the most valuable."*
> —Francis Bacon

Conflict

You may be surprised to see conflict on the list. ("Conflict strategies" may be a more useful term to use.) Organizations that support creative thinking and action honor individuals having a mature, adult way of dealing with their emotions. A high amount of conflict contributes to a lack of innovation success.

Let's see what this might look like. Director A has done something that Director B does not like. And, as a good businessperson, Director B keeps this upset to himself and his team and does not share or discuss it with Director A.

Director A requests information from Director B. And because of this earlier upset, Director B gives this request a low priority. Rather than responding with 100 percent, 60 percent of the needed information is given.

Then, Director B needs some final numbers from Director A to build a business plan. Director A gives this a low priority. You can see what happens. Director A, wanting to get even, is less likely to give as much as 60 percent effort to the request. Director A wants to balance the scorecard.

The effects of this conflict snowball until the two directors and their teams are giving each other minimal information, resulting in inefficient use of time and resources, not to mention the impact on morale!

SCORECARD	
DIRECTOR A	**DIRECTOR B**

Both directors were not supported in terms of working with their emotions. If they had, Director B would have felt comfortable giving productive feedback at the first instance of his dissatisfaction and Director A would be open to hearing it. Both would have acted to bring the misunderstanding to light so it could be understood and addressed.

When conflict is high, people protect their turf and infer less-than-positive meanings about the actions of others. Grapevine gossip flourishes and morale dips seriously low.

What's a leader to do?

Find some strategies for working with your own emotions first. (Yes, you have them.) Then insist that your team become educated in and practice emotional skills related to recognizing and communicating them with win-win outcomes in mind. Call a time-out every now and then to review your process.

Debate

Debate is about hearing different viewpoints from different voices. Honoring those viewpoints is important.

Debate might be better termed as discussion where all parties involved have an opportunity to share their perceptions of an event, situation, or challenge in a nonthreatening way. Debate centers on the idea, rather than the person behind the idea.

Where there is little debate or discussion, people keep their views to themselves. They are less likely to become involved and share information openly. Important bits of information that could make or break an innovation are not offered up. One-sided decisions result that overlook the full scope of information available for optimum decision making.

What's a leader to do?

Collect information from all parties in a safe way, and then bring the team together to have a conversation around the different viewpoints. Investigate "dialoguing" and how to use it. Or use the exercises in this book and hold a conversation about creativity in your group as a starter experience.

Risk Taking

As Bob McAlpine of Type Resources often says, there is no comfort in the growth zone and no growth in the comfort zone. Creative thinking for innovation involves "trying things on for size" before committing to new actions.

While working with an major telecommunications firm's engineering group, I heard the following statement again and again: "Sure, innovation here requires risks. And we are encouraged to take risks...as long as they are successful."

"No idea is so outlandish that it should not be considered with a searching but at the same time steady eye."
—Winston Churchill

Successfully working with risk involves learning from failure and milking every ounce of data regarding decisions and actions (e.g. who, what, were, when, why, how, feelings, interactions and so on) to create success. Reexamining the process and outcomes of failures typifies the adulthood phase of the creating cycle.

When risking is unwelcome people play it safe. They are afraid to suggest anything that may harm their status.

What's a leader to do?

Find a "safe" risk area for you and your team to take. Monitor successes and failures and learn from them. It may be a risk, for example, to have your team members decide how to accomplish a challenge rather than for you to tell them how to do it. Experiment. See how they use their problem-solving capabilities on one small challenge. And then monitor the results. If you frame the risk as a pilot test, then it is even safer.

When there is idea support, open communication, and a structure available to deal with conflict in an adult way, then the tolerance levels for risk and learning from risk are higher. Each attempt is valued for the fruit it will later bear. And you'll be amazed at the energy shift!

"The only sure way to avoid mistakes is to have no new ideas."
—Albert Einstein

Why Didn't Awareness of My Creativity Emerge before Now?

If you have been wondering why your creativity has not necessarily been appreciated or acknowledged, it could be for one of many reasons.

1. Your environment may not have the above factors in place. This could have occurred during your upbringing, in school, at work, or anywhere else that you interacted with others.

2. Those in authority and with influence—teachers, parents, peer groups, siblings—may have had different styles of creating than you; rather than encouraging your uniqueness, they requested, nurtured, and nudged you to be creative just like them!

3. Your creations may not have been evaluated by other people as novel and appropriate because their criteria were different from your own.

4. You may have been shown the "right way of doing things" that suppressed your natural inclinations.

5. You didn't understand that creativity is an inherent condition of our species.

6. You couldn't identify with people who are culturally identified as being creative.

7. High levels of creativity are the only examples you have, not day-to-day creativity.

8. Creativity was pointed out as something that "special" people have, and you may not think of yourself as a "special" person.

9. It never occurred to you to think of yourself as a creative person.

An Anthropologist's Definition of Creativity

Years ago, as an undergraduate anthropology major studying at the State University of New York College at Buffalo and its Center for Studies in Creativity, I asked one of my professors for her definition of creativity.

"Dr. Nash," I asked. "As an anthropologist, how would you define creativity?"

She looked at me, placed her hand on her hip, and smirked. Then she replied, "Well, Marci, creativity is bad manners."

"What?" I responded, shocked to hear her answer. "What do you mean?"

"Simple. Imagine doing something creative at the dinner table. What happens? You get your hand slapped. That's what creativity is—bad manners."

With that, she shook her head and walked away.

Perhaps in the past that's what happened to you-you got your hand slapped for doing what comes naturally to actualize and sustain fulfilling change.

In the following pages we will explore the different styles of creating in such a way that you will be able to determine what comes effortlessly for you and what requires work. Both aspects are important to nurture your creative abilities and outputs. Why? Because in this world there are two kinds of teachers—the mentor and the tormentor. Through both we grow into awareness when we pay attention.

Let's begin.

Notes

2

Discovering Your Creative Voice

Discovering Your Creative Voice

"Voice" is used metaphorically to describe an energy pattern revealed when expressing opinions, beliefs, values and desires. Each individual's voice represents his or her unique energy pattern for motivation, cognitive processing and experiencing life.

When we use our voice we create the future. We ask someone to bring us a glass of water, for example, and in so doing, create a future that includes either getting or not getting the glass of water.

By knowing our own voice we can better understand ourselves. Knowing about others' voices helps alleviate knee-jerk blaming that often occurs when our needs are not met. By familiarizing yourself with "voice" you begin to shift focus away from the 'things happen to me' reactive attitude toward the more progressive "I make things happen."

Knowing about Creative Voice Is Important

Knowing your voice is a good beginning from which to acknowledge your creativity. Once you know your voice, you can also more easily tune into, understand, and encourage others'.

As a facilitator, coach, and mentor, knowing your voice puts a context around the way you manage and interact socially. It gives you keys to the motivation, ideas, and processes you use to actualize change. And it provides avenues to explore to trigger and welcome the contributions of others. Knowing your voice gives you an edge in helping people get and give their best.

The learning curve for voice generally follows this pattern:

1. *My voice is the only voice, and I am right.* Before we know about voice, we think that only our way is the right way to perceive and act.

2. *I know all voices are valuable. Mine is the best.* As we get to know about voice, we begin to affirm our strengths and see how they may not have been affirmed by others. So we proudly display how our way of thinking and acting is better than the others are.

3. *My voice is different from hers. I wonder if that's why she suggests what she does.* The further we investigate voice, the more we appreciate and seek to understand rather than judge.

4. *My voice is one of many. I need to hear what the others have to say for a fuller picture.* Here we see a complementarity and balance in the different energies.

5. *Our voices are all so different. What are some ways that we can maximize our shared expertise?* The greatest challenge of all is how to tap, welcome, and help other people to share the breadth of perspectives available to make better decisions faster.

When your voice is well known to you, your capacity for hearing, feeling, and seeing the perspectives of others increases. By honoring others' voices, you can tune into their wisdom and appreciate their gifts, especially when they are different from your own. As a result, new perspectives are more easily shared, challenge and involvement activities meet a variety of needs, conflict strategies are more accessible and problem-solving activities are more productive. Basically, leadership and teamwork are easier, and greater levels of success are attained and sustained when different voices are welcomed and encouraged.

In essence, knowing your voice helps you to facilitate, nurture, inspire, and welcome creative contributions in yourself and in others. It also gives you the freedom and strength to grow beyond yourself.

Voice is your expression of energy. It is influenced by where you are in the cycle of creating, your environment, your emotional state, your physical state, your motivations, how well you exhibit culturally appropriate creativity, how your brain works, and how well you are able to use messages from your unconscious.

So let's simplify it for clarity, understanding, and easy access. What follows is a beginning based on four time-tested human motivational voices.

Temperament Patterns

What Is Temperament?

Temperament is a systemic approach to understanding patterns in human behavior. Basically, temperament patterns describe ways in which human personalities interact with the environment to satisfy needs. This includes our inherent need to create.

A Little History

The concept of temperament was developed by ancient Greek and classical German writers and psychologists. Taking a holistic view of the human community, individuals such as Hippocrates (450 B.C.), Paracelsus (Middle Ages), Kretschmer (1925), and Spranger (1928) perceived humans as a total system seeking survival in four different and complementary ways. David Keirsey (1998, 1984), a modern psychologist, inspired by these thought leaders, developed the temperament theory that is used today.

What motivates you to move forward? What roles do you naturally assume? What are your typical behaviors? How do you satisfy your creative need for improvement, development, performance, or correction? In short, what's your energy frequency? What kinds of information do you attract, repel, or not even notice? What drives your creativity?

One way to access your drives is to look at the fifteen basic urges (see page 11). Another is to consider the temperament patterns and decide which pattern best fits your life experience. In essence, temperament provides a label for understanding some of the many voices of creativity. With this knowledge you may easily move forward to improve your creating capabilities, use other voices as needed, and have productive dialogue with your colleagues.

What You Need to Know about Temperament Theory

1. Temperament demonstrates a system of human behavior apparent in four specific and unique patterns.

2. Temperament is inborn. It is revealed through themes that emanate from one's core values. Each of us has aspiring within us one of the driving temperament themes.

3. Temperament remains constant. It unfolds over time through the process of physical, emotional, spiritual, and psychological development.

4. Temperament drives behavior. Our activities cluster into patterns that organize around meeting the needs and core values of our temperament.

5. Temperament governs how we grow, how we vary, and how we adapt to meet our needs.

6. Temperament is a pattern of energy that is expressed best when the core needs are being serviced through their associated core values. Stress occurs when the core needs are not being met. Another stressor kicks in when values associated with those needs are not being honored, voiced, or acted upon.

7. We each have a predisposition to one of the four temperament themes. This one theme directs our adaptation to environmental effects. We also develop coping strategies and learn skills associated with the other temperament themes to meet our needs for survival and for creativity.

Temperament Is Dynamic, Not Static; Influencing, Not Limiting*

Temperament is a dynamic pattern, always open to influence from the environment. We come into the world with a predisposition, our *true self*, but growth does not stop with the predisposition. We are free to behave and develop in other ways. We can and do behave in situations in a variety of ways; this is our *contextual self*.

Consider skills, for example. Our temperament pattern will influence which skills we are drawn to develop and which ones we develop more easily, namely, our talents. However, we can and do develop skills that go with any temperament in a given situation, and over time they become an aspect of our *developed self*.

Neither the *developed self* nor the *true self* determines what we do in a given situation. That is the role of our *contextual self*—to act according to the needs of the moment, choosing whether or not to be responsive to the influences of the *true self* and *developed self*.

* Used and adapted with permission, from Linda V. Berens, *Understanding Yourself and Others: An Introduction to Temperament - 2.0* (Huntington Beach, Calif.: Telos Publications, 2000), page 5.

Looking at Temperament Patterns

Our brain is constantly making, breaking, and sustaining patterns. We learn how to interact successfully with our environment through repeated sequences of events.

For example, we learn that a baby smiles after we pick him up, change his diaper, and play with him for a while. This pattern repeats. When the pattern is broken and the baby doesn't smile, we wonder what went wrong. We make meaning out of the baby's change of behavior that fits our expectation. And we adapt. We may hold the infant longer, coo louder, pay special attention to the diapering process, play a little longer, maybe sing a song—until we see that smile again.

From the baby's point of view, he learns that when you enter the room he will be picked up, changed, and played with. He smiles. Then, one day, he is handled a little differently. He doesn't smile when he sees you next. What do you do? Pay him more attention. He then learns that you pay more attention to him and play longer when there is no smile. The baby learns what patterns of behavior help him to get what he wants.

Temperaments are patterns too—patterns of energy that cluster around one main theme or core need. In a sense, temperaments can be classified as different energy frequencies. Like magnets, each of the four temperaments interprets situations from it's own frequency level. Each temperament voice contributes to the whole in valuable ways.

What wonderful creatures we humans are. We repeat things we like and prefer not to repeat things we don't. We notice what matches our frequencies and miss noticing those that do not.

Mentor or tormentor—both may lead to the creation of something new and appropriate.

How Temperament Influences Creativity

Different schools of psychological thought suggest the best mood and environment for people to express their creativity. For example, Sigmund Freud said that creativity is facilitated when conflict exists. Eric Fromm and Abraham Maslow wrote that creativity is facilitated when no conflict exists. Both are right.

Let's think about creativity as actualizing and sustaining fulfilling change. And let's use temperament theory to approach an understanding of what motivates people to do that.

When one's temperament pattern's core needs and values are being met, an individual has the capacity to more fully express his or her true nature.

When the core needs and values are not being met, the individual will do whatever he or she can to balance the energy to create equilibrium.

Self-Discovery through Learning the Four Temperament Patterns—Part I

Let's begin the exploration of your temperament theme experientially through reflection or conversation. Capture your impressions, memories, frameworks, and values for each of the following questions. Then read the responses representing the four temperament perspectives that follow.

1. What is your personal definition of creativity? How might you tell a ten-year-old about creativity?

2. When are you at your creative best?

3. How do you know that you have been creative?

4. When do you tell others that they have been creative?

5. When you initiate a change, what is the nature of that change? And how do you go about doing it?

6. What stops you from being creative?

Now let's compare your responses to those listed on the following pages. See which one most closely matches your experience and outlook. As you read through them, you may recognize the patterns of people you know. Keep track of these associations, perhaps by writing people's names or initials in the margins next to each response.

Response A

1. Creativity, hmm. Creativity is doing something new with something old. Like using an ice cube to move a big piece of machinery. A big ice cube. I did that once. Instead of hiring people and machinery when the boss said we needed to move a large manufacturing gizmo, I hired a guy with a forklift. I got a huge block of ice, hoisted our big machine on the ice block, and pushed it to the place it needed to be. When the ice melted, the machine was in place. Now that's creative, or maybe it's just using my smarts.

2. I'm at my creative best when in a "situation." I don't plan it. I do what needs to be done to meet the needs of the situation. If I planned it, it wouldn't be as challenging or exciting. Like the time I needed a small piercing object to fix something under the hood of my car. All I could find was my earring. So I used that. It worked. My friends thought I was being wasteful because my earring broke in the process. It got the job done though.

3. I know I've been creative when I do something differently than anyone else ever has. When I've solved a problem in a fresh way.

4. When do I tell others they have been creative? When they make me laugh or surprise me by putting things together in a way I have never thought of or seen before. Well-executed events, dance, or art impresses me very much. Demonstrated skill in performance amazes me.

5. The changes I initiate are variations on what has taken place before. When I meet the needs of the situation in a new way, I'm kind of proud of myself, pat myself on the back, and move on.

6. Rules stop me from being creative. If I'm expected to follow the rules exactly as they are set out again and again, then I feel stifled and uncreative. I need room to maneuver and, to tell you the truth, will go outside the rules if they get in my way. Better to ask for forgiveness than ask for permission, right?

Response B

1. Creativity is something others have and I don't. I suppose it's "out of the box" thinking. I don't do that. Not often. My ideas are responsible and practical. I answer a question or solve a problem in specific ways that have been proven to work. I enjoy smooth operations and systematize whatever needs organizing to help that to happen.

2. Sometimes I do little jobs around the house—like building a fence or gardening. Doing these brings me great pleasure and I know it helps my family too.

3. How do I know when I've been creative? Sometimes I like to experiment with procedures, like trying a new recipe at home or tweaking the supply chain at work to find greater efficiencies. When other people tell me I've been creative, I thank them and then usually shrug it off. Basically, I'm just doing what I do.

4. I tell other people they are creative when they do things I would never do or see things the way I do not. Sure, they are creative, but I'll tell you that doesn't mean there's any rhyme or reason to what they are doing. It's not always a positive term for me.

5. When I initiate a change it's for practical reasons and usually it's to help things run more efficiently and with greater economy of effort. Chaotic environments and waste annoy me. When I see them, I am compelled to organize and streamline.

6. What stops me from being creative? I don't paint or do modern dance or write poetry or anything like that. There's not enough time. The solutions I come up with are ones that work. I don't think that's creative so much as problem-solving.

Response C

1. Creativity is a human capacity to see things differently than how they appear. To challenge assumptions and develop a theory of how things might be if certain paths are followed, given the physics of the situation.

2. I am at my creative best when I have time to embrace systemic truths. When I envision the potential outcomes of comparable strategies to move forward in light of a challenge or opportunity.

3. I know I have been creative when two thoughts collapse into a third, newer thought and each maintains its individual vigor. When I see the ideas I have been considering put into action, I know I have been successful. Others praise my insight when I put forward a notion that significantly alters the approach to solving a problem. When I redirect the definition of the problem to access its core assumption, others applaud (sometimes silently) my forethought.

4. I rarely tell others they have been creative. I deduce the logic in their actions and value their expertise in the matter. To me, it's a function of necessary circumstances including learning, imagination, and evaluation. In sum, good thinking.

5. Initiating a change is done with reason. Improvement, innovation, and insight drive the need for change. When I do move on making a change, it is based on a systemic change in perception many times.

6. What stops me from innovating? Lack of time, I suppose. And lack of good strategic support. Many times people do not understand why I am proposing what I propose, and I spend more time than I like explaining the rationale. Why can't more people be more competent?

Response D

1. Creativity is true self-expression, a free and harmonious interpretation of life. It's being the best you can be.

2. I am at my creative best when I encourage, mentor, or facilitate others' growth through personal discovery of meaning.

3. I know I have been creative when others have grown, developed, and learned more about themselves and their chosen path in the world. This applies to myself as well.

4. When people are inspiring and expressing their uniqueness authentically, I tell them they are creative. Honestly, I know that all people are creative because they have within them the life force and the potential.

If they would only know it and give themselves permission to discover that life is a journey for their and our creative purposes. Sometimes, I tell them they are creative to inspire them.

5. The changes I often initiate are changes in relationships. I do what I can to help people get along in harmony, to dissolve the boundaries between people and have their soul needs met as well. I guess when I am creative, people grow as a result—they see the meaning in things. When I help others actualize their potential, that's where my creativity lies. It's so rewarding.

6. What stops me from being creative is when I feel like I am not being true to my values or being dishonest or incongruent. This includes honoring others' needs. I don't like being told to be creative about something or with someone I care little about.

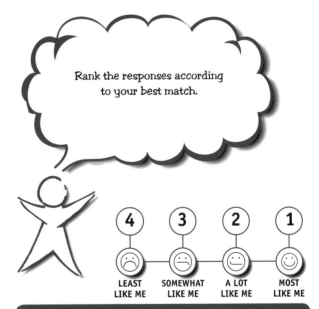

Rank the responses according to your best match.

| 4 | 3 | 2 | 1 |
| LEAST LIKE ME | SOMEWHAT LIKE ME | A LOT LIKE ME | MOST LIKE ME |

Rank the Responses

RESPONSE D	RESPONSE B
RESPONSE C	RESPONSE A

See bottom of page 36 for quick results.

Self-Discovery through Learning the Four Temperament Patterns—Part II

An underlying premise accepted by many creativity researchers today is that most everyone is creative—each in his or her own way.

These definitions are a collection of thoughts from well-known people as well as researchers in the field. Imagine it is your job to teach others about creativity. Which seven quotes would you use?

Some Definitions of Creativity

○ *"Creativity comes from having an inquisitive mind, from being easily bored, from wanting to challenge the status quo."*
Twyla Tharp

○ *"Creativity comes from accepting that you're not safe, from being absolutely aware, and from letting go of control."*
Madeleine L'Engle

○ *"Everything is relevant; making things relevant is the creative process."*
W. J. J. Gordon

○ *"Inspiration is the impact of a fact on a well-prepared mind."*
Louis Pasteur

○ *"Creativity is not simply originality and unlimited freedom. There is much more to it than that. Creativity also poses restrictions. While it uses methods other than those of ordinary thinking it must not be in disagreement with ordinary thinking—or rather, it must be something that, sooner or later, ordinary thinking will understand, accept, and appreciate. Otherwise the result will be bizarre and not creative."*
Silvano Arieti

○ *"Creativity involves breaking out of established patterns in order to look at things in a different way."*
Edward de Bono

○ *"Creativity is the ability to initiate change."*
Michael Kirton

○ *"...to the extent that a person makes, invents, thinks of something that is new to him, he may be said to have performed a creative act."*
Margaret Mead

○ *"Creativity is one of the major means by which the human being liberates himself from the fetters not only of his conditioned responses, but also of his usual choices."*
Silvano Arieti

○ *"Creativity is a process that results in novelty which is accepted as useful, tenable, or satisfying by a significant group of others at some point in time."*
M. I. Stein

○ *"When we are involved in [creative work], we feel that we are living more fully than during the rest of our life."*
Mihaly Csikszentmahalyi

○ *"A problem well stated is half solved."*
John Dewey

○ *"Creativity is the ability to see relationships where none exist."*
Thomas Disch

○ *"It is good to have an end to journey toward; but it is the journey that matters, in the end."*
Ursula K. Le Guin

○ *"If you obey all the rules, you miss all the fun."*
Katherine Hepburn

○ *"Originality is nothing but judicious imitation."*
Voltaire

○ *"To me, success can be achieved through repeated failure and introspection. In fact, success represents 1 percent of your work and results from 99 percent that is called failure."*
Soichiro Honda

○ *"Creative activity could be described as a type of learning process where teacher and pupil are located in the same individual."*
Arthur Koestler

○ *"Without deviation, progress is not possible."*
Frank Zappa

○ *"Creativity is 1 percent inspiration and 99 percent perspiration."*
Thomas Edison

Now that you've selected seven, eliminate two.

Of the five remaining, select three.

Which are your top three definitions or quotes and your overall "message" about creativity?

1.

2.

3.

My "Message" about Creativity...

How would someone close to you choose to teach others about creativity? Consider your partner, your boss, your colleagues, your children, or the teachers of your children. Many times people begin to explore creativity in groups without fully appreciating that others around them may consider creativity totally differently.

Making Some Sense of the Quotations Exercise

Different people select different quotes as being the "right" ones for them. This exercise introduces different attitudes toward creativity, highlighting four different outlooks.

Each outlook represents a unique energy frequency. Each is a contributing voice. All are valuable.

Outlook A:
Artisan Temperament Pattern

Freedom, impact, and action drive Artisans. They figure out a situation and skillfully do what is necessary to get the desired immediate results. People of this temperament pattern generate options for responding to direct needs. They trust their impulses and perform skillfully using whatever tools they have on hand—be they computers, theories or hammers.

Creativity for the Artisan is challenge, fun, and freedom. The Artisan's creativity modifies an already existing idea to suit a new purpose or use.

Outlook B:
Guardian Temperament Pattern

Guardians get the right things to the right people at the right time under budget. They like operations and events to run smoothly and efficiently. People of this temperament pattern like to make things easier for others in practical ways. They make sure everything is taken care of so things go right and don't go wrong.

Creativity for the Guardian is incremental change—sometimes so gradual that it often goes unnoticed and unacknowledged. Aimed at building upon past successes sequentially, the Guardian is motivated to fit in and acts as an experienced cautionary advisor.

Examples of creativity definitions that match the Artisan temperament pattern:

"Without deviation, progress is not possible."

Frank Zappa

"Originality is nothing but judicious imitation."

Voltaire

"If you obey all the rules, you miss all the fun."

Katherine Hepburn

"Creativity is one of the major means by which the human being liberates himself from the fetters not only of his conditioned responses, but also of his usual choices."

Silvano Arieti

"Creativity comes from having an inquisitive mind, from being easily bored, from wanting to challenge the status quo."

Twyla Tharp

From your original selection of seven, how many of these Artisan quotes did you choose? _____

Examples of creativity definitions that match the Guardian temperament pattern:

"Creativity comes from accepting that you're not safe, from being absolutely aware, and from letting go of control."

Madeleine L'Engle

"Inspiration is the impact of a fact on a well-prepared mind."

Louis Pasteur

"Creativity is 1 percent inspiration and 99 percent perspiration."

Thomas Edison

"Creativity is not simply originality and unlimited freedom. There is much more to it than that. Creativity also poses restrictions. While it uses methods other than those of ordinary thinking it must not be in disagreement with ordinary thinking—or rather, it must be something that, sooner or later, ordinary thinking will understand, accept, and appreciate. Otherwise the result will be bizarre and not creative."

Silvano Arieti

"To me, success can be achieved through repeated failure and introspection. In fact, success represents 1 percent of your work and results from 99 percent that is called failure."

Soichiro Honda

From your original selection of seven, how many of these Guardian quotes did you choose? _____

Outlook C:
Rational Temperament Pattern

Rationals abstractly analyze situations and ponder previously unthought-of potentials. They conceptualize and explain probabilities and the factors that influence them from a variety of perspectives. People of this temperament pattern like to question assumptions. In so doing they test their own competence as well as the capabilities of others. Research and analysis support their development of concepts and ideas.

Creativity for the Rational is like an equation composed of multidimensional considerations for strategic vision and goal accomplishment. And then it continues as the Rational finds the precise words to succinctly articulate those concepts.

Examples of creativity definitions that match the Rational temperament pattern:

"Creativity involves breaking out of established patterns in order to look at things in a different way."

Edward de Bono

"Creativity is the ability to initiate change."

Michael Kirton

"Creativity is a process that results in novelty which is accepted as useful, tenable, or satisfying by a significant group of others at some point in time."

M. I. Stein

"A problem well stated is half solved."

John Dewey

"Creativity is the ability to see relationships where none exist."

Thomas Disch

From your original selection of seven, how many of these Rational quotes did you choose? ____

Outlook D:
Idealist Temperament Pattern

Idealists build bridges between people. They delight in acting as catalysts for others' growth. People of this temperament pattern approach life empathically. They are driven to resolve issues that are deeper than what seems apparent to others and do it by moving to another level of abstraction, often using symbols as unifiers.

Creativity for the Idealist is the expression of one's unique identity and the synergy in working together to produce something greater than one person could. The Idealist finds new ways to help people relate and produce harmoniously so each person's stated (and unstated) needs are met and surpassed.

Examples of creativity definitions that match the Idealist temperament pattern:

"When we are involved in [creative work], we feel that we are living more fully than during the rest of our life."

Mihaly Csikszentmihalyi

"It is good to have an end to journey toward; but it is the journey that matters, in the end."

Ursula K. Le Guin

"Creative activity could be described as a type of learning process where teacher and pupil are located in the same individual."

Arthur Koestler

"Everything is relevant; making things relevant is the creative process."

W. J. J. Gordon

"...to the extent that a person makes, invents, thinks of something that is new to him, he may be said to have performed a creative act."

Margaret Mead

From your original selection of seven, how many of these Idealist quotes did you choose? ____

Number of Quotes I Chose

ARTISAN _____

GUARDIAN _____

RATIONAL _____

IDEALIST _____

Summary

- Did you choose the same responses on page 31 as you did for the definitions?

- Do you have a sense of which of the temperaments are most like you and least like you?

- Descriptions of each of the four temperament patterns follow on the next few pages. (The thumbnail descriptions on the next page are followed by fuller descriptions.) Read through the ones that match you the most, and then the others, to decide which one is your best-fit temperament pattern.

If all your choices are in one temperament, then you strongly identify with that energy pattern.

If your choices are in two different temperaments, your self-awareness is strong and you are growing through skill in and practice using a second energy pattern.

If all your choices are in different temperaments, you may be unsure of your temperament pattern, or you may have matured into appreciating and using the different energies available to you.

Look at the temperament you did not choose. What does this tell you about yourself and where you may look to grow creatively? Pay attention to this growth area for you.

If you did not select two temperaments, also pay attention. You may be so focused and successful in what you do that an energy-balancing shock may occur to encourage you to grow in other areas.

"It's not enough to visualize a positive result; it's much better to plan how you are going to get there."
—Shane Murphy

NOTE

The descriptions on pages 37–45 and the Temperament Targets on pages 48–49 are used, with permission, from Linda V. Berens, *Understanding Yourself and Others: An Introduction to Temperament 2.0* (Huntington Beach, Calif.: Telos Publications, 2000).

Connecting Response Summaries (from Page 31) to Temperament

RESPONSE D—IDEALIST
Creativity is self-expression. My being creative involves me as a catalyst or facilitator toward my own and others' self-actualization and in supporting the development of a unified harmonious whole.

RESPONSE B—GUARDIAN
Creativity is frivolous play. So I generally don't like to consider creativity. For me to be creative, though, I need to stabilize chaotic conditions for reasons of safety and security—one step at a time.

RESPONSE C—RATIONAL
Creativity is vision. My creativity involves me competently applying analysis, strategy, and hypotheses to access, realize, and apply the multidimensional qualities of truth.

RESPONSE A—ARTISAN
Creativity is variation and boundary breaking. My take on creativity is that I troubleshoot for action and impact depending on what the situation requires.

As you read through the following descriptions, use this page as a reference to select your best-fit temperament pattern.

Thumbnails
The Four Temperament Patterns

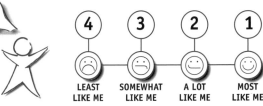

4	3	2	1
☹	😐	🙂	😊
LEAST LIKE ME	SOMEWHAT LIKE ME	A LOT LIKE ME	MOST LIKE ME

IDEALIST
Needs and Values

The Idealist's core needs are for the meaning and significance that come from having a sense of purpose and working toward some greater good. Idealists need to have a sense of unique identity. They value unity, self-actualization, and authenticity. Idealists prefer cooperative interactions with a focus on ethics and morality. They tend to trust their intuitions and impressions first and then seek to find the logic and the data to support them. Given their need for empathic relationships, they learn more easily when they can relate to the instructor and the group.

Talents

Idealists tend to be gifted at unifying diverse peoples and helping individuals realize their potential. They build bridges between people through empathy and clarification of deeper issues. They use these same skills to help people work through difficulties. Thus, they can make excellent mediators, helping people and companies solve conflicts through mutual cooperation. If working on a global level, Idealists will champion a cause. If working on an individual level, they will focus on growth and development of the person.

GUARDIAN
Needs and Values

The Guardian's core needs are for group membership and responsibility. Guardians need to know they are doing the responsible thing. They value stability, security, and a sense of community. They trust hierarchy and authority and may be surprised when others go against these social structures. Guardians prefer cooperative actions with a focus on standards and norms. Their orientation is to their past experiences, and they like things sequenced and structured. Guardians tend to look for the practical applications of what they are learning.

Talents

Guardians are usually talented at logistics and at maintaining useful traditions. They masterfully get the right things, in the right place, at the right time, in the right quantity, in the right quality, to the right people, and not to the wrong people. Guardians know how things have always been done, and so they anticipate where things can go wrong. They have a knack for attending to rules, procedures, and protocol. They make sure the correct information is assembled and presented to the right people.

RATIONAL
Needs and Values

The Rational's core needs are for mastery of concepts, knowledge, and competence. Rationals want to understand the operating principles of the universe and to learn or even develop theories for everything. They value expertise, logical consistency, concepts, and ideas and seek progress. Rationals tend toward pragmatic, utilitarian actions with a technology focus. They trust logic above all else. They tend to be skeptical and highly value precision in language. Their learning style is conceptual, and Rationals want to know the underlying principles that generate the details and facts rather than the details alone.

Talents

Rationals prefer using their gifts of strategic analysis to approach all situations. They constantly examine the relationship of the means to the overall vision and goal. No strangers to complexity, theories, and models, they like to think of all possible contingencies and develop multiple plans for handling them. They abstractly analyze a situation and consider previously unthought-of possibilities. Research, analysis, searching for patterns, and developing hypotheses are quite likely to be their natural modus operandi.

ARTISAN
Needs and Values

The Artisan's core needs are to have the freedom to act without hindrance and to see a marked result from action. Artisans highly value aesthetics, whether in nature or art. Their energies are focused on skillful performance, variety, and stimulation. They tend toward pragmatic, utilitarian actions with a focus on technique. They trust their impulses and have a drive to action. Artisans learn best experientially and when they see the relevance of what they are learning to what they are doing. They enjoy hands-on, applied learning with a fast pace and freedom to explore.

Talents

Artisans tend to be gifted at employing the available means to accomplish an end. Their creativity is revealed by the variety of solutions they come up with. They are talented at using tools, whether the tool be language, theories, a paintbrush, or a computer. Artisans tune into immediate sensory information and vary their actions according to the needs of the moment. They are gifted at tactics. They can easily read the situation at hand, instantly make decisions, and, if needed, take actions to achieve the desired outcome.

The Artisan Temperament

Artisans...

Want the freedom to choose the next act. Seek to have impact, to get results. Want to be graceful, bold, and impressive. Generally are excited and optimistic. Are absorbed in the action of the moment. Are oriented toward the present. Seek adventure and stimulation. Hunger for spontaneity. Trust impulses, luck, and their ability to solve any problem they run into. Think in terms of variation. Have the ability to notice and describe rich detail, constantly seeking relevant information. Like freedom to move, festivities, and games. Are natural negotiators. Seize opportunities. Are gifted tacticians, deciding the best move to make in the moment, the expedient action to take. Are frequently drawn to all kinds of work that requires variation on a theme.

PORTRAIT

For the Artisan, **life is a process** of making instantaneous decisions among an array of options.

Born with a **predisposition** for keen observation of the specific and the concrete in the present moment, Artisans tend to focus on the immediate and to be captured by whatever is happening and do whatever is expedient. They **excel** at astute observation of human behavior and are skilled at seizing opportunities and predicting the moves others will make in the short run. They often are skillful in crisis and emergency situations, able to see exactly what's needed and respond with whatever is at hand, without the concerns for competence or propriety that might inhibit other types. Such a **focus** gives them a talent for improvisation, fitting pieces together, blending, meshing, and remodeling. They are masters at variation, both for the fun of it and for practical problem solving.

Artisans **value** freedom and pragmatism above all else. As a result, they often appear to avoid ties, plans, commitments, or obligations that can get in the way of being spontaneous. This enables them to be tolerant and easy-going in most situations and often to rely on

the situation itself to structure their time and responses. Because of their adaptability, they can often behave like chameleons and respond to the behavioral cues from any type of person in any situation. Their pragmatic perspective leads them to do whatever is useful in order to get the greatest result with the least effort. And yet they may devote a lot of time and effort to achieving perfection in whatever is theirs to achieve. Their power orientation expresses itself in proceeding to action, thereby taking control of a situation.

In an energetic mood, Artisans crave activity and the freedom to act on the needs of the moment in a spontaneous way. Dull routine and structure put them to sleep or force them to "act out" if they cannot escape. They prefer **activities** with an immediate or near-term payoff or those that impact themselves or others. The payoff or impact can be tangible or take the form of feelings of risk for themselves or others. Since Artisans are the ultimate pragmatists, everything, including people, theories, and ideas, can be tools for reaching the exhilaration that comes with the execution of a perfect act, an act full of grace, dexterity, or finesse.

Artisans are apt to show a cool exterior, masking a general **mood** of excitement. They **seek** autonomy, tactical one-upsmanship, and competition in social situations and adopt a fraternal camaraderie with those who play with them on the "team."

Often Artisans insist on negotiation over objects or issues. Their basic cynical **point of view** appears to be that "people are only in it for what they can get out of it." Although generally optimistic, they are not disillusioned when people act in their own interest rather than for the common good.

Artisans place a high value on competence that shows in actual performance and is not just claimed by a degree or by position. They most **admire** people of great skill, the cool or flamboyant virtuoso, hero, high roller, adventurer, inventor, and so on. They despise awkwardness, meekness, and cowardliness, such as that found in "stool pigeons" and "chickens." Their chief internal enemy is boredom. They are **stressed** by wordiness, abstraction, uneventful routine, restraint, and lockstep procedure. They **do their best** in an open atmosphere or a loosely structured one that affords competition, freedom, opportunity, variation, and change. They love helping people by problem solving, fixing things, and making things happen.

They are a **culture's foremost** tacticians. They focus on what can be done now to achieve impossible goals.

SELF-PORTRAIT

As an Artisan...

I must be doing something. I cannot tolerate being bored and I get bored easily. Wherever I am, I find something to do. I need variety and stimulation. It is important that I have freedom. Any situation that is confining will make me miserable, and I will do whatever it takes to change my circumstances. I love to make an impact and do the unpredictable. I live for this moment; the past is gone and the future will take care of itself. I want to squeeze the most I can out of life.

I am very adaptable and take great pride in doing many different things. I often am described as a chameleon because I fit in so many different contexts. I have my own style and do my own thing, but I know how to play the game of life. I love a challenge and will often do something just to prove that I can. I want to prove it to others, but it is even more important to prove it to myself.

I like things to look good in an aesthetic sense. I am very aware of my surrounding environment, and anything that detracts from the setting spoils the whole experience for me. I have a natural sense of style and composition, and I know when something lacks a pleasing quality. It doesn't have to be beautiful, just aesthetically fluid.

I believe I can do anything if I have the opportunity to try. I learn best by doing, not studying. I like to jump right in and start. I work best when I can start with something and then change or vary it to suit the situation better. I am likely to do things no one else has thought of or dared to try. I am great at finding a way to do things. Usually it is not the conventional way, but it is expeditious and effective. It gets the job done!

I am in my element when there is a crisis or problem to be solved. Leave me alone so I can get to it and in no time I have the situation under control. I seem to instinctively know just what to do. I quickly assess the situation and act; it is not a long contemplative process. I just do it naturally. I can feel opportunity in my gut, and when I respond I usually am right on target. When I neglect my instincts I usually pay the price.

I am impressed when people are really skilled at something, and I love it when people notice when I show skill at something. I have tool "intelligence." I just seem to know how things operate, and I have the dexterity to make them work well—whether I'm driving a car, flipping pancakes, or setting the VCR. I am rarely clumsy, and I consciously work on my own individual style and presence.

Sometimes people think I am frivolous and irresponsible. On the contrary, I am serious about enjoying life in all of its capacities. I do have fun, but I also set goals and challenges for myself and work hard to achieve them. I have strong personal convictions, but I don't impose them on others, and I don't respond positively when others impose their convictions on me. I only appear irresponsible when I am in a confining situation. In an attempt to free myself of the trapped feeling, I may sometimes let others down. But I have learned to maintain commitments by incorporating some sense of freedom into the agreements I make with others. I am reliable and loyal when my freedom is not compromised. I will test the limits of others, but I do have a keen sense of just how far I can go before I jeopardize a relationship.

I am interested in what other people want because then it makes it easy for me to interact with them. I love to make an impact on people, and when I know what hits a chord with them I can quickly move our interaction along. I am good at knowing what to say and when to say it.

What I need from others:

I need others to give me space. I enjoy people, but I find too many expectations confining. I want to do things, not just think or talk about them. I want to be appreciated for my troubleshooting talents by being relieved of constraints on my freedom when there is no crisis. I want my free-spirit ways to be seen as a viable and responsible way to live life.

How others perceive me:

Other people see me as fun, quick, and a risk taker. They believe things come to me easily and that I am lucky. They often see me as a maverick or free spirit. They think I am a lot of fun to be around, but they want me to prove that I am reliable.

The Guardian Temperament

SNAPSHOT

Guardians...

Want to fit in, to have membership. Hunger for responsibility, accountability, and predictability. Tend to be generous, to serve, and to do their duty. Establish and maintain institutions and standard operating procedures. Tend to protect and preserve, to stand guard and warn. Look to the past and tradition. Foster enculturation with ceremonies and rules. Trust contracts and authority. Want security and stability. Think in terms of what is conventional, comparisons, associations, and discrete elements. Generally are serious and concerned, fatalistic. Are skilled at ensuring that things, information, and people are in the right place, in the right amounts, in the right quality, at the right time. Frequently gravitate toward business and commerce.

PORTRAIT

For the Guardian, **life is a process** of responsibly cultivating and preserving resources and relationships.

Guardians are born with a **predisposition** for observing and preserving the concrete "realities" of the present. Those "realities" may be rituals, rites, traditions, conventions, manners, facts, relationships, material, institutions, or life itself. Their **focus** is on the present and the past and how to improve what exists without losing the best from days gone by. With such a focus, Guardians **excel** at noticing when something required or agreed upon is not done and then following up to make sure it happens. Regulatory activities within society such as conserving, policing, guarding, counting, stabilizing, and ritualizing often come under their jurisdiction. They recognize that establishing and articulating the rules, sanctions, standard operating procedures, timelines, predictable routines, and protocol makes things easier for people and institutions.

Above all others, Guardians **value** the presence of order, lawfulness, security, propriety, bonds, and contracts. **Activities** that foster these principles keep life simple and ensure the continuance of the world as it is known. Likewise, the virtues of dependability, responsibility, obedience, compliance, and cooperation are necessary in their world, as these virtues add up to everyone contributing his or her fair share to the common good. As those who tend to make constant comparisons, Guardians are often concerned about everyone carrying a fair portion of the load for benefits received. Their power orientation is expressed in adherence to roles and support of the groups to which they belong.

Guardians can frequently portray a **mood** of concern. While they see themselves as optimistic, the unknowns of the future invariably disrupt their world and give them plenty of experiences that can sometimes foster a pessimistic **point of view**. They turn their logistical talents to preparing for the worst so the best can happen.

Guardians **seek** affiliation within hierarchies and social structures with clearly defined roles, responsibilities, and lines of authority. These structures provide security and pose the least threat of disruption to a system. From the Guardians' point of view, it is nice to know one can get the work done without disruption and, therefore, earn one's reward in a stable world.

Guardians like to be included in what's going on. Thus, they find membership in family, groups, and organizations satisfying. They often view organizations as either families or armies united for some useful purpose. This can lead to Guardians taking maternal, paternal, or authoritative roles in relation to others.

Guardians **admire** those with common sense, as well as those with legitimate authority, empowered by degrees, position, divine right, or hard work. A particular favorite is the person who worked his or her way up through the ranks, pulling their fair weight all the way.

Abandonment, exclusion, disrespect for authority, dereliction, and disobedience, all of which threaten the common bond, are particularly offensive and **stressful** to Guardians. They **do their best** when allowed to take on responsibility and when given appreciation and direction from authority. Guardians can demonstrate an incredible capacity for constancy, caretaking, and achievement in such an atmosphere.

The Guardians are a **culture's foremost** overseers and providers and seek to support families, work groups, schools, government, and all kinds of organizations to ensure continuity.

SELF-PORTRAIT

As a Guardian...

I am first and foremost a responsible person. I believe it is important for all of us to contribute to society as best we can so things will run as smoothly as possible. I have a strong sense of duty and loyalty to my family, friends, colleagues, and community. It is important for me and the people close to me to be safe and comfortable.

I am constantly aware of all of the things that need to be done, and I feel uncomfortable if things are not getting accomplished. I tend to stick to a schedule and familiar routines so I am certain to fit everything into my day. I spend much of my time making sure other people have all they need to be comfortable or to accomplish their tasks. Sometimes I get overwhelmed by all of the work I must get done, especially when others assume I will do things without asking if I have the time. It is difficult for me to ask for help, but I am learning to say "no" sometimes.

I have many roles in my life that influence what I do. I pay attention to how people are related to one another in terms of history, experiences, hierarchy, and types of relationships. It is clear to me that my roles come with particular responsibilities, norms, and standards of appropriate behaviors. I am offended and disappointed when people show disrespect for my roles or do not live up to the expectations of their own roles. We all have roles to play in the grand scheme of things; that is what keeps the world going.

I rely on my past experiences to guide me. I am always looking for the best and most efficient way to do things. I can barely tolerate waste. I believe there is a "tried and true" best way to do things and to do otherwise challenges common sense. I have lots of how-tos and how-not-tos that can save time and energy.

I tend to appreciate family and cultural traditions. I have many stories of family, friends, and colleagues and rich remembrances of times we have spent together. Life's milestones of birth, graduation, marriage, promotion, retirement, and death are important events I acknowledge and participate in as a means of maintaining the relationships I have with other people in my life. It is also important to other people when I am there to support them in these important moments.

I believe it is important to be prepared, work hard, and be helpful to others. I prefer to have things planned out in advance so I can avoid negative consequences. I dislike surprises, and I do not like changing a plan just for the sake of change. If there is truly a more efficient way of doing something, I want to be shown; otherwise, I am going to stick to what I have done in the past. I expect others to keep their word and act responsibly. I focus on accomplishments, so I like to be able to focus on a task until it is complete. I am generally thorough and have a clear sense of the beginning, middle, and end of a project.

I need a clear description of what is expected of me, the desired goal, a suggested procedure, available resources, and who is in authority anytime there is a task or project for me to do. One of my natural skills is putting stabilizing structures in place that will make things easier. I develop new procedures by comparing a new task to a task I have done in the past. I am good at demonstrating how things are done so others can learn from my experience. I believe in earning my accomplishments through hard work, diligence, and effort. Often my contributions go unnoticed by others, when just a simple thank-you would increase my morale considerably.

What I need from others:

I need to be appreciated for the simple ways I support others day to day. A sincere thank-you or a special gesture that will make things easier for me goes a long way. I like to be asked to be included in projects and events even though I may not always have time to participate. When people follow through on commitments and fulfill their responsibilities in a timely manner, it is more than a courtesy; it demonstrates their respect for me. I love it when people ask for my experience and support.

How others perceive me:

Other people see me as organized, courteous, responsible, and loyal. They know I am someone they can count on to help out in whatever way I can. Sometimes people think I am too structured and organized and not spontaneous enough. People generally describe me as a good student, spouse, parent, friend, or coworker.

The Rational Temperament

```
╔═══════════════════════════════╗
        SNAPSHOT

       Rationals...

Want knowledge and to be competent, to
achieve. Seek to understand how the world
and things in it work. Are theory oriented.
See everything as conditional and relative. Are
oriented to the infinite. Trust logic and reason.
Want to have a rationale for everything. Are
skeptical. Think in terms of differences, delin-
eating categories, definitions, structures, and
functions. Hunger for precision, especially in
thought and language. Are skilled at long-
range planning, inventing, designing, and
defining. Generally are calm. Foster individu-
alism. Frequently gravitate toward technology
and the sciences. Well suited for engineering
and devising strategy, whether in the social or
physical sciences.
╚═══════════════════════════════╝
```

PORTRAIT

For the Rational, **life is a process** of acquiring knowl-edge and competencies for their own sake or for the political, pragmatic, or strategic advantage such knowl-edge can give an individual or group.

Born with a **predisposition** for the complex, Ratio-nals tend to focus on patterns and "think systems," both technical and social, and move with ease from the big picture to the minute details of ideas or situations. With such a versatile **focus,** they often **excel** at design, schematizing, reasoning, strategizing, analysis, synthe-sis, forecasting, trend analysis, logic, and problem solv-ing. They are adept at seeing the basic principles and unformed possibilities, which leads to visioning and inventing. They are among the world's chief innovators, some driven to implementation of the visions and others driven to designs.

Rationals place a high **value** on competence, coher-ence, and quality. They engage in **activities** primarily because they might learn from them, rather than for deep

significance, for duty, or for enjoyment. Their power orien-tation expresses itself in a search for strategic advantage.

Rationals' prevailing **mood** is one of tranquility. They **seek** to identify and solve problems and enigmas. Sometimes their absorption in the abstract or the future can lead them to seem distant or aloof. They are often competitive and independent and appear to have little regard for common bonds. Bonding for them comes in the form of a shared interest or project. When in a nurtur-ing role, they tend to focus on the competence and intel-lectual development of those whom they contact.

Rationals come into a situation with an almost immediate understanding of the overall system, how it functions and the factors at work. There are always many factors and levels to consider, often with no easy, or at least no easily articulated, answers. Figuring out a system's specifics is often perceived as time better spent elsewhere. Learning means understanding the process of learning, and Rationals are constantly searching for knowledge that is abstract yet explicit. This gives them the power to act in a logical, more objective way that is still tailored to a goal or situation. When a field of study is thoroughly digested, Rationals can explain how they know what they know, when they knew it, and how that knowledge can be extended. Figuring something out means finding more to explore at a deeper level, with their eagerness to explore new or controversial areas tem-pered by the need for verification, proof, or performance. They cannot help but play with ideas and test them. With expertise, Rationals can introduce radical and insightful changes with ease. Rationals appear naturally curious. With their analytical and skeptical **point of view**, they can find themselves doubting anything and everything. Rationals have a high tolerance for complexity and are often surprised by others' resistances to problem solving. Their independence of thought leads to a need for auton-omy in the workplace.

They most **admire** will power and genius, the wiz-ards and inventors of the world, and they despise redun-dancy, incompetence, and weak will. They are their own worst critics and are often **stressed** by a fear of incompe-tence, loss of control, and helplessness. Rigid, routine, dull environments offend them and may drive them away. They **do their best** in situations that stimulate them intel-lectually and that allow them to have control over their learning and expression of their ideas. They can enjoy being challenged and critiqued on their own ground, taking such constructive criticisms as evidence that the critic has truly understood their project.

They are a **culture's foremost** visionaries and pioneers and seek to contribute their strategy, design, and invention.

SELF-PORTRAIT

As a Rational...

I am a perpetual learner. I am constantly in search of answers—fundamental truths—to help me improve and to achieve, and I am never completely satisfied with the answers because there is always more complexity, more questions to explore, and more avenues for progress. Logic and reason are mainstays. I am interested in the logic behind logic and the thinking behind thinking. I want to know why things are the way they are and why things work the way they do. I have a natural inclination to create or launch something that has never been done and enter territory unknown.

I am a natural systems thinker looking for leverage points in the system. I notice what others accept as assumptions in everyday life and question the premise and merit of those assumptions. I have a sense that human destiny is to promote progress. I have an inherent understanding of "natural law" and use that knowledge to consider and improve the way things are done. Elegant ideas and theories that explain the aesthetic beauty of natural law can offer a lifetime of stimulation. Elegance elicits efficiency and precision in a system, changing and improving its quality in a way that often goes unrecognized by society.

Self-mastery is a motivating force in life. I set my own standards, which are undoubtedly high, and achieve them. I do not rely on others for appraisal of my work, but I do like to be acknowledged for innovative contributions. My work is my play, having fun while challenging myself. Expertise and full knowledge of a profession or area of interest are very important. I aspire to be precise in all things, particularly in defining ideas and how I think of the words that express them.

Incompetence is my nemesis. It makes me feel stupid and like a failure. To avoid it, I strive for competency in all that I do. My strategy is to understand the underlying principles, the inherent assumptions, and the methodology behind something so I can improve my capabilities. I will continuously improve my skills, striving for perfection—perfection, in my mind, being the highest level at which I can achieve my intended purpose.

Problem solving comes naturally to me. I view the universe as a myriad of problems to solve. I do not accept anything on face value without some skepticism. I will take something apart in order to discover what must be hidden there that will explain what it is or how it works. When I have a problem to solve, I look for many other examples. I compare the examples, looking for distinctions and for what is missing. I determine or design a structure that will help to analyze the problem. I systematically initiate a change and run a test until I successfully solve the problem. I have a high tolerance for ambiguity and uncertainty, so I can easily consider many alternatives and think conditionally (if this, then that) in a search for solutions. A problem will often need to be completely rethought or designed with different assumptions in order to make it solvable.

Ideas are independent entities. They are meant to be challenged, modified, and redefined. I may have a great amount of conviction about an idea and speak in a way such that others believe I am certain it is the truth, yet I am quick to discard an idea once it is proven false. Of course, this requires a solid, logically consistent argument. I can discuss, critique, analyze, and hypothesize about any idea or theory, but I am most satisfied when the topic is within my area of expertise. I expect others to challenge my ideas, but I can be offended when others don't acknowledge the logical process of how my ideas were formed.

I prefer to direct my own life, living according to my own standards. I often pay secondary attention to the customary and conventional, except in important situations. Relationships must fit into a particular structure in the larger scheme of things. I am usually drawn to people who share a common interest in an area of my expertise. I interact with them for intellectual stimulation and to test my ideas. I have a tendency to treat people as just another variable to consider.

What I need from others:

Allow me to think for myself and give me room to be creative. I want to be taken seriously. Don't rush me if you want quality. Work with me to meet long-term goals, even if they don't seem to have an immediate payoff.

How others perceive me:

Generally I am perceived as intelligent. Others may also view me as lacking emotion, or they misinterpret what emotion I do show. They often view me as having particular talents rather than seeing my talents as intrinsic to who I am.

The Idealist Temperament

SNAPSHOT

Idealists...

Want to be authentic, benevolent, and empathic. Search for identity, meaning, and significance. Are relationship oriented, particularly valuing meaningful relationships. Are romantic and idealistic, wanting to make the world a better place. Look to the future. Trust their intuition, imagination, impressions. Focus on developing potential, fostering and facilitating growth through coaching, teaching, counseling, communicating. Generally are enthusiastic. Think in terms of integration and similarities and look for universals. Are gifted in the use of metaphors to bridge different perspectives. Are diplomatic. Frequently are drawn to work that inspires and develops people and relationships.

PORTRAIT

For Idealists, **life is a process** of cultivating relationships, pursuing self-actualization, and developing the potentials of those around them.

Born with a **predisposition** for the abstract, global and personal, Idealists tend to **focus** on human potential, ethics, culture, quality of life, metaphysics, and personal growth. With such a focus, they often **excel** at communication, especially metaphor and imaginative narrative. Relating to others empathically, they have a keen ability to reflect and anticipate unspoken issues and intentions of others. They likewise excel at giving "strokes," interacting enthusiastically, personalizing the impersonal, sharing in participatory leadership, and empowering and facilitating growth in those with whom they come in contact. Thus they appear to be natural catalysts of group formations and interaction.

They place a high **value** on authenticity and integrity in people, relationships, and organizations. They engage in **activities** because they are meaningful, rather than because they are routine, mandatory, efficient, or entertaining. The power orientation of Idealists

expresses itself in a search for fame, recognition, or personal impact upon society.

They are apt to exude warmth and a general **mood** of enthusiasm. They **seek** affiliation, harmony, and cooperation in social situations and often adopt a nurturing role toward those with whom they come in contact. Believing in the fundamental goodness of humankind, they maintain a generally optimistic, credulous, receptive, and accepting **point of view** toward the world.

Idealists come into a situation with an immediate impression of what's going on within and between the people. They take in the experience of the group and receive insights into the dynamics at work long before others do and usually beyond what others perceive. These insights are often vague impressions, although some will be quite powerful. Exploring relationships in all their forms is part of the human experience for them. They can call things as they see them or intervene in a creative way, acting as catalysts for growth. Ethical considerations and the impact on the web of relationships are part of empathizing with others. They enter, maintain, and leave relationships with their eyes wide open. Idealists cannot help but explore their feelings and how they feel about those feelings—feelings mean values. Idealists operate out of their values and intuitive perceptions and are often surprised when others lack awareness of the deep issues below the surface, from the past and for the future. They usually have a sense of where a person will be in the future. Idealists may show a different side in work environments, setting boundaries with an awareness of what they can afford to care about. They constantly balance seemingly contradictory needs for unity and empathy with others with their need for their own unique identity.

They most **admire** people of great integrity and commitment, the messiahs and sages of the world, and shun or despise the wishy-washy, the mundane, and the fake. They are **stressed** by the impersonal and the impervious and can suffer sometimes excruciating alienation in situations where their needs for relationship, significance, and esteem are not met. A divisive, argumentative, competitive atmosphere offends them and brings out their desire to rescue any victims or leave the scene. They can be troubled by a loss of their ability to experience or express unconditional positive regard. They **do their best** in environments that convey such positive regard, recognize their uniqueness, and provide validation, interaction, receptivity, and support.

They are a **culture's foremost** humanists and focus primarily on the meanings of humanity's past and the possibilities for its future.

SELF-PORTRAIT

As an Idealist...

I believe people and relationships are the most important aspects of my life. I am naturally empathic. When I interact with people, it is important for me to step inside their skin and see out through their eyes. This gives me confidence in how I can best help that person grow. I believe we are meant to lead meaningful and purposeful lives, and I like to act as a catalyst for helping other people identify their life purpose and what is meaningful to them. It is easy for me to inspire, appreciate, and reveal the best in others. I am a good listener and a good friend or mentor.

I view all individuals as having a unique identity with special gifts to contribute to the universe. It is important that every person be nurtured for who they are, not what others want of them. I will defend the right of anyone to do what he or she believes as long as no one else comes to harm, and likewise I will act in accordance with my own beliefs.

I respect myself and others when they are authentic. I respect people who show their true self and do not wear false fronts. It is easy for me to see the deep motivation and inner workings behind what people do and say. So when a person says or does something incongruent with what I see, it is difficult for me to believe the person. Occasionally, what I see inside the person is incorrect, but usually my insight is correct. Often others are not even aware of their own incongruity, and that is when I go to work. I provide emotional support and listen to their life stories. I have a talent for subtly drawing people out. In the process they gain insight into their own beliefs, gifts, meaning, and purpose. Sometimes I want people to grow when they don't want to or are not ready. It is physically painful for me to see potential in another person who is not able or willing to actualize that potential. Maturity and practice help me know when it is appropriate to push someone and when it is not.

I envision an ideal world where every individual is self-actualized, contributing his or her gifts and reaping satisfaction, and where we all live in harmonious community. In support of this, I am often dedicated to causes that will bring about change to the quality of life in a deep way. I utilize my natural talents as a counselor and diplomat to bring together different perspectives. I have a gift for communicating complex images of purpose and vision through metaphor that allows each person to visualize his or her own meaning and contribution.

I am particularly aware of the ethical merits of actions and beliefs. Because it is so easy for me to imagine how words and actions will affect people, I am constantly on guard to ensure people will not be negatively affected. I will go to great lengths to thwart what I believe to be unethical behavior, and it is very difficult for people who have behaved unethically to regain my trust and respect.

Passion, romance, images, dreams, beliefs, intuition, and ideals are all dimensions of what it is to be me. At times I am disappointed that individuals, groups, communities, and situations don't live up to my idealized expectations. I like to hope that somehow they can live up to those idealized expectations. I always, even in the darkest moments, have some hopefulness that if we all learn from each other and work together, we can overcome our shortcomings and attain the ideal. We are a unified whole, ever interconnected. What happens to others happens to me.

What I need from others:

A personal connection is imperative for me. I must feel that other people are acting authentically, and I must feel they will accept me if I act authentically. I expect open discourse and personal sharing. I want to tell my stories as well as listen to theirs. I need some feedback that they believe in me and my life purpose. I look for a willingness to stand together in the face of conflict and misunderstanding with the belief that working through it will only strengthen our bond.

How others perceive me:

Other people view me as a people person, someone who demonstrates empathy easily and makes others feel good about who they are. They commend my communication skills and say I am a natural teacher, counselor, and mentor. They also believe I wish for too much, and they are afraid they may not be able to live up to the ideal image I have of them. They may describe me as imaginative, idealistic, mysterious, intuitive, gullible, friendly, empowering, committed, and genuine.

Temperament and Creativity in Action

A Case Study

In a workshop using temperament to help people appreciate their different styles of creativity, I asked four groups—one of each temperament pattern—to join together.

The Setup

To each group I gave the same supplies and the same task. The task was to make a toy for a child using the supplies provided and to be prepared to present the toy in fifteen minutes. The supplies included colored paper clips, aluminum pie plates, plastic straws, wooden Popsicle® sticks, colored yarn, and scissors.

What Happened

The Artisans (creativity is challenge, fun, and freedom) looked at what they got and immediately left the room. On seeing this, I was deliberate in reminding them they needed to be back in fifteen minutes. The last one out the door said, "Okay."

The Rationals (creativity is strategic vision) surveyed the materials, clustered their chairs in a tight circle, and began to discuss and debate.

The Guardians (creativity is incremental change) also surveyed the materials and began to share how they used each in the past, careful not to touch anything lest it become disorganized, until they consensually agreed on a toy to make.

The Idealists (creativity is self-expression) immediately began handling all the items individually, playing with them, delighting in them. Like children themselves, they individually explored the potentials and contributed ideas freely and easily in what looked like a playroom setting. Together they laughed and giggled, all while "doing their own thing."

For fifteen minutes I observed the different approaches each temperament pattern took—except for the Artisans because they were out of the room.

Of the four, the Guardians finished their task first. Together they decided exactly what toy they would make, made it, and bundled the remaining sup-

plies together. They presented me with their unused materials in the original packaging. Then they waited for the fifteen minutes to be up. There were five minutes remaining.

While this was happening I noticed the Idealists still at play, inventing, reinventing, sharing, and contributing more ideas to their "playmates."

And the Rationals? Well, they were talking. I walked over to their cluster and reminded them that we needed to see their toy in five minutes. They did their best to ignore my interruption. I persevered and they began to interact with the supplies, somewhat reluctantly.

When the time for the task was over, the Artisans burst into the room carrying a big cardboard box decorated with giftwrap and inflated balloons of many colors. The Guardians sat quietly. The Rationals showed intrigue and disgust. The Idealists kept playing.

What were the toys? The Artisans presented first. They showed us the box, as a magician would demonstrate that there is nothing up his sleeve. Teasingly slow, they began to unwrap it, inciting great curiosity from all who watched. "Good," they said. "Now that we have your attention…" The Artisans explained that a good child's toy invites curiosity and wonder. They said the mystery behind what's in the box is as much a part of the play as the contents itself. Then, in one skillful pour, they dumped the contents of the box on the floor for all to see. There were all the materials, in a pile, colors and textures intermixed in a collection of sensory delight. As the finale to their presentation, the Artisans reminded us that for a child to truly enjoy a toy, the child must see and play with and experiment with and engage in all the wondrous things in front of him.

The Guardians presented next. They showed us how they assembled the straws to the length of a fishing pole, strung the pole with a strand of colored yarn, and affixed a paper clip to the end of the yarn. On the paperclip hung an aluminum fish. They said that this toy was a prototype for a fishpond game—a prototype because they would never give a young child something that might be dangerous, like a paperclip that may be opened and hurt someone or aluminum with sharp edges. They told us they thought their toy was boring, even though it was colorful and simple in execution. One Guardian mentioned having an important childhood memory of fishing with her father and how she goes fishing now with her children. At this point, one of the Idealists blurted, "Hey! We didn't think of that one!" And the rest of their group giggled.

Then the Idealists presented. They each, individually, demonstrated different ways a child could experience aspects of herself by the way she interacted with the different materials. They agreed that playing with the child was important as was helping her to make up stories to go with each of the creations as they built them. Some examples of their toys: passion blow straws to send kisses long distance to loved ones, pie-plate hats that could be tied onto the head with colored yarn as protectors against scary people. Popsicle stick drumsticks for beating on drums made from aluminum pie plates sealed together with the paperclips inside. As they demonstrated the last of their multiple applications, they eventually all stood and danced to the percussive rhythm of their new "tambourine."

Finally the Rationals presented, harrumphing a little as they did. The spokesperson announced that they had more or less agreed that it was useless to put a toy together for a child. Instead, they agreed, more or less, that the child must learn how to play with each of the items individually, and then in combination, considering the different aspects presented by each item, and that they, the Rationals, would show the child how to do this. As a result of the interaction, the child would know more about the interplay of color, texture, and shape.

Four different outlooks, four different temperament patterns, four different ways of demonstrating creativity. The bottom-line definition of creativity is coming up with something new and useful. All the temperament groups did that. By the end of the workshop, all could see their own style of approaching a creative task and marveled at how others did it so differently. There were big "ahas" all around.

Key Learnings from the Workshop about Temperament Motivations in Generating Ideas

When you look for good ideas, what are you really looking for?

- Artisans want ideas that make best use of what is at hand, break boundaries, and can be acted upon immediately.

- Guardians want ideas that work, are safe, can be planned and easily implemented, and at the same time conserve resources.

- Rationals want ideas that efficiently integrate and use new knowledge.

- Idealists want ideas that stretch and develop human potential as well as honor the people involved.

Needs and Outcomes

You interact with people on a daily basis whose natural energy falls predominantly in one of the four temperament energy patterns. This case study, as well as the information provided leading to it, demonstrates the different needs and outcomes you might expect from engaging in creative activities with these people.

If you are involving a team of mixed temperaments in an idea-generating or creative problem-solving session, here are some of the expectations they might bring with them.

"Our result must include an order, a procedure, and demonstrate efficiency. It must also build from other successful endeavors."

GUARDIAN

"Our result must have impact, be immediately doable, and involve a modicum of risk."

ARTISAN

"Our result must align with important values and ethics."

IDEALIST

"Our result must include another perspective of truth and provide intellectual challenge."

RATIONAL

To dig deeper, gain greater insights, make extended connections, and more fully explore the dynamics of the motivations behind each of the four temperament patterns, take a look at the Temperament Targets™ on the following two pages.

The Temperament Targets™ display an interrelated group of characteristics meant to reflect the essence of the represented temperament. A particular individual may find a few characteristics on his or her own target that he or she does not identify with, but overall, the characteristics on that target provide a fairly accurate description for that person. Likewise, an individual may find a few characteristics on other targets he or she identifies with, but one target will offer a more comprehensive description. In general, all of us experience most of the characteristics listed on these targets at times. But if we ask what a particular characteristic means to an individual of each of the four temperaments, we discover that for one temperament, that characteristic is well defined and articulated with passion. It is revered, trusted, and utilized by that individual in a way different from the others. Essentially, it is who that person is, not just something he or she does.

The Graphic Representation

The concentric ring formation is best visualized as a sphere, with the needs being the inner core from which all else emanates. The values, talents, and behaviors are the surest ways in which the core needs are met and expressed.

Needs

The needs represent the basic psychological needs of the temperament, the driving force. Individuals, unconsciously and consciously, seek every avenue to have these needs met. When these needs are met, the individual is energized and light of spirit. When these needs are not met, the individual is drained of energy and suffers dissatisfaction or stress.

Awareness of our psychological needs helps identify what motivates or inspires us and gives clues as to what may bring the greatest personal satisfaction.

Our core needs are often invisible to us and to others. These are so much the essence of who we are, it does not occur to us to name them. We assume these are the same needs of all human beings, so it is assumed we need not discuss them. It would be like announcing, "My name is…, and I am a human being," every time you meet someone new.

Values

The values are not just beliefs but what an individual considers innately worthwhile. The values provide sustenance. The energy expended on them comes back in an increased amount and satisfies the core needs.

Awareness of our values helps us understand why particular things have great importance for us. This may also give us clues about what we assume others will consider important. Energy can be increased through the expression of our values.

Our values are usually known to us, but we may choose not to convey them openly. Sometimes others can guess our values by observing our actions. We are likely to assume others share our values, but experience quickly proves otherwise.

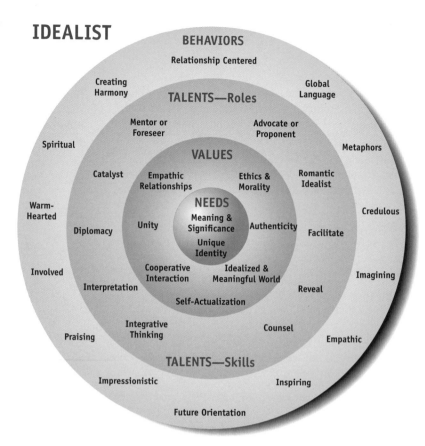

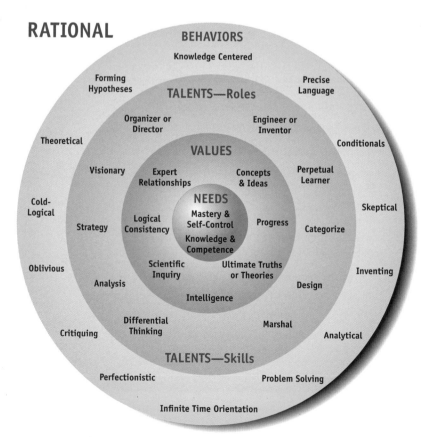

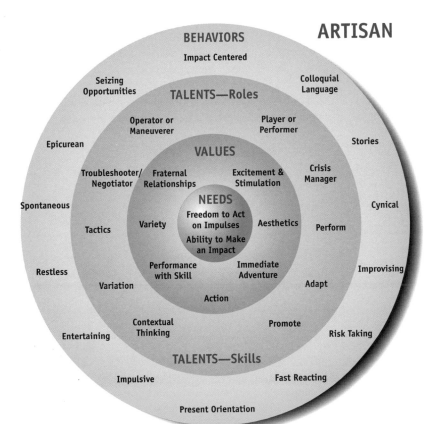

Talents

The talents are the natural gifts and abilities. Regardless of occupation or training, these roles and skills can be identified in the personal and work lives of the individuals. It is not just that they can do these things, but they cannot *not* do them. These talents require minimal energy output and result in high quality performance, one equation for self-esteem.

Awareness of our talents helps us identify our natural abilities, those roles and skills that capitalize on our innate assets. Engaging our talents can reduce stress and provide the greatest opportunity for satisfaction.

Our talents are often better known to our friends and colleagues than to ourselves because they observe the talents we take for granted. Because we use our talents with such ease, we assume everyone can do the same as we do. But others observe our ease and commend our talent because they appreciate what hard work it would be for them to do the same.

Behaviors

The behaviors are everyday actions we can observe or hear an individual demonstrate. These behaviors have a direct line to meeting the core needs.

Awareness of our behaviors helps us understand why we do and say things that may seem very different from or very similar to what others around us do or say. It can also help us know what things will satisfy our core needs.

Our behaviors are observable by ourselves and others, yet we may not recognize how important they are to who we are. We tend to take these behaviors for granted, and others are likely to notice them.

Parallel Construction

It is helpful for the sake of comparison to know that the Temperament Targets™ are designed in parallel fashion. The placement of each word on a target corresponds to a particular theme. For example, in the six o'clock position of the "Behaviors" ring is the "time orientation." This is true for all four targets.

The Purpose

It is useful to know ourselves, important to value ourselves, and imperative to value others. All endeavors have the greatest potential for success when all four temperament perspectives are taken into account. The intent of these targets is to promote a view of the individual that seeks the collaboration of others. Use them to know yourself and shift your perspective to understand others.

The Words: Meanings and Usage

For definitions of how these words are intended to be used, please see Appendix B: Glossary for the Temperament Targets™.

Using Temperament to Inspire Creativity

> Before you go about inspiring the creativity of others, you first must know exactly what you are inspiring.

What is creativity to you? What are you attempting to accomplish?

- To use "out of the box" thinking?
- To set and hold the climate for personal expression?
- To consider alternative probabilities?
- To embrace a new vision?
- To experience freedom and fun?
- To come up with new workable ideas?

All of these, you say? That's a big task to accomplish in one session.

Quick Tips

Encourage creativity in others by affirming their gifts and giving tasks and challenges that speak to their voices or interests. This is more easily accomplished when you are clear about and appreciate your own gifts.

For easier understanding and application, let's break it down into bite-sized pieces using the Intrinsic Motivation Theory of Creativity—engaging aspects of others in tasks they like or are interested in—as a base. Also, let's keep in mind that creativity is the spark of life with which each of us is born. When we tap creativity in others and ourselves, what we are essentially doing is tapping into the human spirit.

> Here's how the human spirit is tapped in each of the four temperaments and how each of the temperaments contributes to our survival.

IDEALIST

Championing a cause, encouraging others, unifying diverse factions, improving relationships among people, inspiring others, revitalizing morale, interpreting trends from a human dimension, empathizing with others, developing human potential, seeking common ground, mediating disputes.

Idealists want to make a difference in meaningful ways. They synthesize and harmonize the human spirit to maximize group synergy and output.

GUARDIAN

Assessing situations for safety and security, sequencing processes, getting the right amount to the right people and not the wrong amount to the wrong people, enforcing procedures, stabilizing chaos, specifying resources, protecting group accord and progress, organizing people and things, making plans more efficient.

Guardians structure and standardize the human spirit to maximize its cohesion and efficient use for improvements.

RATIONAL

Analyzing systems, building prototypes, defining challenges, searching for systemic inefficiencies, designing models, conceptualizing potentials, classifying competencies, questioning ideas, forecasting, exploring probabilities, visioning futures, hypothesizing, deducing rudiments of global truths, inventing strategies.

Rationals understand the human spirit from a conceptual base. They identify the variables, systems, and ideas used to model theories for consideration.

ARTISAN

Adapting to the needs of a situation, performing with skill and panache, negotiating agreements, entertaining others through speech and action, making things happen, responding to the needs of the moment, improvising and troubleshooting, varying applications.

Artisans manipulate opportunities in the immediate environment (including people) to produce impactful and simple solutions. They cater to the sensual experience of the human spirit.

Each temperament has its own voice that makes specific contributions to our system of creative survival. Put the four energies together—synthesizing and harmonizing, structuring and standardizing, sensually impacting, and conceptually understanding the nature of the human spirit—and you have the human creative experience in total.

How to Use This Information

To encourage creativity in others, identify who does what most naturally and

1. Encourage them to engage in activities that require that focus.

2. Help them to stretch, learn, and use skills associated with the other temperament patterns in a physically and psychologically safe environment.

Long-Term Commitment

Influencing the creation of the desired climate supports people doing their best work.

To seriously actualize and sustain a fulfilling change for creativity, allow yourself a process pattern, method, system, or structure for staying aware of what you are doing. Check your progress in honoring the temperament themes in each of the nine "climate" factor areas: challenge and involvement, trust and openness, freedom, idea support, humor and playfulness, idea time, conflict, debate, and risk taking (pages 19–22).

Review the suggestions accompanying the factor descriptions entitled "What's a leader to do?" and begin a program to encourage and sustain the environment. Nothing prevents successful execution and implementation of initiatives more than lack of committed follow-through. Be careful. Be wise.

Grant yourself patience. Changing behaviors takes time and encouraging reinforcement.

Walk the talk. Actions speak louder than words.

Do your best to determine the temperament patterns of the individuals you would like to support you. Use the descriptions of the Temperament patterns to put together a presentation and rationale for support in each temperament's voice. Remember to list the benefits in all four temperament languages. Your presentation may look something like this:

By improving the day-to-day climate in our organization, division, unit, office, we will improve morale, create new knowledge, pro-vide greater opportunities for breakthrough, and use our time efficiently and effectively when problem solving and decision making.

What You're Up Against

Before we discuss tools to encourage creative expression, incremental change, boundary breaking, and perspective shifting, we need to examine some fundamental truths about creativity.

Creativity, besides inspiring growth and progress, also connotes destruction and death. Recall the myth of Persephone and the underworld. As an allegory of the farmers' experience of the growth cycle from barrenness to fertility, this myth reminds us that there is death, and there is life afterward.

To embrace the new, the old must be let go. Endings foster new beginnings. Each new occurrence holds the potential for infinite new possibilities.

George Land shows us this cycle in his book *Breakpoint and Beyond* (1992). A revered researcher of general systems, Land has simply and elegantly identified a three-phase common theme of growth.

Phase 1: Exploring and Inventing

Confusion and a willingness to explore result in risking, reaching out, and inventing.

Examples:

A seedling sends out roots to explore the environment for nutrients.

A new relationship begins with dating.

An entrepreneur who sees an opportunity for new business hangs her shingle on the door.

Phase 2: Repeating and Improving

Control and order are emphasized. Patterns are duplicated. Specialization and incremental improvements occur.

Examples:

After finding nutrients, the seedling grows into a tree as cell replication occurs and specialized genetic coding causes branches and leaves to emerge.

The couple decides to commit to their relationship. They become comfortable with each other and the roles each has assumed in maintaining their connection.

The entrepreneur has met with success in her endeavor and finds ways to standardize and improve her offerings, including hiring staff and establishing production and delivery schedules, to support the continuation of her successful business.

Phase 3: Maturing and Transforming

Old patterns break down, leading to discomfort and confusion with a strong emotional pull to return to the past. Anxiety about the future prevails. This phase is also known as "when the rules change."

Examples:

A drought hits the area of the tree. It dies.

One of the partners in the relationship wants to maintain what they have; the other wants to explore other options. Due to their disagreement on direction, their compatibility suffers and the relationship ends.

Conditions in the environment have shifted consumers away from using the product made by the company. Competition increases as others in the industry offer the same product as well as greater customer satisfaction at a lower price. The company goes out of business.

Based on these observable constants on all known levels of existence, Land supports the notion of death being the end. He goes on to show that organisms, relationships, or businesses that shift with the signals of Phase 3 do so by directing energy toward a new Phase 1—the afterlife, so to speak.

New Phase 1: Exploring and Inventing

Old patterns are reviewed and some are salvaged while others let go. Refocusing of the vision occurs. Information and resources are gathered as new methods are piloted. New people are partnered with. The shift in energy invites invention and innovation.

Examples:

Low water levels trigger the tree's genetic programming to produce seeds that later scatter.

Free from a confining relationship, both former partners appreciate the wisdom of their experience and eventually enter new relationships with other people.

Rather than totally "throw in the towel," the entrepreneur surveys her market, benchmarks what her successful competitors are doing, and initiates strategic alliances with a company in another business sector.

Bottom-Line Message

Growth can and does occur when we pay attention and shift our energy when the rules change. Two business examples of this are taking place as this book is being written. There is controversy over an Internet site from which people can download music at no cost—signaling a rule change to the music industry. Another example is an Internet player and new software that are threatening the way phone companies receive revenues from long-distance calling. Watch how (or if) these industries shift their energies to work with the new rules.

On a simplistic level, dealing with your creativity means that you must let go of some old thinking, some previous notions, and some seemingly unconscious patterning. Consider that you are in Phase 2 and the rules are changing. If you maintain your current course, endings are imminent. Some of the traps of Phase 2 thinking are accepting our assumptions as truth, defending routines, blaming others, controlling people, hoarding resources, and engaging in competition so others lose.

To help shift your energy, focus and attention, you need to metaphorically "step up to the plate" with courage to embrace the unknown. And you must also be prepared to decide which of your patterns serve you and which no longer do. You must eliminate or replace the latter in some way, perhaps by making friends with the obstacles that keep you from initiating something new and relevant and finding out from those obstacles just where your areas of growth lie.

One assumption I am making is that you are looking for ways to enliven your own creativity as well as the creativity of others. Consider this: You are the one who is ultimately responsible for making that happen.

"If it is to be, it is up to me."
—Anonymous

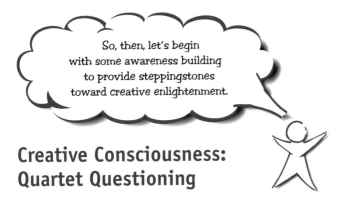

So, then, let's begin with some awareness building to provide steppingstones toward creative enlightenment.

Creative Consciousness: Quartet Questioning

What follows is a walk-through for you to use to inspire emerging creative energies. It can be used to enter a new Phase 1 (in Land's theory) or when you feel blocked.

These questions are facilitative triggers based on the wisdom of the different temperament voices. As you begin the exercise, imagine you are interacting with a guide from each temperament. These questions represent a balanced and whole approach for creative inspiration.

Each of us has one prevailing temperament pattern or theme. And each of the questions, though specifically identified with one of the four, does not preclude value when approached from another temperament perspective. Each response will assist your creative development and help you to overcome some blocks to your development, outlook, and learning. You may find some questions more challenging to respond to. This is natural. Persevere rather than leave a response blank.

One way to interact with these questions is to write your responses down in a free-flow manner without any concern about them being right or wrong. All responses are valuable.

- When you have completed the entire set, begin to review, add to, and modify what you have.

- Mark with a star those responses that you find exciting, compelling, and involving enough for you to want to move forward on.

- Then, commit to acting on one.

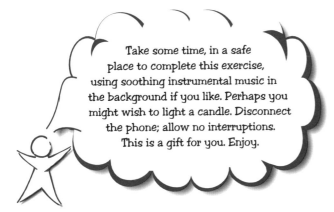

Take some time, in a safe place to complete this exercise, using soothing instrumental music in the background if you like. Perhaps you might wish to light a candle. Disconnect the phone; allow no interruptions. This is a gift for you. Enjoy.

Questions to Inspire Emerging Creative Energies

How might I stimulate and vary my environment for needed energy?

How might I recognize and find new options within the current context?

What new activities might I engage in?

In what ways might I organize and stabilize chaotic situations and securely proceed?

In what ways might I be included effectively in creative activities?

What roles might I assume as a creative person?

In what ways might I innovate to fully understand the system at hand?

In what ways might I reconfirm my competencies?

What new projects might I initiate?

In what ways might I appreciate and affirm others?

In what ways might I feel nurtured and appreciated?

What new searches might inspire me?

These facilitative questions help you become aware of your creating patterns as well as invite you to increase your perceptions and willingness to explore areas you might otherwise ignore. In essence, they will help you bridge from Phase 3 to new Phase 1.

You may wish to revisit your earlier reflections on pages 8–11 for the purpose of comparison, synthesis, and assistance. Some actions listed in "Getting to Specifics" (see page 8) may trigger your thinking about ways to move on your desire. By reviewing your ranking of the basic human urges, you may find the theme of your current area of new Phase 1 growth.

Clues for Understanding Others' Fears about Creating

People of different temperament energies were asked to respond to this question: What is your greatest fear about your being creative? Here's a sampling of their responses.

> *"What moves men of genius, or rather what inspires their work, is not new ideas, but their obsession with the idea that what has already been said is still not enough."*
> **—Eugene Delacroix**

IDEALIST

Lack of unique personal meaning. This lack of meaning is experienced through insincerity, betrayal, and lack of integrity. Idealists fear not being recognized for their gifts.

Some questions for Idealists to consider:

- How might I nurture my true personal expression?
- How might others appreciate and nurture me?
- What new search might inspire me?

GUARDIAN

Lack of belonging and responsibility. When Guardians sense this lack, they talk about experiences of abandonment, insubordination, and not belonging. Guardians fear not being of useful service to others.

Some questions for Guardians to consider:

- How might I organize and stabilize chaotic situations and securely proceed?
- How might I be appreciated and included in creative activities?
- What new roles might I consider for myself as a creative group member?

RATIONAL

Lack of competence. When Rationals talk about this lack, they say they experience it as powerlessness, ineptitude, and lack of knowledge. Rationals fear not having knowledge.

Some questions for Rationals to consider:

- How might I innovate on an intellectual plane, to fully understand the system at hand?
- How might I reconfirm my competencies?
- What new projects might I initiate?

ARTISAN

Lack of freedom and opportunity. When Artisans sense this lack, they talk about boredom, constraints, and lack of impact. Artisans fear not having an impact.

Some questions for Artisans to consider:

- How might I stimulate and vary my environment for needed energy?
- How might I recognize and find new options within the current context?
- What new activities might I engage in?

The opposites of fear are confidence, faith, and courage. These questions are provided for you to help shift from a less desirable to a more desirable emotion.

Use these as beginning points to appreciate your own obstacles as well as barriers affecting others. These facilitative questions are offered to help you overcome obstacles. Feel free to use them for yourself and also when in conversation with others.

> *"Teachers open the door, but you must enter yourself."*
> **—Chinese proverb**

Summary of Learnings

Applying Temperament and Creativity to Yourself and Someone You Like: A Colleague, Partner, Child, or Friend

Your Temperament Voice of Creativity	His/Her Temperament Voice of Creativity
My temperament pattern (from pages 29–45)	**His/her temperament pattern** (from pages 29-45)
How my temperament pattern considers creativity (from page 36)	**How his/her temperament pattern considers creativity** (from pages 36)
What my temperament pattern looks for in creative ideas (from page 47)	**What his/her temperament pattern looks for in creative ideas** (from page 47)
What my temperament pattern wants in the way of creative outcomes (from page 47)	**What his/her temperament pattern wants in the way of creative outcomes** (from page 47)
My temperament pattern's contribution to the "human spirit" (from page 50)	**His/her temperament pattern's contribution to the "human spirit"** (from page 50)
What my temperament pattern fears about being creative (from page 54)	**What his/her temperament pattern fears about being creative** (from page 54)

How might we work together to honor our different creative energies?

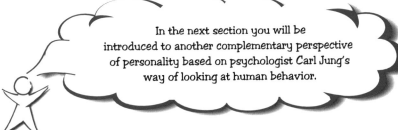

In the next section you will be introduced to another complementary perspective of personality based on psychologist Carl Jung's way of looking at human behavior.

Notes

3

Jung's Theory of Psychological Type

Jung's Theory of Psychological Type

More Ways to Discover Your Creative Voice

Temperament energy is one way to consider creative voice. The wisdom of Swiss psychologist Carl Jung reveals another.

Both frameworks offer important leads for recognizing and inspiring creativity. Each gives important clues for tools to use when leading an idea-generating session or looking for "creative" ideas.

In this section you will be introduced to Jung's theory of the cognitive processes of psychological type and shown how they interact to maintain balance. These processes, and their development over time, lend insights to creative activity. They contain within them the seeds of the stirrings, the little voices, and the glimpses of truth from which we can choose to transform and create.

Real-world examples of the processes in action are given at the end of the section for you to more fully appreciate these unique perspectives.

Introduction

Dr. Jung's book *Psychological Types* was first published in 1921. Instruments have been developed to help individuals find where they fit within his theory. The Myers Briggs Type Indicator® (MBTI®) is one. If you have already used it and know your personality type code, then the following information will refresh and add to your knowledge.

If you have yet to be exposed to psychological type theory, then use the information that follows to find how you express and experience life using this theory. Match your energy pattern, as you know it, with what is presented. Qualified professionals in psychological type have an ethic to give more weight to a person's self-assessment than to what the MBTI reports. So pay attention and honor your self-assessment.

Here are a few basics about psychological type theory:

1. It comes from Carl Jung's theory of personality.

2. All people are drawn to use, or prefer, certain cognitive processes for accessing information and making decisions.

3. Cognitive process preferences are dichotomous. We have a natural pull to use one of the pair of each dichotomy more so than the other.

4. Cognitive process preferences are innate. Environment impacts their development.

5. Cognitive process preferences are not the same as ability or skill. Consider them instead as antenna for attracting and emitting certain energy frequency information.

6. The cognitive processes interact in a dynamic fashion for balance in our personal energy system.

7. As we age, we are inclined to develop an ability to tune into other frequencies in addition to our natural cognitive process preferences.

8. All cognitive processes are valuable.

9. We can and do develop skills associated with our nonpreferences. The lifelong innate push for development encourages this to happen.

10. We are born unconscious and continue to become more conscious as we grow and experience life on this planet. Jung called this "individuation."

11. The drive for individuation is innate.

12. The more we become aware of our cognitive process preferences and development, the better able we are to choose which we use.

The Processes of Our Energy System

Jung's theory proposes that human behavior is not random but patterned according to how we access information and make decisions. We engage in both of these cognitive processes in one of two orientations. One is experienced when introverting; the other, when extraverting.

Introverting Processes

When introverting, we reflect, consider, think, and mentally review. All of us engage in introverting activities some of the time. When we introvert, we often personalize the events in our environment. The world comes to meet us. And sometimes our awareness is universal.

We introvert primarily in four ways:

• By mentally recalling past experiences.

• By foreseeing future implications.

• By analyzing based on closely held principles of truth.

• By valuing using a ranking of importance.

Which of the processes is used at what time varies from individual to individual.

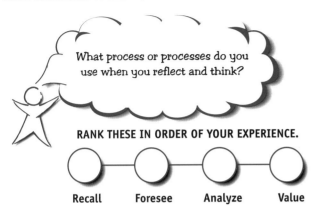

Extraverting Processes

Using the extraverting orientation, we interact with others and things in our environment. Here we engage with the world outside of ourselves. All of us use these processes some of the time. We use extraverted energy to go out to meet the world.

When we use the extraverting processes, we do so primarily in four ways:

- By fully experiencing the moment.
- By inferring global potentials and meanings.
- By structuring things and processes.
- By harmonizing people according to their needs.

Notice that in each of the four processes the focus is external, in our immediate and particular environment.

Two people extraverting may be quite similar in that they actively engage in conversation to initiate some action. However, what they talk about and their specific actions may be quite different depending on which of the extraverting processes they are using.

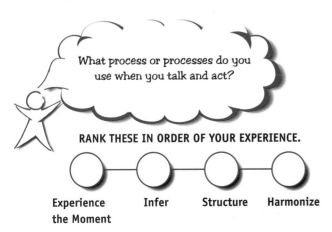

Summary

We use cognitive processes in both the extraverting and introverting orientations. When we extravert, we talk and participate with people and things in an active way. When we introvert, we are quiet and reflective and internally active. We do both naturally.

Creative Stirring

Stirrings for creative activity come from both worlds—inner and outer.

An external event may trigger an inner consciousness. New thinking occurs that may lead to a heightened awareness.

For example, while conducting business as usual, the stock market suddenly nosedives. This external event impacts Stan's values surrounding how he invested his personal resources for future security. He begins to recognize his true values. Whereas before he thought his priority was all about money and material gains, he now sees how the relationships he has in his life are the most important things for him to maintain. The outer event triggered a new personal awareness.

An outer-world event may trigger an outer-world response.

Stan's main competitor has just re-introduced a product line they both carry. He reviews how his advertising budget is spent and restructures his ad for a better placement and greater targeted attention. He also hires salespeople on contract to generate more sales and establishes a measure to gauge the effectiveness of this program.

Alternatively, an internal wish may provoke a desire to make changes in the world outside.

Ever since he was a boy, Stan has had a dream of walking the Great Wall of China. Now middle-aged, Stan wants to realize his dream. He starts to walk on a daily basis to get into shape and begins to study Chinese so he'll have some comfort when he finally makes the trip. His new activities change the organization of his day and lead him to meet new people.

An inner stirring may inspire internal change.

Stan's partner, Stella, brings home materials related to personality type from a weekend workshop.

When Stan reads the materials, something clicks with him about how the two of them communicate. He learns about his natural tendencies to speak first and ask questions later and how this affects Stella's naturally quiet demeanor. Stan learns to appreciate Stella's silences and begins to consider being a little more thoughtful himself. In his reveries he discovers new memories and lessons from people important to him that otherwise would not have come to mind. He begins to pay more attention to the other people around him too and to consider what he offers to them by way of learning.

In and out, out and in, out and out, in and in—which one of the orientations provides the first trumpet call, the stirring, the glimpse? All. Actualizing and sustaining fulfilling change engages each.

Finding out which is your favorite orientation is a good first step to inspire the creative spark in yourself and others. Let's decide which of these two orientations predominates for you. Once you know, you can more easily shift to the other to gain greater insights for action.

Favorite Orientation

Our favorite orientation is the one we seek out and enjoy. We prefer it because using it energizes us.

What happens with your energy when you spend more time introverting? What happens to your energy when you spend more time extraverting?

People who favor introverting say that when they spend an excessive amount of time extraverting, they become tired and stressed. They tell us they do their best work when they have time to reflect and incubate about ideas.

Those who favor extraverting report that they get antsy when in the introverting orientation for too long. They say they become uncomfortable with silence and fill "dead air."

Jung wrote that we balance our energy by both extraverting and introverting, and it is not necessarily a fifty-fifty split.

When involved in idea-generating activities, make sure to tap both introverting and extraverting orientations.

> **Give a percentage ranking to each orientation. Where do you feel your natural preferences are?**
>
> My Orientations: Extraverting _____ % Introverting _____ %
>
> **Which would you say is your favorite orientation?**

Culturally, it may seem more appropriate to engage in one orientation rather than the other. This is disappointing. It places a value on one being the "better" one or the "right" one. When you were a child, which of the two was valued more in your family? At school? And now, at work?

Fortunately, Jung and the MBTI developers give equal value to both. The value of extraverting is interaction and engagement. The value of introverting is reflection and consideration.

Knowing that people have different orientation preferences is a big help when leading idea-generating sessions. As an example, people with introverting preferences tend to like to write their thoughts. They claim to need some time to think before expressing options. People with extraverting preferences tend to express their options as they are thinking them.

Voices of Cognitive Processes

Within the orientations we use different cognitive processes. Each one resonates to a unique frequency and offers a different pattern of mental activity.

Some of these processes form perceptions. Others form conclusions.

Each process holds a different kind of energy, and when we use it, we align with information and make decisions that vibrate in its same frequency.

For simplicity, let's consider each cognitive process as a different voice. Let's use the voice metaphor to examine the whole collection of cognitive processes described by Jung.

A Brief Explanation of the Cognitive Processes
The Perceiving Processes

In total, four cognitive processes are used to access information. These are clustered into two groupings around the kind of information sought.

Two cognitive processes resonate with information that is concrete, tangible, specific. The other two attract and transmit information that is abstract, patterned, and general. We use each, one more than the others.

To enter the world of self-discovery using this system, pay attention to which one of the four perceiving processes is more natural for you. Ask yourself, "Where is the first place I go to notice and share information about my reality?"

Concrete Perceiving Processes

Of the two concrete perceiving processes, one is accessed when introverting; the other, when extraverting. Although their theme of concreteness is shared, the frequency vibrations of concreteness are unique.

Using one process, we access concrete information externally. That is, using extraverted Sensing (coded as Se), we

- experience the moment and the swirl of information available.
- actively interact with textures, smells, sensations, people, colors, and tangible evidence in our immediate surroundings.
- create based on what's needed now.
- rely on being adaptable to fit the external context.

Using the other process, we access concrete information stored internally. Using introverted Sensing (coded as Si), we

- compare what we are experiencing with what we already specifically know.
- rely on benchmark memories to guide our understanding and appreciation of the present.
- create based on past successes and failures.
- remember details and impressions.

Both processes involve perceiving information that is concrete, tangible, and in the present. The first experiences stimulation from the world outside while the second recalls from inner memory.

Someone who speaks in the Se voice may be so in the moment that neither the past nor the future holds much allure. Despite a plan to execute an idea, Se information might totally alter the person's role as he or she sees fit to deal with the situation at hand. Things change.

In response to a new idea, the Se voice may say, "Sure, why not?" fully expecting to act in the moment to actualize it.

A person speaking in the Si voice remembers almost everything, even without taking notes. The Si voice recalls promises others made three years ago—and those that were kept.

In response to a new idea, the Si voice may say, "We tried that before and here's what happened," fully expecting the same to happen again.

Abstract Perceiving Processes

As in the concrete process descriptions, there is a pattern in abstract perceiving as well. One abstract perceiving process is extraverted; the other, introverted. Both have unique frequencies.

When we use the external abstract process, extraverted iNtuiting (coded as Ne), we

- journey from the present moment into abstract patterns and potentials to infer what might be.
- leap to generalizable insights about the meaning of the moment.
- create theories of what might be behind the stimulus in front of us.
- see relationships between elements in our surroundings and easily share our "whole," or big picture, in an idealized conceptual way.

The internal abstract perceiving process is almost devoid of tangible reality. It holds instead conceptual inner connections and associations. When we use the internal abstract process of introverted iNtuiting (coded as Ni), we

- perceive true symbolic meaning arising out of a place we can pinpoint.
- holistically attune to images, ideas, notions, concepts, and archetypal patterns all floating and streaming inside our knowing.
- create conceptual systems.
- foresee the future, with certainty, often far removed from time and space from current reality as experienced by others.

Both processes share a focus on potentials, futures, and concepts. The first experiences stimulation from the world outside and generates new abstract ideas for what might be in the external world. The second process perceives internally from a richness of symbolic associations. It's like both are different shades of blue.

When using extraverted iNtuiting (Ne), we generate limitless future potentials based on current conditions. Options of future promise are offered up sometimes in a popcorn-like fashion with one or many ideas bouncing off of each other in rapid succession.

When asked to consider a new idea, the Ne voice may respond with, "Oh, how about…" fully expecting to generate additional ideas.

When using introverted iNtuiting (Ni), we connect disparate information and conceptualize future outcomes. We may also be insistent that before a project can begin, the vision must be articulated in terms of the long-range goal or objective.

Give introverted iNtuiting (Ni) a new idea to consider and this voice may respond by saying either "yes" or "no," fully expecting you to know how this announces its match to his or her internal vision.

So we have four different perceiving processes, each a different voice, each valuable. Each is looking to match and represent its natural energies. And each is active in you at different levels of intensity.

By theory, one energizes you more and has for a long time. And because of development, the others may have become more active recently. Can you discern which of the four prevails for you?

Rank these in order of which you do first, second, third, and fourth. If you find this challenging, read the following section and chart first and compare yourself to the examples given. Then come back and do the ranking as best you can.

◯ **Extraverted Sensing (Se)** interacts with the richness of the tangible moment in a questioning way.

◯ **Introverted Sensing (Si)** compares an event against a set of established personal past experiences.

◯ **Extraverted iNtuiting (Ne)** generates global potentials for the future in a questioning way.

◯ **Introverted iNtuiting (Ni)** accesses future visions and conceptual symbols.

The Perceiving Processes in the Real World

Let's see what these voices are like on a nice day in the park. Imagine them encountering a tree. How might the perceptions vary?

Using **Extraverted Sensing (Se),** we see the tree and experience the variety of colors, distinct textures, smells, shapes, and size of the tree, reveling in the coolness of its shade.

Using **Introverted Sensing (Si)**, we see the tree and remember other trees just like this—including the one in our childhood backyard, and how it grew from a mere sapling into a grand specimen of tree, and the games we played.

Using **Extraverted iNtuiting (Ne)**, we see the tree and enthusiastically begin to generate ideas to improve on the idea of "tree" and what else trees might be used for or what else might be trees in relationship to other natural phenomena.

Using **Introverted iNtuiting (Ni)**, we see the tree, its symbolism, and what it offers. We recognize it as a conceptual clue as an integrated whole within a larger world.

Now let's move the voices into the boardroom at budget time. Imagine that they are working together to set the budget for the coming year.

Using **Extraverted Sensing (Se)**, we focus on the current data, what is happening now, and what is immediately needed.

Using **Introverted Sensing (Si)**, we pay attention to budget recommendations based on last year's successes and lessons learned.

Using **Extraverted iNtuiting (Ne)**, we generate unorthodox budget options for opportunities the organization may explore.

Using **Introverted iNtuiting (Ni)**, we recommend budget considerations for the long-range future aligned with our vision for the group and the organization.

The chart* on the next page shows each of the four perceiving processes in more depth.

---

*The chart has been taken, with permission, from Linda V. Berens, *Dynamics of Personality Type: Understanding and Applying Jung's Cognitive Processes* (Huntington Beach, Calif.: Telos Publications, 2000).

Essential Characteristics of the Perceiving Processes

Extraverted Sensing **Se**
—**Experiencing**
—**Doing**
—**Observing and Responding**
—**Adapting and Varying**
—*Present*

• Current perceptions vividly capturing attention
• Paying attention to what stands out and is impactful
• Becoming aware of rich sensory details

• Noticing what's happening "now" as it changes
• Scanning the current situation for relevant information

• Energy going to more and new stimulation

• Focusing on possibilities for action
• Talking about things to do, actions to take
• Asking for specific details to perceive the pattern
• Reading minimal nonverbal cues
• Seeking aesthetic purity and pleasure in experiences
• Attention turning outward to more sensory input

• Living an experience

"This is what is."
"What's next?"

Extraverted iNtuiting **Ne**
—**Inferring**
—**Hypothesizing**
—**Seeing Potentials**
—**Wondering and Brainstorming**
—*Emergent*

• Current perceptions sparking alternatives
• Paying attention to relationships and connections
• Becoming aware of patterns, implications, and meanings
• Noticing metacommunications and what is not said
• Scanning the current situation for what might possibly be
• Energy going to interactions to generate more possibilities
• Focusing on multiple aspects of the whole context
• Talking about possibilities, new ideas, meanings
• Asking, "Have you thought about . . . ?"
• Reading the meanings of a situation
• Seeking more possibilities, ideas, options
• Attention turning outward to more relationships and meanings
• Interpreting an experience

"This is what might be."
"It could be this or this or this or . . ."

Introverted Sensing **Si**
—**Recalling**
—**Linking**
—**Comparing and Contrasting**
—**Noticing Match and Mismatch**
—*Past*

• Current perceptions eliciting stored impressions

• Paying attention to similarities and differences
• Becoming aware of differences from what was
• Noticing discrepancies
• Scanning memory bank for related information
• Energy staying with the recalled image
• Focusing on past successes (or failures)
• Talking about past experiences
• Asking for history or prior experience
• Reading lessons from the past
• Seeking to avoid mistakes made before
• Attention turning inward to images of past impressions

• Reliving an experience

"This is how it has always been."
"This reminds me of . . ."

Introverted iNtuiting **Ni**
—**Foreseeing**
—**Conceptualizing**
—**Understanding Complex Patterns**
—**Synthesizing and Symbolizing**
—*Future*

• Current perceptions sparking insights into complex situations
• Paying attention to future implications
• Becoming aware of universal meanings and symbols
• Noticing whole patterns or systems
• Scanning internal images for insights
• Energy staying with the vision
• Focusing on depth of understanding
• Talking about the future and the meaning
• Asking, "What is the goal?"
• Reading the future and the potential in others
• Seeking innovative ideas or universal symbols
• Attention turning inward to images forming of the future
• Imagining and anticipating an experience

"This is how it will be."
"Aha, that's it!"

When generating ideas in groups, a variety of energies prevails. Each energy pattern is a voice of creativity—past, present, future, and forever. Think back to a time when people in an idea session were generating all these different kinds of ideas: here-and-now actualities, future potentials, past successes, and far future concepts? Now you know where these different perspectives came from.

Four voices, all aligned with their natural energies, contributing from the whole of human perception. Open your ears; hear the wisdom. Now that you know about these voices, you can begin to distinguish them. Now that you know them, you can feel how yours is one of many.

Consider shifting your perspective momentarily. Do you know what happens when you do? You open the door for another kind of personal creativity. Imagine perceiving differently, if only for a short period of time.

> To illustrate the importance of understanding your dynamic pattern of creative voices, let's try them on for size.

TIP In brainstorming activities, engage all four of the perceiving processes.

You are doing your best to position a new idea for acceptance by others, so you want to point out its features.

Using the Si voice you say...

Using the Se voice you say...

Using the Ne voice you say...

Using the Ni voice you say...

In creativity, many times the focus is on generating ideas. By doing the preceding exercise, you began to tap into the different ways people articulate informational energies that attract them to pay attention.

Generally, when we ideate, we use these four perceiving processes. Using this information you can easily adapt, modify, and add facilitative questions that get at all these four voices.

The downfall of many idea-generating sessions is that new ideas generated are evaluated by the same criteria we always use.

Decision making in creativity is critical. We spend a lot of time developing new considerations and then go back to the same old ways of reaching conclusions. Consider this: creativity also implies making decisions differently.

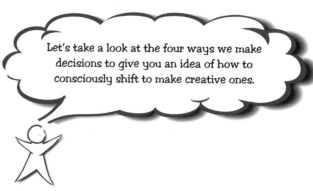

> Let's take a look at the four ways we make decisions to give you an idea of how to consciously shift to make creative ones.

The Judging Processes

Jung proposed that as well as having perceiving processes, we also have decision-making or judging processes.

There are four different and valuable ways in which we conclude about what we perceive. These judging energies are clustered into two groups:

- Decisions based on detached principles, discerning order and structure

- Decisions based on personal and social significance, discerning values and worth

Detached Judging Processes

As we saw in the perceiving processes, one judging process is accessed when introverting; the other, while extraverting. Both are used to make detached decisions and each has its own frequency.

The introverting objective judging process, introverted Thinking (coded as Ti), focuses us to

- internally analyze our external perceptions.

- consistently classify information within clear categories and principles.

- create definitions and frameworks for clarity of understanding.

- want to know how things work.

The extraverting objective judging process, extraverted Thinking (coded as Te), attracts us to

- externally structure our internal perceptions into logical and measurable steps and stages.

- objectively organize the things and the people in our environment to meet a goal.

- create measures for standardization and evaluation of success.

- plan goals and manage resources (including people) to meet them.

Do you hear the different voices? Do you see the differences? One is analyzing internally for accurate consistency; the other structures the external world with measures for accomplishing goals.

Someone speaking with the Ti voice makes decisions based on analyzing consistency with frameworks. Ti decision making is more of a checks-and-balances process, evaluating information according to an internal structure or logic. Information, rather than being judged good or bad, is categorized and subcategorized into unique compartments of truth.

How might someone using the Ti voice respond to deciding about a new idea? Likely, he or she asks for some time to consider it, seeking to better understand the categories involved, and fully expecting you to be category literate and open to questions.

When we use the Te voice, our approach is different. Te voices logical evaluation as opinion and shares it easily. Te decision making compartmentalizes, orders, and structures information using the principles of standards and accomplishment.

When faced with a new idea, someone using the Te voice will likely respond by stating standardizing ways to measure its success, fully expecting you to agree with Te's clean, objective logic.

Personal Judging Processes

We make decisions in other ways too, based on the values of importance and worth. And, as with all the others, one occurs with an introverted orientation; the other, with an extraverted one. As with all the others, the energy frequencies of each is quite unique.

When we use the internal personal process of introverted Feeling (coded as Fi), we

- internally evaluate external conditions by checking for ethical congruency.

- make decisions based on importance.

- create commitment for what is good for all.

- prioritize based on what we want and what is really important.

When we use the external personal process of extraverted Feeling (coded as Fe), we

- consider our decisions in terms of how others may respond and react.

- are concerned about others' welfare.

- create harmonious connections among and between people.

- help people realize what they need to do for their own good.

Both of these processes vibrate to a different frequency and both are anchored in using a value-ranking system for making decisions, either with an internal locus (good for me) or an external one (good for others).

When using the Fi voice, decision making includes considerations of beliefs, attitudes, and especially core values of what is universally right and wrong, good and bad. Fi helps us develop loyalties to decisions that are congruent with our sense of who we are and what we believe. This extends as well to organizational beliefs and attitudes as revealed through decisions made.

In response to a new idea, someone speaking the Fi voice will likely request time to consider it and ask questions about the intentionality of the idea to see how it aligns with universal or organizational values, fully expecting you to commit to it if it supports the value system in place.

When we use the Fe voice, we focus outward to the people, the environment, and on how well they match societal or cultural beliefs about rightness and wrongness. Attending to the needs of others supersedes the consideration of self. Connecting with others is important as well. Someone speaking the Fe voice likely asks people to talk about themselves to keep the conversation going, to stay connected with them, and to find more ways to adjust to their needs.

How might a person speaking the Fe voice respond to a new idea? He or she may first want to check with others to find out how they feel, fully expecting you to want to do the same.

We have four different judging frequencies, each a different voice, each valuable. Each is looking to match and represent its natural energies. And each one is active in us to some degree of intensity. One prevails in you. Can you discern which it is?

Rank these in order of which you do first, second, third, and fourth. If you find this challenging, read the following section and chart first and compare yourself to the examples given. Then come back and do the ranking as best you can.

○ **Introverted Thinking (Ti)** internally analyzes for consistency.

○ **Extraverted Thinking (Te)** externally organizes to accomplish objectives.

○ **Introverted Feeling (Fi)** internally considers congruency with values.

○ **Extraverted Feeling (Fe)** externally connects with others to serve their needs.

The Judging Processes in the Real World

Let's see what these voices are like on a beautiful day in the park. Imagine them encountering a tree. How might the decisions about it vary?

Using **Introverted Thinking (Ti)**, we classify the kind of tree it is.

Using **Extraverted Thinking (Te)**, we set a goal to come back to the park to see it again next autumn.

Using **Introverted Feeling (Fi)**, we immediately like or dislike the tree.

Using **Extraverted Feeling (Fe)**, we make a mental note to show this tree to our friend because we know how much our friend likes trees.

Now let's go to budget time. The four voices must decide on the budget for the coming year.

Using **Introverted Thinking (Ti)**, we analyze the consistency or fit of each recommendation with the goals and mission of the organization.

Using **Extraverted Thinking (Te)**, we structure, organize, and prioritize each recommendation and then evaluate each proposal on a "doable" basis.

Using **Introverted Feeling (Fi)**, we consider the good and bad aspects of each recommendation based on its congruence with our sense of the values of the organization.

Using **Extraverted Feeling (Fe)**, we appraise each proposal for its appropriateness of meeting the needs of the organization, its customers, and its suppliers.

The chart* on the next page shows each of the four judging processes in more depth.

---

*The chart has been taken, with permission, from Linda V. Berens, *Dynamics of Personality Type: Understanding and Applying Jung's Cognitive Processes* (Huntington Beach, Calif., Telos Publications, 2000).

Essential Characteristics of the Judging Processes

Extraverted Thinking **Te**
- —Being Organized
- —Coordinating and Sequencing
- —Segmenting
- —Checking Against Criteria
- —*Particular to What Is Here and Now*

- Talking about the steps to get things done
- Asking Socratic questions to clarify logic or make a point
- Evaluating priorities in reaching a goal
- Deciding about sequence, hierarchy, schedule
- Determining the required resources to achieve a goal
- Being guided by organizing principles and criteria
- Convincing with logical arguments
- Noticing the component parts and what's missing
- Focusing on cause and effect
- Looking for logic
- Searching for efficient organization
- Seeking to establish order and efficiency
- Organizing an experience

"This is how to do it."
"People do . . ."

Extraverted Feeling **Fe**
- —Being Considerate
- —Adjusting and Accommodating
- —Affirming
- —Checking Appropriateness
- —*Particular to What Is Here and Now*

- Talking about personal details
- Asking questions to find out what others need

- Evaluating appropriateness
- Deciding about what is friendly, nice, mean
- Determining what others want
- Being guided by harmonizing the group
- Convincing with self-disclosure and warmth
- Noticing what's important to others
- Focusing on consideration of others
- Looking for unexpressed wants and needs
- Searching for connection and affirmation
- Seeking to establish rapport and stay in touch
- Relating through an experience

"This is what we need."
"We do . . ."

Introverted Thinking **Ti**
- —Principles
- —Categorizing and Classifying
- —Analyzing
- —Checking Consistency
- —*Universal*

- Asking what is wrong, how something's not working
- Looking for concise, clear explanations
- Evaluating accuracy and internal consistency
- Deciding what kind of object something is
- Determining the defining characteristics
- Being guided by the reasons things work
- Convincing with clear, precise definitions

- Noticing inconsistencies and imprecision
- Focusing on thorough analysis, seeing all the angles
- Talking about how things match a model or blueprint

- Searching for a "leverage point" to fix things
- Seeking to solve problems
- Analyzing and critiquing an experience

"This is why . . ."
"It does. . ."

Introverted Feeling **Fi**
- —Values
- —Harmonizing and Clarifying
- —Reconciling
- —Checking Congruency
- —*Universal*

- Talking about likes, dislikes, and what's important
- Asking, "Is it worth standing up for?"
- Evaluating priorities according to values
- Deciding about what is important
- Determining the essence of what's important
- Being guided by strong convictions
- Convincing with rightness/wrongness or goodness/badness
- Noticing incongruities and phoniness
- Focusing on authenticity, living out values
- Looking for intrinsic values, something worth believing in
- Searching for people, ideas, or actions worth promoting
- Seeking to establish loyalty and commitment
- Valuing an experience

"This is important."
"I (or you) do . . ."

The Challenge of Decision Making in Teams

Ever wonder why team decision making can be so challenging? Generally, we use our perceiving processes to generate ideas. Because they are the mental functions for accessing information, it's an easy "go with the flow" experience. Then it's time to put the brakes on to evaluate the ideas. When this massive energy shift occurs, we engage our judging processes. A different mood prevails. It's like sailing in a way. When we use our perceiving processes, we are in a boat on a calm lake enjoying the sun and water. When our judging processes engage, it's like docking the boat in stormy conditions.

Each of us depends on our decision-making process because it works for us. Of course, we believe that our process should work for everyone else too. With this tension among the voices, decision making in groups becomes sometimes animated, discordant, and tedious. Politics come into play as each person jockeys for positions of influence in one way or another. Human behavior is the greatest form of entertainment, and decision making is no laughing matter.

Each voice in decision making offers a different set of considerations for evaluating ideas. Four voices, all aligned with their natural energies, contributing from the whole of human judgment. Rather than fight to be right, open your ears and pay attention to the wisdoms. Now that you know about the variations in ways people decide, you can appreciate how your method is one of many.

Consider each voice a teacher, each voice a learner. We all have something important to share from our unique set of experiences and energies.

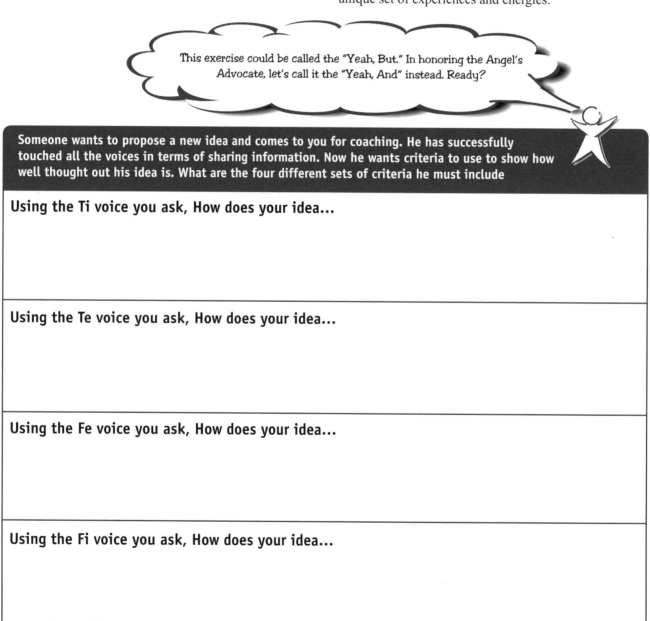

This exercise could be called the "Yeah, But." In honoring the Angel's Advocate, let's call it the "Yeah, And" instead. Ready?

Someone wants to propose a new idea and comes to you for coaching. He has successfully touched all the voices in terms of sharing information. Now he wants criteria to use to show how well thought out his idea is. What are the four different sets of criteria he must include

Using the Ti voice you ask, How does your idea...

Using the Te voice you ask, How does your idea...

Using the Fe voice you ask, How does your idea...

Using the Fi voice you ask, How does your idea...

Understanding Your Pattern of Processes

Why This Is Important

What we know about the perceiving and judging cognitive processes helps in idea generating. Our knowledge helps us understand the dynamics of the people sitting around the table and gives us insights into ways to inspire the creative stirrings from each person involved.

The movement between judging and perceiving, perceiving and judging is fast, sometimes split-second. To honor the energies and give them time to be heard we need to look at a freeze frame. Instead of generating an idea and then immediately judging it, hold off. Let the perceiving processes have full rein. Access the present, the past, the future, and forever for new ideas. Then call the judging processes into play. Use each of the four to analyze, structure, value, and harmonize the ideas' worth. This, of course, will lead to more idea generating. That's another story.

Each pairing of a judging and perceiving process yields a unique awareness. We interpret experiences through their dynamic interplay. We access information and form conclusions that resonate with particular energy patterns. It is important for you to do some figuring for yourself before proceeding to the next few pages to see a demonstration of each pairings awareness. Throughout this section you have been led to identify your best-fit personality type using the Jungian cognitive processes. Let's collect that information so it's all on one page.

Self-Selections

My favorite orientation _____
(from p. 59)

My first-place perceiving process _____
(from p. 62)

My first-place judging process _____
(from p. 66)

Now read the examples of how each pairing dynamic—there are sixteen in all—find problems or challenges and suggest solutions. The context is a retail setting. Each combination of voices is speaking about what actions should be taken to improve or change the business. Which of the different viewpoints is the right one?

All are. Each of these sixteen voices has a valuable and correct viewpoint. You can encourage people's creativity by hearing and affirming their voices and wisdom.

Now, reread the one (or ones) that matches your self-selections. Then read the short description* of that type theme on pages 72 and 73. The MBTI type codes are included for those who know them and the overlap with the temperaments is provided for your easy identification. Remembering your temperament pattern will help you find the type description that matches your self-assessment.

Digging Deeper

The patterns of the preferences, or voices, are really "where it's at," creatively and holistically speaking. Why? Because we all perceive something and we all make decisions about what we perceive. The following tables give you an example of the voices and their frequency awarenesses. They are meant to give you some indication of the different perspectives you are working with when leading an idea-generating session.

The Patterns of Our Voices

The pattern of your preferences for using these voices represents the way your mind is naturally organized. This pattern is not a combination of characteristics like different colors of paint mixed together or connected building blocks. The pattern of organization exists from the beginning. Your pattern of voices is sometimes referred to as your personality type or *best-fit type*.

Finding Your Best-Fit Type Pattern**

Best-fit type refers to the personality type pattern that you decide fits you best. No one description or pattern will be a perfect match to all of who you are. Your personality is rich and complex, and a "type" or type pattern cannot adequately express all of that richness.

---

* These "snapshots" are taken, with permission, from Linda V. Berens and Dario Nardi, *The 16 Personality Types: Descriptions for Self-Discovery* (Huntington Beach, Calif.: Telos Publications, 1998).

** If after reading the following sections you are still having trouble deciding on a best-fit personality type, refer to *The 16 Personality Types: Descriptions for Self-Discovery* for further clarification.

Foreseer Developer

MBTI® Type Code: INFJ

Ni—Foresee, Fe—Harmonize

Images of the future give meaning in terms
of meeting people's developmental needs.

"With all the e-business now, people are dissociated from each other and need to find ways to relate and interact. It's only human. Our vision includes helping people to develop their interpersonal awareness and give them meaning they can relate to on a more global level so they will frequent our sites."

Harmonizer Clarifier

MBTI® Type Code: INFP

Fi—Value, Ne—Infer

Personal beliefs and loyalties are
used to infer future patterns.

"I'm fine with the way things are, more or less. What scares me is that we might lose sight of what's really important—the proper recognition of all the work people put in to make this company a success. It's one of our company's values. I think each person needs to find ways to personally commit to it because if we don't walk our talk, we will have no sound ethical grounding in what we consider right and wrong practices. It's important that our decisions are aligned with what we value—that they show we mean what we say."

IDEALIST

Envisioner Mentor

MBTI® Type Code: ENFJ

Fe—Harmonize, Ni—Foresee

Other people's needs are met with
regard to their future potential.

"A lot of the jobs around here are dead-ended. There's no training, no development, no growth. This is what's holding us back from competing with the other retailers in our sector. Let's get some programs going to better equip our staff with the skills they will need not only for today but for the uncertainties of tomorrow. It's for their own good and, in the long term, ours as well."

Discoverer Advocate

MBTI® Type Code: ENFP

Ne—Infer, Fi—Value

Patterns and future trends are considered
and their importance evaluated.

"We can make a difference one customer at a time. Our products pollute. Let's have waste receptacles and recycling mechanisms available at each of our outlets globally. We can teach other retailers how true we are to our values of longevity and clean living by setting the example and walking the talk. Then, we can..."

Conceptualizer Director

MBTI® Type Code: INTJ

Ni—Foresee, Te—Structure

Images of the future bring to mind
strategic plans to accomplish goals.

"Within the next ten years, retailing, as we know it today, will be obsolete. We need to reorganize our resource base, including financing options to allow more R&D for developing leading-edge systems and practices for the future of retail business."

Designer Theorizer

MBTI® Type Code: INTP

Ti—Analyze, Ne—Infer

Inconsistencies in decision making are noticed
and generalized to patterns for the future.

"It seems to me that the decisions we make don't fit the mission of our organization. If we continue to ignore our foundational framework, we are going to lose our position in the marketplace. We need each decision to pass the test of how well it fits our mission. If it doesn't, then we'll need to modify the decision so it does fit. Either that or change the mission, which, for many good reasons, I don't think is a good idea. Then again..."

RATIONAL

Strategist Mobilizer

MBTI® Type Code: ENTJ

Te—Structure, Ni—Foresee

The efficiency of procedures is positioned according
to the long-range strategic plan or vision.

"Our sales figures show we've slowed down in the past eight months. We're right on target. Shifting to accommodate the year '05 plan means we'll continue to float at this level for the next quarter at least. We should start looking at the end of next quarter and see what we can do to start maximizing our profitabilities and begin integrating the new direction into our communications."

Explorer Inventor

MBTI® Type Code: ENTP

Ne—Infer, Ti—Analyze

Patterns and future trends are considered
and their inconsistencies analyzed.

"We tell people we are their prime source for these products, and you know what? In three years they won't need what we offer. We need to generate new business using other products and even incorporate new services. Let's make our products into services and extend our reach and our business that way. Let's come up with ideas for alternative forms of revenue from new and unusual alliances."

Planner Inspector
MBTI® Type Code: ISTJ
Si—Recall, Te—Structure
Concrete data from the past are considered in light of how a procedure may be more efficiently organized.

"Remember that sales were down last year and that our return policy was inefficiently organized. We need to re-evaluate our criteria for returns and exemptions and then restructure our process to entice consumers to purchase additional items when they return a good."

Protector Supporter
MBTI® Type Code: ISFJ
Si—Recall, Fe—Harmonize
Concrete data from the past are considered in light of how people's personal needs may be met.

"Remember that some people were dissatisfied with our return policy. So let's talk to the people to find out what they would like and reorganize our system to make them happy with our service."

GUARDIAN

Implementor Supervisor
MBTI® Type Code: ESTJ
Te—Structure, Si—Recall
The efficiency of procedures is compared to past successes and failures.

"Our sales figures show we've slowed down in the past eight months. We should see if this is something industry-wide or particular to our outfit. The last time this happened our management focused on generating new business rather than improving our operating systems—so it's the same problem that didn't go away last time. We should have greater efficiency and better accountability of where time and money are spent."

Facilitator Caretaker
MBTI® Type Code: ESFJ
Fe—Harmonize, Si—Recall
Meeting other people's needs is matched to past successes and failures.

"Our team decision making is awful. We fight all the time. We get stressed even at the mention of a meeting, and it's so important for us to compare notes and fill each other in about what's happening to whom. Why can't people get along? We should find out how other groups accomplish making their decisions while keeping the sanity around the table. The way we're going right now, it's just not right."

Analyzer Operator
MBTI® Type Code: ISTP
Ti—Analyze, Se—Experience
Inconsistencies in decision making are immediately noticed and acted upon.

"We have everything we need to get the job done right and no one needs to get fired. Greater revenues, says management? Okay, let's handle it. What's going on now that's in the way of pushing product harder? What new tactic can we conjure to allure folks into our store? Prizes? Celebrations? Contests? Let's get something going for next month that'll increase product sales."

Composer Producer
MBTI® Type Code: ISFP
Fi—Valuing, Se—Experience
Personal beliefs and loyalties are used to guide immediate action.

"I'm fine with the way things are. Really. I mean if we could make a change somewhere, let's get back to our priorities for making this a good place to work. I'd like to see some fresh paint in the staff cafeteria. A nice color that soothes and relaxes. And different kinds of music and good food too. Maybe a quiet space for people who want to read or have private conversations."

ARTISAN

Promoter Executor
MBTI® Type Code: ESTP
Se—Experience, Ti—Analyze
The present circumstances are considered and the inconsistencies in what is taking place are analyzed.

"Our stores are a mess. They look like they are from the Stone Age. If we wait long enough, it'll be a retro look and that will be hot. Still, in business, besides location, it's the experience of the environment that counts. Let's do some serious impact marketing and upgrade of our locations right away."

Motivator Presenter
MBTI® Type Code: ESFP
Se—Experience, Fi—Valuing
The present situation is considered and the importance of what is taking place is evaluated.

"What's important here is that we workers are happy. The plans for the next two years don't mention anything about dealing with our current day-to-day problems, like they are going away or something. We are working long hours and that impacts how we interact with our customers—who are also tired and overworked. Let's make them feel better by having us feel better and more refreshed."

Foreseer Developer

MBTI® Type Code: INFJ

Ni—Foresee, Fe—Harmonize

Theme is foresight. Use their insights to deal with complexity in issues and people, often with a strong sense of "knowing" before others know themselves. Talents lie in developing and guiding people. Trust their inspirations and visions, using them to help others. Thrive on helping others resolve deep personal and ethical dilemmas. Private and complex, bringing a quiet enthusiasm and industry to projects that are part of their vision.

Harmonizer Clarifier

MBTI® Type Code: INFP

Fi—Value, Ne—Infer

Theme is advocacy and integrity. Talents lie in helping people clarify issues, values, and identity. Support anything that allows the unfolding of the person. Encourage growth and development with quiet enthusiasm. Loyal advocates and champions, caring deeply about their causes and a few special people. Interested in contemplating life's mysteries, virtues, and vices in their search for wholeness. Thrive on healing conflicts, within and between, and taking people to the center of themselves.

IDEALIST

Envisioner Mentor

MBTI® Type Code: ENFJ

Fe—Harmonize, Ni—Foresee

Theme is mentoring, leading people to achieve their potential and become more of who they are. Talents lie in empathizing with profound interpersonal insight and in influencing others to learn, grow, and develop. Lead using their exceptional communication skills, enthusiasm, and warmth to gain cooperation toward meeting the ideals they hold for the individual or the organization. Catalysts who draw out the best in others. Thrive on empathic connections. Frequently called on to help others with personal problems.

Discoverer Advocate

MBTI® Type Code: ENFP

Ne—Infer, Fi—Value

Theme is inspiration, both of themselves and others. Talents lie in grasping profound significance, revealing truths, and motivating others. Very perceptive of others' hidden motives and purposes. Interested in everything about individuals and their stories as long as they are genuine. Contagious enthusiasm for "causes" that further good and develop latent potential and the same zeal for disclosing dishonesty and inauthenticity. Frequently moved to enthusiastically communicate their "message."

Conceptualizer Director

MBTI® Type Code: INTJ

Ni—Foresee, Te—Structure

Theme is strategizing, envisioning, and masterminding. Talents lie in defining goals, creating detailed plans, and outlining contingencies. Devise strategy, give structure, establish complex plans to reach distant goals dictated by a strong vision of what is needed in the long run. Thrive on putting theories to work and are open to any and all ideas that can be integrated into the complex systems they seek to understand. Drive themselves hard to master what is needed to make progress toward goals.

Designer Theorizer

MBTI® Type Code: INTP

Ti—Analyze, Ne—Infer

Theme is designing and configuring. Talents lie in grasping the underlying principles of something and defining its essential qualities. Seek to define precisely and bring coherence to systems based on the pattern of organization that is naturally there. Easily notice inconsistencies. Enjoy elegant theories and models for their own sake and for use in solving technical and human problems. Interested in theorizing, analyzing, and learning. Thrive on exploring, understanding, and explaining how the world works.

RATIONAL

Strategist Mobilizer

MBTI® Type Code: ENTJ

Te—Structure, Ni—Foresee

Theme is directing and mobilizing. Talents lie in developing policy, establishing plans, coordinating and sequencing events, and implementing strategy. Excel at directing others in reaching the goals dictated by their strong vision of the organization. Thrive on marshaling forces to get plans into action. Natural organization builders and almost always find themselves taking charge in ineffective situations. Enjoy creating efficiently structured systems and setting priorities to achieve goals.

Explorer Inventor

MBTI® Type Code: ENTP

Ne—Infer, Ti—Analyze

Theme is inventing, finding ingenious solutions to people and technical problems. Talents lie in developing ideas into functional and innovative applications that are the first of their kind. Thrive on finding new ways to use theories to make systems more efficient and people better off. Hunger for new projects. Have faith in their ability to instantly come up with new approaches that will work. Engineers of human relationships and systems as well as in the more scientific and technological domains.

These 16 "Snapshots" have been taken, with permission, from Berens, L.V. and Nardi, D., *The 16 Personality Types: Descriptions for Self-Discovery* (Huntington Beach, Calif.: Telos Publications, 1999).

Planner Inspector

MBTI® Type Code: ISTJ

Si—Recall, Te—Structure

Theme is planning and monitoring, ensuring predictable quality. Thorough, systematic, and careful. See discrepancies, omissions, and pitfalls. Talents lie in administrating and regulating. Dependable, realistic, and sensible. Want to conserve the resources of the organization, group, family, or culture and persevere toward that goal. Thrive on planning ahead and being prepared. Like helping others through their roles as parent, supervisor, teammate, and community volunteer.

Protector Supporter

MBTI® Type Code: ISFJ

Si—Recall, Fe—Harmonize

Theme is protecting and caretaking, making sure their charges are safe from harm. Talents lie in making sure everything is taken care of so others can succeed and accomplish their goals. Desiring to serve individual needs, often work long hours. Quietly friendly, respectful, unassuming. Thrive on serving quietly without fanfare. Devoted to doing whatever is necessary to ensure shelter and safety, warning about pitfalls and dangers and supporting along the way.

GUARDIAN

Implementor Supervisor

MBTI® Type Code: ESTJ

Te—Structure, Si—Recall

Theme is supervising, with an eye to the traditions and regulations of the group. Responsible, hardworking, and efficient. Interested in ensuring that standards are met, resources conserved, and consequences delivered. Talents lie in bringing order, structure, and completion. Want to keep order so the organization, group, family, or culture will be preserved. Thrive on organizing and following through with commitments and teaching others how to be successful.

Facilitator Caretaker

MBTI® Type Code: ESFJ

Fe—Harmonize, Si—Recall

Theme is providing, ensuring that physical needs are met. Talents lie in supporting others and supplying them with what they need. Genuinely concerned about the welfare of others, making sure they are comfortable and involved. Use their sociability to nurture established institutions. Warm, considerate, thoughtful, friendly. Want to please and maintain harmonious relationships. Thrive on helping others and bringing people together.

Analyzer Operator

MBTI® Type Code: ISTP

Ti—Analyze, Se—Experience

Theme is action-driven problem solving. Talents lie in operating all kinds of tools and instruments and using frameworks for solving problems. Keen observers of the environment, they are a storehouse of data and facts relevant to analyzing and solving problems. Thrive on challenging situations and having the freedom to craft clever solutions and do whatever it takes to fix things and make them work. Take pride in their skill and virtuosity, which they seem to effortlessly acquire.

Composer Producer

MBTI® Type Code: ISFP

Fi—Valuing, Se—Experience

Theme is composing, using whatever is at hand to get a harmonious, aesthetic result. Talents lie in combining, varying, and improvising, frequently in the arts but also in business and elsewhere. With their senses keenly tuned in they become totally absorbed in the action of the moment, finding just what fits the situation or the composition. Thrive on having the freedom to vary what they do until they get just the right effect. Take action to help others and demonstrate values. Kind and sensitive to the suffering of others.

ARTISAN

Promoter Executor

MBTI® Type Code: ESTP

Se—Experience, Ti—Analyze

Theme is promoting. Talents lie in persuading others and expediting to make things happen. Have an engaging, winning style that others are drawn to. Adept at picking up on minimal nonverbal cues. Anticipate the actions and reactions of others and thus win their confidence. Like the excitement and challenge of negotiating, selling, making deals, arbitrating, and in general, achieving the impossible. Thrive on action and the freedom to use all resources at hand to get desired outcomes.

Motivator Presenter

MBTI® Type Code: ESFP

Se—Experience, Fi—Valuing

Theme is performance. Warm, charming, and witty. Want to impact and help others, to evoke their enjoyment, and to stimulate them to act. Want to make a difference and do something meaningful. Often masterful at showmanship, entertaining, motivating, and presenting. Thrive on social interaction, joyful living, and the challenge of the unknown. Like helping people get what they want and need, facilitating them to get results.

These 16 "Snapshots" have been taken, with permission, from Berens, L.V. and Nardi, D., *The 16 Personality Types: Descriptions for Self-Discovery* (Huntington Beach, Calif.: Telos Publications, 1999).

Eight Voices of Creativity

"Cracking the Code"*

It is important to remember that the four-letter type code is more than the sum of four letters. It results from how we answer questions along four dichotomies, Extraversion-Introversion, Sensing-iNtuiting, Thinking-Feeling, and Judging-Perceiving. While on the surface, these dichotomies can be described generally, they are not separate parts or traits. In the development of the MBTI, it was assumed that reporting preferences for one over the other of each dichotomy would give us an idea of the pattern of cognitive processes of the personality and thus reveal Jung's psychological type patterns. Use the table on the next page to remind you of the kinds of processes and what the letters mean.

One can "crack the code" in a mechanical fashion, and for some people this is necessary for them to understand how the processes are structured in a hierarchy.

What follows is a step-by-step process for converting the MBTI type code into the pattern of processes represented by that code.

1. Look at the last letter of the code. It tells you which one of the two middle letters is extraverted. If it is J, then that tells you that the T or F in the code is used in the external world.

   • TJ in the code indicates extraverted Thinking is the preferred process of judgment for that type pattern.

   • FJ in the code indicates extraverted Feeling is the preferred process of judgment for that type pattern.

   (Some people say that *J* "points to" the letter just next to it.)

   If it is P, then that tells you that the S or N in the code is used in the external world.

   • S_P in the code indicates extraverted Sensing is the preferred process of perception for that type pattern.

   • N_P in the code indicates extraverted iNtuiting is the preferred process of perception for that type pattern.

   (Some people say that *P* "points to" the previous letter.)

2. Now that you have determined which process is extraverted, know that the remaining middle letter in the code is introverted.

3. Now look at the first letter in the code. If it is an E, then the extraverted process identified in step 1 is the leading-role process (dominant). If it is an I, then the introverted process identified in step 2 is the leading-role process (dominant).

4. The other middle letter is the supporting-role process (auxiliary).

5. The dichotomous opposite of the supporting-role process will be the relief-role process (tertiary).

6. The dichotomous opposite of the leading role process will be the aspirational-role process (inferior).

7. To get the shadow processes (in the fifth through eighth columns of the table), just take the hierarchical sequence of the primary processes and reverse the attitude (extraverted or introverted) of the process.

"There are sixteen personality types. Each type represents a unique predictable pattern of how our cognitive processes are used in everyday life."
—Linda V. Berens

Our Unique Patterns of Behavior**

Our best-fit type predicts which of the creative voices we are inclined to use naturally. And we are free to use whatever creative voice works to meet the challenges of a situation. Since we have innate preferences, we are likely to respond more automatically using one or two of these creative voices.

In What Ways Are You Creative?

Now it's time for you to interpret your creating energies based on the Jungian cognitive processes. The table to the right shows the sixteen types so you can tell which are your dominant or leading process, auxiliary or supporting process, tertiary or relief process, and inferior or aspirational process. Each one of these is a different creative voice and holds a different energy in your consciousness. That is, access to these processes is available in a descending order.

As a facilitator, coach, and mentor, knowing your voice gives you an advantage in working with others. You are aware of your natural energies and are very well aware that the energies of others may be different.

*, ** These sections have been taken, with permission, from Linda V. Berens, *Dynamics of Personality Type: Understanding and Applying Jung's Cognitive Processes* (Huntington Beach, Calif.: Telos Publications, 2000).

We each have a leading voice that develops from the ages of 6 to 12; a supporting voice, from 12 to 20; a relief voice, from 20 to 35; and an aspirational voice, from 35 to 55. In this stage theory proposed by Harold Grant, we understand that the leading voice continues to lead throughout one's life and that the others develop and hold their relative position as we grow with life experience.

In the shaded part of the table are the functions that are usually more outside of our consciousness. When they are active, it's as if we suddenly glimpse another frequency. To engage in these requires great energy and effort, so we usually choose not to use these processes. When we are asked to use one of them, we often ask for clarifications or for a question to be restated.

ROLES AND ORDER OF OUR USE OF THE COGNITIVE PROCESSES

MBTI Type Code	1st Leading	2nd Support	3rd Relief	4th Aspirational	5th Opposing	6th Critical Parent	7th Deceiving	8th Devilish
ARTISAN								
ESTP	Se	Ti	Fe	Ni	Si	Te	Fi	Ne
ESFP	Se	Fi	Te	Ni	Si	Fe	Ti	Ne
ISTP	Ti	Se	Ni	Fe	Te	Si	Ne	Fi
ISFP	Fi	Se	Ni	Te	Fe	Si	Ne	Ti
GUARDIAN								
ESTJ	Te	Si	Ne	Fi	Ti	Se	Ni	Fe
ESFJ	Fe	Si	Ne	Ti	Fi	Se	Ni	Te
ISTJ	Si	Te	Fi	Ne	Se	Ti	Fe	Ni
ISFJ	Si	Fe	Ti	Ne	Se	Fi	Te	Ni
RATIONAL								
ENTJ	Te	Ni	Se	Fi	Ti	Ne	Si	Fe
ENTP	Ne	Ti	Fe	Si	Ni	Te	Fi	Se
INTJ	Ni	Te	Fi	Se	Ne	Ti	Fe	Si
INTP	Ti	Ne	Si	Fe	Te	Ni	Se	Fi
IDEALIST								
ENFJ	Fe	Ni	Se	Ti	Fi	Ne	Si	Te
ENFP	Ne	Fi	Te	Si	Ni	Fe	Ti	Se
INFJ	Ni	Fe	Ti	Se	Ne	Fi	Te	Si
INFP	Fi	Ne	Si	Te	Fe	Ni	Se	Ti

KEY PHRASES

Perceiving Functions
Se—What is now/experience in the moment
Si—What was/recall
Ne—What might be/infer
Ni—What it represents/foresee

Judging Functions
Te—Evaluate and structure using measurable principles
Ti—Analyze for understanding
Fe—Evaluate and harmonize people according to their needs
Fi—Personally value

For fuller descriptions of the perceiving functions, see page 63. The fuller descriptions of the judging functions are on page 67.

The meanings behind the roles of all the eight voice positions are given on page 80. Before you go there, find your type on the preceding table, notice the order of the processes, and then fill in the table on page 77 that describes the order in which you use the conscious cognitive processes according to the theory.

Now, let's make the first translation using the conscious processes. Write the description of your processes in words and phrases to make them real for you. Use the key phrases provided at the bottom of page 75. Here are examples for you to use.

MY PERSONALITY TYPE CODE: I   S   T   P

Processes	My Energy Patterns	Role of My Process
Ti	Analyze for understanding	Leading
Se	What is now	Supporting
Ni	What it represents	Relief
Fe	Evaluate and harmonize people according to their needs	Aspirational

This generally outlines the process I use on a day-to-day level. In a sentence format, it looks like this:

Summary Statement
When I enter a new situation, first I analyze to understand what is happening in the current situation. I imagine what it represents and then harmonize people according to their needs.

Let's see how someone else might do this exercise. Here's Tony.

MY PERSONALITY TYPE CODE: E   N   T   J

Processes	My Energy Patterns	Role of My Process
Te	Structure using measurable principles	Leading
Ni	What it represents	Supporting
Se	What is now	Relief
Fi	Personally value it	Aspirational

Summary Statement
When I enter a new situation, I evaluate its structure using measurable principles in light of how I foresee it advancing my vision. I pay attention to what is happening in the current context and place a personal value on it.

And let's use another example for some variety. Here's Peter.

MY PERSONALITY TYPE CODE: E N F P

Processes	My Energy Patterns	Role of My Process
Ne	What might be	Leading
Fi	Personally value it	Supporting
Te	Structure	Relief
Si	What was	Aspirational

Summary Statement

When I encounter a new situation, I first generate options of what might be. I choose one that aligns with my personal values and then create a structure to actualize the best potential. After, I consider how I might have done something like this in the past.

Now, you do yours. Fill in the table, and then write your summary sentence below.

MY PERSONALITY TYPE CODE:

Processes	My Energy Patterns	Role of My Process
		Leading
		Supporting
		Relief
		Aspirational

Summary Statement

Now do it again for a friend, colleague, partner, or child. Choose someone you like. You may wish to use the individual you selected for the temperament summary exercise on page 55.

HIS OR HER PERSONALITY TYPE CODE: ☐ ☐ ☐ ☐

Processes	His or Her Energy Patterns	Role of His/Her Process
		Leading
		Supporting
		Relief
		Aspirational

Summary Statement

And here's another one for someone with whom you may be experiencing some tension.

HIS OR HER PERSONALITY TYPE CODE: ☐ ☐ ☐ ☐

Processes	His or Her Energy Patterns	Role of His/Her Process
		Leading
		Supporting
		Relief
		Aspirational

Summary Statement

Conscious Cognitive Process Insights and "Ahas"

1. How are your energy patterns the same as or different from the others you selected?

2. What new awareness do you have about your relationships with these individuals?

3. How is your day-to-day creative energy sparked?

4. How is their day-to-day creative energy sparked?

5. What other insights or connections come to mind?

Roles of the Creative Voices*

In these patterns of creative voices, one voice has a stronger pull than the other ones. That is, one of these creative voices is dominant or plays a leading role. It is a stronger attractor than the others are.

The primary creative voices are those used in the first four roles. These creative voices tend to emerge and develop at different times in our lives. During these times we are drawn to activities that use these processes. Then, learning the content and the skills that engage these processes is often nearly effortless. We find our interest is drawn to them and our interest is pulled away from things we were drawn to before.

The Leading Voice

The voice that plays the leading role is the one that usually develops early in childhood. We tend to engage in this process first, trusting it to solve our problems and help us be successful. Being the most trusted and most used, it usually has an adult, mature quality to it. While we are likely to engage in it rather automatically and effortlessly, we have much more conscious control over it. The energy cost for using it is very low. Much like in the movies, the leading role has a heroic quality as it can get us out of difficult situations. However, we can sometimes "turn up the volume" on this process and become overbearing and domineering. Then it takes on a negative dominating quality.

The Supporting Voice

Our supporting voice is how we are helpful to others as well as supportive of ourselves. Once we have developed some facility with our leading creative voice, we are likely to engage a different process in supporting role behavior. In its most positive form, it can be quite like a nurturing parent. In its more negative aspect, it can be overprotective and stunting rather than helpful. When the leading role process is an extraverted one, the supporting role process is introverted. When the leading role process is an introverted one, the supporting role process is extraverted and may be quite active and visible as it provides a way of dealing with the outer world.

The Relief Voice

The relief voice gives us a way to energize and recharge ourselves. It serves as backup to the supporting voice and often works in tandem with it. When we are younger, we might not engage in the process that plays this role very much unless our life circumstances require it or make it hard to use the supporting voice process. Usually, in young adulthood we are drawn to activities that draw upon this process. It is how we are playful and childlike. In its most negative expression, this is how we become childish. Then it has an unsettling quality, and we can use it to distract ourselves and others, getting us off target.

The Aspirational Voice

The aspirational voice usually doesn't develop until around midlife. We often first experience it in its negative aspect, projecting our "shoulds," fears, and negativities onto others. The qualities of these fears reflect the process that plays this role, so we are likely to look immature when we engage in the process that plays this role. There is often a fairly high energy cost for using it—even when we acquire the skill to do so. As we learn to trust it and develop it, the idealistic role process provides a bridge to balance in our lives. Often our sense of purpose, inspiration, and ideals have the qualities of the process that plays this role.

As you can see, these processes are weighted. That is, we are energized by spending more time using both the leading and support processes than the other two. When we must use the relief and aspirational processes, the energy cost is must greater. As a result, we prefer to use these on a less frequent basis. Yes, we learn skills associated with each of the preferences and become more comfortable using them after a while. Remember the learning curve of mastering them?

The Shadow Processes**

The other four cognitive processes, or voices, operate more on the boundaries of our awareness. It is as if they are in the shadows and come forward only under certain circumstances. They are like the "spear carrier" in the theater—an unknown, coming on to the stage, bearing a "spear." We often experience them in a negative way, yet when we are open to them, they can be quite positive.

The Opposing Voice

The opposing voice is often how we get stubborn and argumentative—refusing to "play" and join in whatever is going on at the time. It might be easy for us to develop skill in the process that plays this role, but we are likely to be more narrow in our application of this skill, and it will likely take more energy to use it extensively. In its positive aspect, it provides a shadow or depth to our leading process, backing it up and enabling us to be more persistent in pursuit of our goals.

The Critical Parent Voice

The critical parent voice is how we find weak spots and can immobilize and demoralize ourselves and others. This process is often sporadic in its appearance and emerges more often under stressful conditions when something important is at risk. When it does appear, it can go on and on. To access its positive side of discovery, we must learn to appreciate its presence and be open to it. Then it has an almost magical quality and can provide a profound sense of knowing and wisdom.

The Deceiving Voice

The deceiving voice fools us into thinking something is important to do or pay attention to. The process that fills this role is often not trusted or seen as worthy of attention, for when we do pay attention to it, we may make mistakes in perception or judgment. It can paralyze and double bind us. Yet this role can have a positive side as it provides comic relief. Then we can laugh at ourselves. It can be refreshing and join with the relief role as we recharge ourselves through play.

The Devilish Voice

The devilish voice can be quite negative. Using the process that plays this role, we might become destructive of ourselves or others. Actions (or inactions) taken when we engage the process that plays this role are often regretted later. Usually, we are unaware of how to use the process that fills this role and it just erupts and imposes itself rather unconsciously. Yet when we are open to the process that plays the devilish role, it becomes transformative. It gives us the impetus to create something new—to make lemonade out of lemons, rather than lament their sourness.

Now, let's see how knowing your shadow processes can assist your creative development.

*, ** These sections have been adapted, with permission, from Linda V. Berens, *Dynamics of Personality Type: Understanding and Applying Jung's Cognitive Processes* (Huntington Beach, Calif.: Telos Publications, 2000).

Now, use the shaded functions from page 75 to find areas of personal growth by identifying the shadow processes using the same format.

MY PERSONALITY TYPE CODE: I S T P

Processes	My Energy Patterns	Role of My Process
Te	Structure using measurable principles	Opposing
Si	What was	Critical Parent
Ne	What might be	Deceiving
Fi	Personally value	Devilish

**Summary Statement—To fully use my creating capabilities
I must grant myself patience and give myself permission to:**

Use structures and measures (rather than avoid them) and pull into awareness the learnings from my past. (Te, Si)
Generate alternative future potentials and spin-offs, in a good way, and discover what I personally value. (Ne, Fi)

Now, use the shaded processes to find areas of personal growth using the same format for Tony.

MY PERSONALITY TYPE CODE: E N T J

Processes	My Energy Patterns	Role of My Process
Ti	Analyze for understanding	Opposing
Ne	What might be	Critical Parent
Si	What was	Deceiving
Fe	Evaluate and harmonize people according to their needs	Devilish

**Summary Statement—To fully use my creating capabilities
I must grant myself patience and give myself permission to:**

Analyze to understand and generate potentials of what might be (different from the vision). (Ti, Ne)
Pay attention to what has already happened and evaluate and harmonize people according to their needs. (Si, Fe)

Now, use the shaded processes to find areas of personal growth using the same format for Peter.

MY PERSONALITY TYPE CODE: E N F P

Processes	My Energy Patterns	Role of My Process
Ni	What it represents	Opposing
Fe	Harmonize people	Critical Parent
Ti	Analyze for understanding	Deceiving
Se	What is now	Devilish

**Summary Statement—To fully use my creating capabilities
I must grant myself patience and give myself permission to:**

Allow the symbol of the experience to have meaning for me and make an effort to evaluate and
harmonize the people around me, according to their needs (not my own). (Ni, Fe)
Analyze the situation for understanding and pay close attention and stay with what is happening now. (Ti, Se)

Here's one for you.

MY PERSONALITY TYPE CODE:

Processes	My Energy Patterns	Role of My Process
		Opposing
		Critical Parent
		Deceiving
		Devilish

**Summary Statement—To fully use my creating capabilities
I must grant myself patience and give myself permission to:**

Here's one for the person that you like from page 78.

	HIS OR HER PERSONALITY TYPE CODE:					
Processes	**His or Her Energy Patterns**					**Role of His/Her Process**
						Opposing
						Critical Parent
						Deceiving
						Devilish

Summary Statement—To fully use his or her creating capabilities
he or she must grant patience and give him or herself permission to:

And here's one for the person with whom you are experiencing some tension, from page 78.

	HIS OR HER PERSONALITY TYPE CODE:					
Processes	**His or Her Energy Patterns**					**Role of His/Her Process**
						Opposing
						Critical Parent
						Deceiving
						Devilish

Summary Statement—To fully use his or her creating capabilities
he or she must grant patience and give him or herself permission to:

Shadow Process Insights and "Ahas"

1. How are your energy patterns the same or different from the others you selected?

2. Which, if any, of your conscious cognitive processes (page 77) are shadow processes of theirs (page 83)? How might this information help you to understand the others?

3. Which, if any, of your shadow processes (page 83) are conscious cognitive processes of the others (page 78)? How might this information help you to understand your relationships with them?

4. In what ways might the individuals you selected inspire your creativity just by being who they are? Refer to the sections in Jung's theory of psychological type, starting on page 58, for information about your areas of creative growth.

5. How might you consciously inspire creativity in others by being who you are? Refer to the sections in Jung's theory of psychological type starting on page 58 for information about your conscious gifts.

To more fully appreciate the impact of this information in helping to understand your creative energies, write down your energies in the table on page 87. Here's an example.

MY PERSONALITY TYPE CODE: I S T P

Processes	Stirrings, notions, and glimpses of the creative spark appear when I challenge, change, or improve:	Role of My Process
Ti	How things work	Leading
Se	The immediate environment	Supporting
Ni	Conceptual images of the ideal future	Relief
Fe	Ways to harmonize according to others' needs	Aspirational
Te	Ways to structure and organize	Opposing
Si	Procedures that have worked/not worked in the past	Critical Parent
Ne	Potentials of what might be	Deceiving
Fi	The importance of a personal value	Devilish

Here is an example of how this is real for me.

Here's my story.

The stirrings of this book, for example, came when a personal value was violated (Fi) because I read in the MBTI manual that only some types were considered creative. From there, I challenged my understanding of how creativity works and how type works (Ti) and began to marry the frameworks together. I moved into action in my immediate environment by giving a workshop for my local chapter on type and creativity (Se) to impact how people understood and harmonized around the notion of creativity (Fe). All the while, since the initial stirring, I had an image of the future in which all types would be valued as creative (Ni).

Internal analysis continued throughout the years (Ti) as did my experiencing different ways to present the material with different groups of people from around the world (Se). Then, when invited to publish my work, I began to cautiously structure and organize how it might all appear in print (Te). That took a lot of time. What stalled me was a recurring memory of past experiences where I had done my best to put my thinking out there for others to consider and was harshly criticized (Si). When the energy balanced again and I moved toward completion, I began to generate further options of where this book may go and what new doors might be open as a result (Ne).

The overall goal for me in writing this book is so that others (Fe) recognize their own creativity and make better choices using what they know about themselves and others utilizing the framework of personality type. Notice that the initial stirring in this instance came for me from Fi, my devilish process.

Ready? Now it's your turn to uncover your creative energies.

MY PERSONALITY TYPE CODE: ☐ ☐ ☐ ☐

Processes	Stirrings, notions, and glimpses of the creative spark appear when I challenge, change, or improve:	Role of My Process
		Leading
		Supporting
		Relief
		Aspirational
		Opposing
		Critical Parent
		Deceiving
		Devilish

List some examples of how this might be real for you.

Write your story.

What sparks creativity in your close friend, colleague, or relative?

HIS OR HER PERSONALITY TYPE CODE: ☐ ☐ ☐ ☐

Processes	Stirrings, notions, and glimpses of the creative spark appear when he or she challenges, changes, or improves:	Role of His/Her Process
		Leading
		Supporting
		Relief
		Aspirational
		Opposing
		Critical Parent
		Deceiving
		Devilish

Can you write an example of his or her story?

And what sparks creativity in someone with whom you are experiencing some tension?

	HIS OR HER PERSONALITY TYPE CODE:		
Processes	**Stirrings, notions, and glimpses of the creative spark appear when I challenge, change, or improve:**	**Role of My Process**	
		Leading	
		Supporting	
		Relief	
		Aspirational	
		Opposing	
		Critical Parent	
		Deceiving	
		Devilish	

Can you write an example of his or her story?

Applying the Eight Voices of Creativity

The eight cognitive processes described by Jung show four perceiving processes (ways of accessing and gathering information) and four judging processes (ways of evaluating and deciding). Each is a different voice; each vibrates with its own frequency. Each is attracted to those things and actions that undulate at the same speed. Each contributes unique and powerful perspectives.

---

*"Every creative person is a duality
or a synthesis of contradictory aptitudes."*
—Carl Jung

---

*"Originality is simply
a fresh pair of eyes."*
—Woodrow Wilson

We can use all eight creative voices, and we have preferences or natural inclinations for some of them. We are naturally inclined to use these eight voices in a pattern.

Let's see how each of the functions might be provoked to spark us to create something new and fulfilling.

How Might You Approach Creating Something New and Meaningful?	The Eight Voices of Creativity
By changing something in the environment—e.g., finding a new use for an old tool or getting new ideas from combining two things in front of you such as an egg and a radio.	**Extraverted Sensing (Se)**
By changing a procedure that has been less than successful in the past—e.g., improving upon the information available in a spreadsheet program.	**Introverted Sensing (Si)**
By changing the pattern of what might be—e.g., generating further new ideas based on current market trends.	**Extraverted iNtuiting (Ne)**
By changing the representation or conceptual vision for a new holistic view—e.g., imagining another direction for perfection.	**Introverted iNtuiting (Ni)**
By changing a goal or structure or organizing principle—e.g., organizing a business system according to new criteria such as customer satisfaction.	**Extraverted Thinking (Te)**
By changing an understanding of how something works and shifting categories—e.g., redefining the function of a pencil.	**Introverted Thinking (Ti)**
By changing the way people harmonize—e.g., appreciating individuals whose cultural values are different from your own.	**Extraverted Feeling (Fe)**
By changing the importance or finding new congruencies with personal values—e.g., finding value and committing to something that before seemed worthless.	**Introverted Feeling (Fi)**

TIP

Engage the wisdom from each cognitive process as best you can—both perceiving and judging—when you are deliberately approaching a task where you want to use creativity for yourself and with groups.

The value of tapping the cognitive process is proven when you begin to consider how you might more easily facilitate and inspire creativity and creative thinking in yourself and others. Once you know what works for you, you are freer to integrate that which is more challenging.

You see, the tools you choose to trigger new thinking and new decision making may be easy for you to use. Those same tools, however, may be quite difficult and challenging for others to use. Imagine, for example, that your leading process is the devilish process of someone you are working with in a creativity session. What kind of energies do you think might emerge? Probably not helpful ones. It would be better to have a selection of varied activities related to the different processes to help you achieve your desired outcome and goal.

You made it. Congratulations! So what's next?
Actually, that's totally up to you.

Some Points to Remember

Creativity is a condition of our species, and the urge to create is an energy extension of our biological imperative to procreate. It's that natural.

Each person is predisposed to certain energies that contribute to his or her creative process. The kind of creating we do can be influenced by many factors, including the cycle of creating, emotional attributes, motivations, cultural expectations, temperament pattern, and cognitive processes—both conscious and outside of consciousness.

So, what's your plan? Now that you know more about creativity in yourself and others, how might you use the information in an impactful, responsible, wise, and meaningful way?

Make some notes in the box to the right to make this plan your own.

Here's something else to consider. Make some time to work with others who are similarly interested in honing their knowledge, skills, and experiences to nurture and produce creative growth. Programs on Creativity are also offered by Temperament Research Institute that you might be interested in attending. The programs work through the concepts of this book in a practical, hands-on, results-oriented way. As well as gaining more access to your creative energies and those of others in a threat-free environment, you will meet and have the opportunity to create a network of like-interested individuals. Who knows where it might lead?

I'd like to...

I plan to...

Notes

SECTION

4

Idea-Generating Setup

Idea-Generating Setup

The Truth about Facilitating Idea Generating

Chances are, you have been participating in, if not leading, idea-generating or brainstorming sessions for years. And it's easy, right? Actually, sometimes the sessions work, sometimes not. For ideational excellence to happen more frequently you must be patient, understanding, and clear about the effective use of tools. You must honor the energies of the people in the room in service of the desired outcomes.

The intent of this section is to help you appreciate what is going on in people's minds and hearts when involved in generating ideas and to give you a firm framework to integrate into your practices. A little history and context building is also included to round out your idea-generating intelligence.

Initially, people tend to be a little wary about contributing in a session. Yes, they are scared, downright nervous.

In business settings, people feel pressure to perform according to the demands of the leader, group, organization, and industry. Politics and petty jealousies creep in to affect the outcome of using creative processes. And past experiences might have been less than positive.

Systemically, idea-generating sessions sometimes open a "can of worms." New ideas are produced with excitement and expectations of change and then nothing happens, causing distrust among the members. Or new ideas are generated only to be vetoed by others who did not participate in the session for unknown reasons. Or people not relevant to the topic are invited, or there is little commitment to the topic and the outcome. The list goes on.

Generally, it is safe to say that some people have had negative experiences in idea-generating sessions. Their voices may not have been welcomed or, in other words, their hands were slapped, resulting in fears for the next session. In a sense, facilitators (trained and untrained), who have passed before you may have unknowingly set you up.

The basic emotion, fear, precedes you. And what is it that people fear? Here's a sampling.

Fears in Idea-Generating Sessions

- Being misunderstood
- Speaking out of turn
- Committing a political faux pas
- Saying something wrong
- Having a creative block
- Lacking originality
- Articulating an idea improperly
- Not pushing the limits enough
- Other people thinking the idea is dumb
- Giving ideas that are not immediately doable
- Limiting yourself
- Being verbally criticized
- Being judged personally
- Feeling vulnerable
- Being rejected
- Being pigeonholed as the idea person
- Being in a "dead" group
- Failing
- Disappointing others
- Not getting honest feedback
- Encountering politics—"not invented here" mentality
- Facing intransigence
- Feeling alone
- Getting noncommittal approval
- Feeling discomfort in receiving feedback
- Not having an idea
- Getting a lecture, i.e., getting punished
- Not being fast enough
- Having an idea accepted but buried
- Being challenged too much
- Not "getting it"
- Nitpicking
- Losing status

Care to add more?

When leading an idea-generating session, not only are you asking for courage to create, you are asking for courage to overcome these fears that evolve over time with experience. Add to this list the fears of the four temperament voices:

- lack of personal meaning, not being recognized (Idealist)

- lack of belonging and responsibility, not being useful to others (Guardian)

- lack of freedom and opportunity, not having an impact (Artisan)

- lack of competence and knowledge, not being challenged intellectually (Rational)

You can see you've got a lot of interpersonal variables to work with.

It's almost like the facilitator is a chariot driver who has to run a race with horses of four different temperaments. As the driver, you need to know each horse well enough to motivate every one to give it's best in order for your team to win.

One "quick fix" for the fears, though not really a solution at all, is to remember that "fear" is an acronym for "false expectations appearing real." In some way it is helpful to reassure all those present to have faith, to trust, and to work with their processes in an environment you set up that is threat free.

Setting the Environment for Idea Generating

Here's a challenge for your creative ability: What are some ways to help an idea-generating environment be one in which people feel free to contribute what comes naturally? How might you make it safer so people can relax enough to let their true ideas percolate and emerge?

One approach I have used successfully is in the design phase. I make sure to include all four temperament pattern concerns in the interplay and outcome. As such, I take the responsibility to make sure the outcome of the session

- personally affirms the uniqueness of each participant in synergistic ways (Idealist)

- demonstrates responsible service to the organization's mission (Guardian)

- seizes opportunities that can result in impactful ideas (Artisan)

- elegantly progresses intelligence (Rational)

These cornerstones make up the framework for the design, as well as the diverging and converging activities described later.

Usually clients' requirements for the session fall within one of these four areas. What I add to the mix is support for the other three.

Another approach to building a safe environment for all to voice their contributions is to include some covert personality type information up-front in a little exercise to help people appreciate their uniqueness and differences. Most of the time it works to relax everyone. It really depends on the team of individuals gathered.

Here's an example. I call this the "Expert Game."* I like to use it as a warmup exercise because it helps to "even the playing field" and brings to immediate awareness a few points. First, each person experiences using the imagination. Second, each experiences asking questions, and third, each person is positioned as an expert worthy of being listened to.

Here's how it works. I ask the group to join together in trios. Then I ask each group of three to decide who will go first, second, and third. At this point they have no idea of what they will be asked to do. I go back to them after a minute to check their progress. Then, I ask for a round of applause for those who volunteered to go first. Why? Because these individuals are true risk takers—they have no idea of the adventure facing them.

> ### Volunteers Wanted for Hazardous Journey
> Small wages. Bitter cold. Route unclear. Frequent periods of complete boredom. Constant danger. Safe return doubtful.**

Then I announce that those going first are experts and I will tell them their area of expertise. For two minutes their colleagues act as interviewers—they are charged to find out whatever they can about the particular area of expertise. Following that will be two more rounds, each with an expert and interviewers, so that all have the experience of both roles. (If the group size does not accommodate trios I ask the people to form pairs.)

---

* Adapted from an exercise shown to me by Marg Delainey, formerly of the Saskatchewan Teachers' Federation at their Summer Institute.

**Adapted from Sir Ernest Shackleton's first Expedition to Antarctica. Thanks to Rolf Smith for sharing this.

Once the procedure has been explained, we go to the exercise. The areas of expertise I commonly use are

- being a psychologist for bees.
- teaching elephants to jump from airplanes.
- fitting silkworms with dentures.

For two minutes each of the experts answers questions from the interviewers. When the round stops, applause is asked for the expert. Then the new area of expertise is introduced and the exercise continues for two minutes.

Then comes the processing. First I ask the participants why they think we did this exercise, what happened?

Mostly they respond with comments like, "It was fun," "We used our imagination," "We found we could make up answers to anything," "A good icebreaker," and so on.

I ask what they have learned about the areas of expertise, making sure to touch base briefly with all the groups for the content of their conversations. Then I point out the differences in their learnings and ask why they think this is so.

The bottom line here is that the topics for each round are the same, and the interviewers and the experts are different from grouping to grouping. Diverse information surfaces as a result.

Then I ask what they liked about the exercise itself and what was challenging for them. I ask for key observations and learnings and also what it was like to be the expert and what it was like being the interviewer. Some say it is easier to ask the questions; for others, responding to the questions is easier.

Again, I emphasize this is natural for some to have an inclination toward asking questions and others to be more motivated to give answers. I then point out what I observed from their intense body language and the levels of laughter.

I ask them if as the interviewer they paid attention to the responses of the expert. Usually they say yes and that these responses triggered more questions for them to ask. I follow with the question, As the expert, did you pay close attention to the questions being asked? Again, the responses generally are yes.

The key point I make here is that we are all experts in the room because each person sitting at the table brings to the group a unique perspective. Each has different experiences, outlooks, and function areas. Each also has a different family situation, educational background, and hobbies. So in our session we must listen intently to what our fellow experts are saying and pay attention to and give value to the different ideational offerings.

Regarding body language, generally what happens is the expert strikes the expert pose. Watch for it when you do it. It's amazing to see how people shift in their seats and assume a "know-it-all" tone of voice. And it's remarkable as well to observe the interviewers' intent and active listening posture.

As for the levels of laughter, this signals that true boundary-breaking thinking is going on. We laugh when we encounter the unexpected, the novel, or a shift in perspective. I encourage laughter in our session because there is a direct connection between laughter (the "ha-ha") and the insight (the "aha").

This exercise works to break the ice and to level the field somewhat. Politics prevail, though at a less intrusive level. And I set myself up as the guardian of the environment and demonstrate people can trust me because I will support each one to use his or her unique voice during the session.

From a temperament pattern perspective, I have spoken to the Idealist theme of affirmation of unique personalities, the Guardian theme of roles and belonging, the Artisan theme of activity and impact, and the Rational theme of expert knowledge. In less than fifteen minutes, the message of all voices being welcome is delivered with impact in a safe, personal, and insightful way.

Working with Ideas

Getting ideas is one part of the idea-generating goal. Following up on the ideas is as important. How you interact with the group or a team is as important as the tools you use to welcome the many creative voices.

The Segal Model of Creative Problem Solving

Idea generating is one stage of the creative process. Generally, what precedes it are these stages:

- **Trumpet Call to Adventure:** Heeding and understanding the challenge for change.

- **Data Scope:** Data collection around that understanding.

- **Defining Challenge:** Articulation of the challenge as understood given the data.

- **Idea Time:** Idea generating.

Following that are these stages:

- **Reality Check:** Evaluating the ideas for breakthrough success.

- **Support and Action:** Composing the solution, getting buy-in for it, testing the solution, and putting it into action.

The process mapped here borrows from years of study synthesized by Osborn, Parnes, and others. The arrows on the outside of the dotted circle show the general process direction. The internal lines connecting the stages show movement of the mind. The Segal Model of Creative Problem Solving is intended for use throughout each phase of the creating cycle (see Cycles of Creating beginning on page 6).

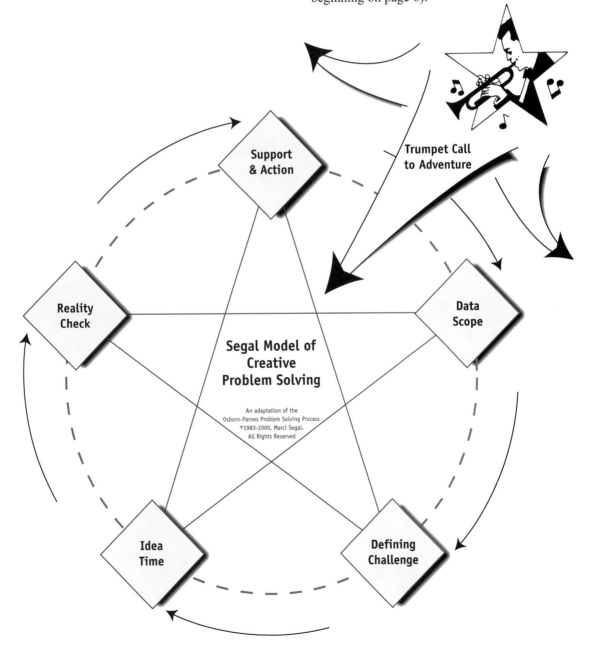

Support & Action

Trumpet Call to Adventure

Reality Check

Data Scope

Segal Model of Creative Problem Solving

An adaptation of the
Osborn-Parnes Problem Solving Process
©1983-2000, Marci Segal.
All Rights Reserved

Idea Time

Defining Challenge

Working with People and Ideas

The four different temperament patterns perceive differently from each other. So the idea-generating outcomes may be interpreted in different ways.

For example, if you are leading a session to find new ways to market pens,

- the Idealist may understand this as a way to let individual talents shine and so may generate ideas for that result.

- the Guardian may understand this challenge as a way to maximize current resource allocations, so ideas to do that will be offered.

- the Artisan may perceive the situation as how to make more of an impact on the distributors and end users so they will feel compelled to buy more pens. Those kinds of ideas will ensue.

- the Rational may sense this challenge as an opportunity to do more research and develop new strategic alliances. The ideas that follow may include trending benchmarks and schema.

Without clear instructions as to the meaning of the topic, your participants may feel misled in terms of their desire to contribute according to their own natural energy. With that comes a lack of trust and a greater likelihood to withdraw and sense that the meeting is a waste of time. Be clear about the topic itself and the definition of success for the time spent together.

Basic Idea Generating

The bottom line to a successful idea-generating process is to honor the voices in the room and to use different thinking styles. That's right, intermix the different temperament patterns as well as the divergent perceiving and convergent judging focuses and activities.

Divergent and convergent thinking is important to understand.

Alex Osborn, the advocate of brainstorming, compared divergent and convergent thinking to driving a car. Imagine, he said, that when you are using divergent thinking, your foot is on the gas pedal, all the way to the floor. There are no obstacles, and the roads are in perfect condition. The ideas flow.

When using convergent thinking, it's as if your foot is on the brake, evaluating, selecting, and judging ideas.

His point was this: it is critical to facilitate creative thinking by honoring both processes and keeping them separate. If you don't, it's as if you had your foot on the gas pedal and the brake at the same time. You wouldn't get very far, and it wouldn't be good for the transmission either.

In essence, from a psychological type perspective, Osborn said to honor the perceiving processes and then honor the judging processes. First, generate information and ideas using Si, Se, Ni, and Ne, and then call on Ti, Te, Fi, and Fe for making decisions.

Divergent thinking. Convergent thinking. Sounds simple, and sometimes it's challenging.

As a facilitator of idea-generating activities, it is your job to ensure both processes take place. First, diverge by listing many options. Second, converge by judging the ideas. Diverge, converge; diverge, converge.

Normally we don't do that. Normally we immediately evaluate the worth of an idea as soon as we hear it.

- Idealists look for congruency with identity and purpose.

- Guardians look for practicality and economy.

- Artisans look for novel impact and variety.

- Rationals look for strategically elegant inroads.

And if the idea offered up does not meet our personal temperament pattern criteria, we are quick to set the idea aside as worthless.

By using divergent and convergent thinking, you are asking people to stretch from their comfort zone. For them to do that, they need to trust you. With the tools provided in this book, along with the right attitude of honoring the many voices of creativity, you will succeed in building trust in your abilities to guide the process for generating new ideas that will become useful. And with that trust will come commitment for doing a good job, confidence in the creativity of yourself and others, competency in using the tools and methods, and capability to use the right techniques at the right time.

Step 1: Divergent Thinking

Here are some examples of divergent thinking triggers:

- List all the uses you can think of for a shoe.

- Generate meanings for a nutshell.

- List all the resources available for your next project.

- Make as many sentences as you can using all of the following words: candle, hope, tissue, egg.

Notice how each is an open-ended exercise. No evaluation is required or asked for. None of the questions asked you to meet any criteria whatsoever. The responses are free from any restriction, even if they are outside the parameters you perceive in the question. That's an important point.

These examples each reflect one of the four different temperament patterns. In order, they are the Artisan, Idealist, Guardian, and Rational.

Generally, though, we unconsciously know there are "right" answers and that there is only one right answer to every question. To truly appreciate the gift of divergent thinking, a change of attitude is required. People need to be open to the idea that there may be many "right" answers.

The goal of using divergent thinking is to generate as many potential "right" answers as possible. In order to do this, the potential "wrong" answers must be included. One of the benefits of using divergent thinking is knowing that in the second phase, during convergent thinking, the best responses will be selected and ideas not worth considering will be left behind, modified, or saved for later.

How do you get outrageous ideas? Ask for them! Research conducted in the '50s showed that when idea-generating participants are asked to generate outrageous ideas, they do. When they are not asked for outrageous ideas, they are not as likely to offer them up. Try it out, and see for yourself.

Step 2: Convergent Thinking

Here are some examples to demonstrate convergent thinking.

- Which shoe idea is the most novel?

- Rank your meanings of the nutshell from the most personally meaningful to the least.

- Select the resources that are most challenging to maintain.

- Of all the sentences you made, which is the most intriguing?

Notice each statement or question asks you to use "narrow-down" thinking. During the convergent stage, we apply critical thinking; that is, we use some criteria to evaluate, select, and analyze the output from the divergent phase.

Each example is based on one of the four temperament patterns. In order, they are the Artisan, Idealist, Guardian, and Rational.

If the divergent output is kept in the verbal realm, only in talking or in conversation, it is quite challenging to do a good job in the convergent stage. As a result, one of the standards for idea generating is to capture the ideas in a way that makes it easy to evaluate the total output later on.

Also, if all the idea generating is conducted interactively, you are pulling only on the extraverting processes—Se, Ne, Te, and Fe. By doing this you get ideas that fit what is (Se), what might be (Ne), how to organize using principles (Te), and how to organize to meet people's needs for harmony and connecting (Fe).

For balance, consider including opportunities for reflection time for the other four voices to be heard—Si, Ni, Ti, and Fi. Factor in occasions to welcome ideas from what was in the past (Si), conceptual considerations and meanings (Ni), framework fit (Ti), and personal values (Fi).

Divergent and Convergent Thinking in the Four Temperament Voices

When asked to respond to triggers, we generate ideas and make decisions that align with our temperament pattern and cognitive processes (see below).

As a rule of thumb, remember these key temperament idea-generating themes:

- Idealists generate and evaluate ideas based on symbolic meaning and integrity.

- Guardians generate and evaluate ideas on tangible improvements based on what has been done before.

- Artisans generate and evaluate ideas for impact and immediate use.

- Rationals generate and evaluate ideas for theoretical strategic elegance that systemically unifies the past, present, future, and forever.

So if you need ideas for cost reductions, whom do you structure your idea-generating session for? For all temperament types! And from each temperament voice you will get a different perspective—all valuable, all filling in the gaps of what might not be said if that voice weren't present.

Divergent and Convergent Thinking in the Eight Cognitive Process Voices

This chart shows how each cognitive process voice may contribute to diverging and converging activities. Use it as a guide to broaden your approach to stimulate creative thinking.

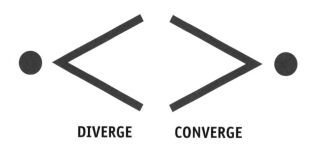

DIVERGE   CONVERGE

PERCEPTION	JUDGMENT
Creative ideas—where they come from. Consider using each of these:	Creative ideas—how they are evaluated. How well do ideas meet these criteria?
Extraverted Sensing (Se) Change what is. • Give new uses and tactics for what is contextually happening now, what's right in front of you.	**Extraverted Thinking (Te)** Improve efficiencies, structures, measurements, and organizing principles. • Demonstrate excellence using provable and profitable standards.
Introverted Sensing (Si) Change what was. • Recombine past elements.	**Introverted Thinking (Ti)** Improve understanding of how something works. • Provide clear categorical shifts.
Extraverted iNtuiting (Ne) Change what might be. • Infer new patterns, potentials, and spin-offs from the current situation.	**Extraverted Feeling (Fe)** Improve harmony among people. • Facilitate cooperation and interpersonal harmony in the outcome.
Introverted iNtuiting (Ni) Change the representation of the future. • Integrate insights to form new concepts.	**Introverted Feeling (Fi)** Align with values, personal and corporate. • Demonstrate commitment to what is truly important to those impacted and involved.

Fuller descriptions of each cognitive process appear on pages 63 and 67. In addition to using this chart, you may find stimuli on those pages to use to facilitate shifting energies to actualize and sustain fulfilling change.

Rules for Idea Generating

Alex Osborn supplied these rules for running idea-generating sessions.

1. Defer Judgment—evaluate later. Convergent thinking is used separate from divergent thinking.

"Defer judgment" also implies that the ideas given are neither affirmed nor critiqued during ideational flow.

Osborn found that when ideas were affirmed, the idea giver felt great and the others involved felt less than great. Affirming ideas adds to the discomfort and fears of the people sitting around the table because others who do not receive a "Good one" or a pat on the back for their contributions sense that their value is less than those who do. He also found that when an idea was critiqued, the idea giver retreated and did not add any more. He witnessed a slower pace and more careful contributions by the others—for fear they may be criticized as well.

How can deferred judgment be practiced?

- Use a flip chart as the group's memory and make sure each idea is written down *verbatim* as the individual offers it.

- If someone affirms an idea, challenge that individual to modify it—to make it even better. If someone critiques the idea, challenge that person to make that criticism into an idea. Don't let people get away with making these judgments!

- As a facilitator, one of the best things you can do to support deferred judgment is to say, "What else?" after each idea is given. In this way, you're being fair to everyone.

- If you are idea generating on your own, deferring judgment is far more challenging because you need to resist the temptation to allow your internal critic to have its say. To overcome this challenge, consider role-playing other temperament voices and freely list what they might say in response to a trigger question. Keep the temperament targets in front of you for assistance. Make sure to keep writing, without stopping, for at least five minutes. (Use an egg timer to keep track.) Additionally, use your other hand to write if really blocked. Experience it. You'll be amazed at the results.

"The best way to get good ideas is to get a lot of ideas"
—Linus Pauling

---

2. Quantity Breeds Quality—the more ideas there are, the better the choice overall, and the greater the potential for breakthrough new ideas.

Some people believe idea generating with others is a waste of time. They already know what needs to be done. Alternatively, some people are not at their best in intensely interactive situations and prefer idea generating when they have time to think and reflect.

Others like idea generating in groups. Idea generating this way involves others who are likely responsible for following through on the idea's implementation, and it gives an opportunity to hear different voices and to share different perspectives. They enjoy the lively interchange of bouncing and connecting ideas.

Regardless of your disposition—however you get your best ideas—make sure to generate at least five more ideas than you think you need. If you are doing the idea-generating on your own, do your best to include how other temperament voices might respond to the trigger question. Consider using the cognitive process chart on the previous page for additional triggers.

To remember that quantity breeds quality, think about professional baseball. Before the batter steps up to home plate, he stays in the batting cage working with different bats. He selects the best bat to use from a selection of bats. If he had only one bat to choose from, he really wouldn't have a choice, would he?

Research conducted in the early '80s (Basadur 1986) showed some interesting results regarding the quantity notion. Groups of individuals in industry were asked to generate ideas regarding improved efficiencies in production. The ideas were then given to industry experts for evaluation. The experts chose the best ideas from all the ones generated. Where did these ideas occur? In the bottom two-thirds of the list. The lesson? Generate many ideas to increase the probability of getting really good ideas and expect them to occur within the bottom two-thirds of your list. Generally ideas that appear first are our knee-jerk responses, culturally accepted, and safe. Once elicited, they make way for fresh thinking and fresh ideas.

3. Seek Combinations—build upon and get inspiration from other ideas.

The human mind is constantly making connections. During idea generating, we honor that process.

In a group setting, it is challenging *not* to make a connection or to springboard from ideas as they emerge. It is sometimes also challenging to bring that connected thought or idea forward. No matter how effectively we know a technique, people continue to resist offering their connections and combinations. Here are some reasons why:

- People are looking for the immediate "right" answer and are unsure if their offering fits the criteria.

- People are nervous about "stealing" another's idea.

- People may sense that by offering their connection, they are "besting" the idea of another, showing that their idea is better.

- The environment is threatening rather than welcoming.

- People don't know it's okay to connect and combine.

So, what's a facilitator to do?

1. Stress the fact that all ideas are welcome and that the ones most worthy will be selected later.

2. Demonstrate how instead of "stealing" ideas, we are building on ideas, honoring our natural processes to connect to our past, present, future, and forever.

3. Tell the group that each idea is a contribution to the "bucket" of ideas. Basically, all ideas offered serve two purposes: they are potential solutions as well as provocations for other new ideas.

4. Build and maintain a safe environment.

5. Tell your participants that building on ideas is welcome and, if they wish, they may acknowledge that they are building on someone else's contribution.

   For example, Jody offers an idea for marketing pens. She offers making a promotion called "express yourself" using the pens during exam week for university students. Mark triggers off of that and says, "Building on Jody's idea, let's market the pens as the first writing device for future corporate presidents, and let's encourage parents to buy these as status symbols for students just entering primary school." Do you see how this works?

6. Provide sticky note pads or other attractive note-taking supplies and encourage people to scribe their ideas as the connections are being made. Then, when there's a lull, these ideas can be added to those already contributed. This technique works well in support of our introverting voices that speak best in reflection.

7. Plan for a balance between interactive time and reflection/incubation time.

4. Use Techniques Deliberately—manage the idea-generating flow by offering different kinds of triggers for thinking differently.

It amazes me that so few people are aware of the myriad techniques available to trigger new ideas. In fact, great mythologies have been constructed around ways to get ideas and who has greater access to them.

The first myth is "I'm not worthy." Some people honestly subscribe to the myth that they are not deserving of getting new ideas.

"My parents are working stiffs" is the second myth. In other words, some people truly believe that because their heritage is from ordinary folk, they do not have the genetic capability for creative greatness.

The third myth is "I must lead an exemplary life so the fates will be good to me." This is related to the "I'm not worthy" syndrome.

Another myth is "I must abuse myself to really get in touch with my creative juices." As a result, people refrain from sleeping, eating, and washing (sometimes). With that, they partake copious amounts of false-euphoric substances to open the channels for idea production.

Of course, impediments do exist to idea generating and true creative expression: stress, tension, tiredness, overwork, pressure to perform, lack of adequate time and, of course, fear.

To overcome these impediments, show your group how each can use a technique to generate different kinds of new ideas. And give everyone a little break from the high pressure. Entertain and rejuvenate.

Some people actively use their imaginations and succeed in getting ideas that are "out of the box" quite effortlessly. Fortunately or unfortunately, these individuals set a standard of expectation for others. Using the imagination is easier for some than for others.

I have learned that Idealists and Rationals are generally more in touch with the imagination than are the Guardians and Artisans. Both Idealists and Rationals have either Ne or Ni as their leading and supporting processes.

As a facilitator, you can make it easier for all to know and access their imaginations by using an exercise that guarantees ideational success. The Expert Game does that, and so does the following nuts-and-bolts example that classifies and provides experience in using the imagination.

Experiencing Imagination

As a child, I became frustrated when teachers would ask me to use my imagination. A precocious student, I asked, "What's the imagination?" and frustrated teachers replied, "Just pretend." Not satisfied with their answer, I followed with, "Pretend what?"

Chances are, some of the people you are working with have a similar outlook. Perhaps they have Se or Si as their leading or supporting processes. Use a concrete example to describe what you want to communicate.

To introduce the imagination in a concrete way, simply tell your group that the imagination is a function of *memory*, and there are two kinds of imagination.

One kind of imagination is called the "reproductive imagination." By using it, we recall something we have already experienced—some learning, some emotion, some sensation, some objects.

Ask your group to imagine a tame horse. Instruct them to see the horse, to hear the horse, to feel the horse, to smell the horse. Then ask for volunteers to describe their horse to the group.

Congratulate the people for meeting with success in using their imaginations. By using it, they have brought a horse, or many horses, into the room.

The second kind of imagination is called the "productive imagination." Using this imagination we create new images.

Ask your group to imagine in-line skates, then imagine their horse on the skates. Ask a few individuals to share their new image of the horse.

What you have done by leading this experience is provided an opportunity for all to successfully use their imaginations.

Using this exercise, you can safely segue into how individuals' imaginations will be honored and encouraged throughout the session. Then you can tell the group that different techniques will be used to trigger thinking away from the habit-bound reactionary style to the off-road excitement of exploration and adventure.

Bonus: By using this exercise you build trust between the group and you as their facilitator.

Summary

Before the session:

- The design for idea generating includes a selection of diverging and converging process tools as well as the promise to meet four different thematic outcomes:

1. Personally affirms the uniqueness of each participant in synergistic ways (Idealist)

2. Demonstrates responsible service to the organization's mission (Guardian)

3. Seizes opportunities that can result in impactful ideas (Artisan)

4. Elegantly progresses intelligence (Rational)

In the session:

- Begin to build a trusting, safe environment using the Expert Game.

- Define success for the meeting.

- Overtly tell the group the different kinds of thinking processes that will be used to achieve the goal for the session: divergent and convergent. And give examples of both.

- Review the rules for brainstorming. Again, give examples. (Please resist telling people there are no bad ideas. There are plenty of bad ideas. Swimming in Lake Ontario during a water warning is one. If you as the facilitator say there are no bad ideas, your people will know you are either very naïve or lying. The trust level will suffer as a result. Instead, suggest to your group that "all ideas are welcome." That's the truth.)

- Tell the group that your role as the facilitator is "the guide by the side" rather than "a sage on the stage." Your job is to make sure all ideas are recorded and to guide both the diverging and converging aspects for creative thinking. You may also make clear that you are working for your client. To do that effectively, check with the individual who "owns" the content outcome from time to time for refined direction, interest, and relevancy.

- Tell the group members that their role is to participate by ideating and evaluating as asked. Note: if one person is the overall decision maker or owner of the ideation results, identify that the role of that individual is to make the decisions. If all are involved in making the decision and all are owners of the outcome, then the converging will be done as a group.

The next section provides you with tools to help you inspire the many voices of creativity in others. Enjoy!

Notes

Tools for Inspiring the Many Voices of Creativity

How to Inspire the Many Voices of Creativity

This sections contains a set of different tools you can use to help people get new ideas. They are positioned to access the different cognitive processes and support the different temperament pattern motivations.

Creativity is more than using tools. Attitude plays a part too. Thoughts are things, in a way—what you think, you manifest. Here's some advice before you enter into your next idea-generating session: Think happy thoughts, know you will tap the creative energies in the room, know you will be successful, and remember to breathe.

Preparing Yourself to Set Up the Session

Do your best to answer these questions before you begin designing:

People—Who is involved and what is important to them?

How might you help them collaborate harmoniously? (Fe)

How might you affirm their importance and welcome their creative contributions? (Fi)

Purpose—What is the ideational task for the session?

What creative framework might you use to get there? (Ti)

How will you measure successful achievement of the objective? (Te)

Environment—What is the context?

What have they tried before and would like repeated? (Si)

What is the current situation and context? (Se)

Future Links—What happens after the session?

In what ways might this session positively impact the individuals, group, team, organization? (Ne)

What best-case scenario emerges when you imagine the future of its success? (Ni)

All of these considerations go into the design of an effective idea-generating session. The answers influence how you will lead it. They can be responded to in any order.

Other design considerations include the following:

- Cyclical voice: Where in the cycle is the project right now—birth, childhood, adulthood, or death (pages 6–8)? In which phase is it best to focus the team's energy? Alternatively, use Land's model (pages 51–52) of exploring and inventing, repeating and improving, maturing and transforming, and new exploring and inventing as your place marker.
- Emotional voice: How are you feeling? What emotions are team members experiencing?
- Motivational voice: What temperament patterns prevail in the team? That is, what creating drives are present?
- Cultural voice: What roles are appropriate and expected of team members involved in the session? And what generally happens in the organization after a creativity session is over?
- Mental voices: How might you integrate the cognitive processes in the session?
- Unconscious voice: What else might you pay attention to?

Leading an idea-generating session takes your commitment, competence, comfort, and confidence. Ways to build these include practicing asking for peer feedback, making mistakes and learning from them, and getting permission. The permission is for yourself to "try things on for size," to build a repertoire, and to modify it as needs change and as you continue to grow in experience.

Helpful Frameworks
Who's Who in Idea Generating*

Client/Decision Maker

- Owns/implements the outcome.
- Hungry for new ideas and new perceptions.
- Joins in generating phases.
- Evaluates and selects ideas during convergent phases.
- Integrates others' thinking into his or her own.

---

* Adapted from Grossman et al, 1988, 174-188

Resource Group

- Contributes ideas.
- Gives ideas from general knowledge and imagination.
- Verbalizes, draws, and records all ideas.
- Trusts the process, trusts the others in the room.
- Is willing to express novel, personal, unpopular points of view.
- Refrains from evaluation, unless asked.

Facilitator

- Checks with decision maker for ideational direction prior to the event.
- Designs and monitors session structure, environment, and process.
- Builds and maintains a safe group environment.
- Leads generating and converging activities.
- Keeps everyone focused.
- Pays attention to group energy and dynamics.
- Keeps ideas flowing.
- Ensures all ideas are recorded.

Setting the Stage

Who might be invited?

As diverse a grouping of people as possible. Have people present who are interested in contributing to the outcome.

How many participants are included?

No less than 6, no more than 12.

What's the topic?

You need to know this in advance to help you to plan.

What kind of ideas are needed?

Does your client want Guardian, Artisan, Rational, or Idealist ideas (p. 47)? Evolutionary? Revolutionary? (p. 16).

Room setup

A boardroom setting is fine. Make sure you have movable chairs. It's better if the room is large enough for people to wander around. A festive atmosphere is nice. Windows help too.

Materials required

Basics include a flip chart, markers, masking tape, and a place to hang the sheets from the flip chart. Each person needs to have paper to write on (or the equivalent computer technology) and a pen or pencil. Sticky notes or index cards are helpful. Nice-to-have items include a timer for you and an attention-getting device. See Support Materials (p. 108) for further suggestions.

Refreshments

At a minimum, have spring water and other beverages available, depending on the time of day and the length of the session. Do not conduct these sessions over a lunch period.

Timing

Allow for warmup, using two or three idea-generating techniques including decision making and then getting feedback. Anywhere from forty-five minutes to three hours. It depends on the outcomes desired. More than three hours of idea generating is exhausting. If you have more than three hours, then also include time for diversionary topic related activities.

Choreography and dynamics

Large group, individual work, pairs, trios, quartets, and so on. Vary these dynamics to keep the session lively. Breaks can also be structured to provide for incubation time. See Choreography (p. 108) for suggestions to keep the session involving.

Leading the Session—A Sample Outline

1. Purpose
   Why are we here doing this now?
2. Definition of success
   How will we know we have accomplished our task?
3. Contract for the room
   How will we conduct ourselves?
4. Introductions
   Who's here? Can also ask about a creative hero, a favorite vacation, and so on.
5. Warmup
   Some creative thinking exercises or brainteasers—might be sharing the results from a presession activity.
6. Tools 1 and 2
   General brainstorming from individual to total group involvement. Diverge. Converge.
7. Tools 3 and 4
   Small groups. Diverge. Converge. Small groups present their highlights.
8. Tools 5 and 6
   Cluster highlights from total group. Theme the cluster of highlights. Select the theme most relevant and exciting to work through. In small groups, work on the themes. Diverge. Converge.
9. Next steps—what happens now?
10. Feedback

TOTAL TIME: Three hours including a break. Fifteen minutes for items 1–5. Forty minutes each for items 6, 7, 8; ten minutes for items 9 and 10.

NOTE: It's your decision whether the first two points are presented by you or by the client.

Choreography to Keep It Involving

1. Large group discussion
2. Small group discussion
3. Team exercise (competition)
4. Trio discussion
5. Paired discussion
6. Role-play
7. Game
8. Individual exercise
9. Simulation
10. Guided imagery
11. Large group exercise
12. Demonstration
13. Seated
14. Standing
15. Moving
16. Showing a videotape
17. Listening to music
18. Breaks
19. Drawing
20. Making magazine picture collages

What else?

Support Materials to Consider Using

- Slides
- Overheads
- Flip chart
- Workbook
- Handout
- Action plan
- Toys
- Session evaluation
- Videotape
- Audiotape
- Video camera
- Sticky notes
- 3"x5" cards
- Posters/magazines
- Presession activity (i.e., creative thinking challenges)
- CDs
- Sticky dots
- Colored markers
- Masking tape
- Timer
- Attention-getting device
- Dictionaries
- Newspapers
- Cookbooks

What else?

Tools

Consider this the beginning of your tool collection or an addition to the one you have already started. What's special about these tools is they bring focus to the motivational energies and cognitive process energies mentioned throughout this book.

Many people ask me how to engage the introverting preferences and how to get creative ideas from Guardians. My sincere wish is that by the time you get to this section, you have already read the previous ones. A rationale is provided there to help you shift your attitude toward embracing a broader nature of creativity and its nature and appearance.

Generally, this kit contains fundamentals for good idea generating. Mix and match them according to your needs and objectives. Timing for the warmup exercises is generally five to fifteen minutes. For the other tools the timing to allow is indicated for each.

The timings provided are approximate and are intended to be used as rough guides for your planning. Size of the group, levels of complexity, and involvement affect how long each tool will actually take. Each session and group is different.

Use the sample outline (p. 107) as a guide for a three hour session. If you have only an hour, consider using the Opportunity Grid^{SM} on page 136.

TOOLS   Table of Contents

Warmup Exercises

Why use warmup exercises? Old patterns of thinking need to be put aside to generate new ideas. Warmup exercises are a great way to introduce fresh thinking and to get yourself and others used to stretching mental muscles.

Most of these can be used both by you alone and with groups, except for the Expert Game, which requires other people to be involved.

Allow about five to fifteen minutes to do the warmup and then, if in a group, time to share the results and process. Any special worksheets or supplies you need to conduct the experiences are listed in the instructions for each exercise.

TOOL #1 **Write Me a Story**

Special Materials:

- Writing paper, pen or pencil, timer, Word Trios + Emotions table

Benefits and Considerations:

- A great way to show how everyone has the capability to be creative; works well to break current mind-set
- Can be used also as personal creativity exercise on a daily basis

How It's Done:

- Set the timer for five minutes only. Randomly select one trio of words by choosing a number from 1 to 25. Write a story or paragraph based on those words, without stopping, making sure that all three words are in the first sentence.

Variations:

1. Add an emotion to your set of words. Randomly choose one from the right-hand column.
2. Relate the story to your topic for idea generating.

Word Trios + Emotions			
Trio Number			**+ Emotions**
1	monumental	temple	exploration	ecstatic
2	shark	air supply	diver	pleased
3	dog	bone	treasure	satisfied
4	wind	kitten	yarn	fearful
5	leap	miscalculation	umbrella	nervous
6	starship	galaxy	discovery	at peace
7	fox-trot	jalapeño	gulp	happy
8	miracle	life	baby	curious
9	zipper	lecture	embarrass	appeased
10	celebration	caviar	champagne	angry
11	strip	lose	poker	tearful
12	sherpa	Himalayas	burden	considerate
13	lazy	meander	raft	hungry
14	rainbow	waterfall	orchids	lovingly
15	luau	hula	ukulele	frustrated
16	bush pilot	caribou	tundra	amused
17	feast	explorer	cannibals	terrified
18	safari	savanna	roaring	excited
19	swells	sail	gate	serene
20	plank	kidnapped	pirates	thirsty
21	quicksand	trapped	sinking	trust
22	explode	test tube	experiment	confidence
23	pants	dance	ants	discover
24	cliff	Rolls Royce	mother-in-law	overcome
25	fan	plan	man	sympathetic

TOOL #2 Common Threads and Connections

Special Materials
- Flip chart, markers

Benefits and Considerations:
- Invites curiosity for the session; people will want to compare results
- Given as a presession activity, allows people reflection time to work on ideas
- Helps people make new connections and stretch their thinking into new patterns; some call it making sense out of nonsense
- Enables facilitator to point out (either directly or in a group debriefing) the different perspectives available in the room to build from for new ideas

How It's Done:

Group:
- Pick three items, concepts, people, or processes at random (examples are given below).
- Ask each person to find the common thread among the three things. Ask them what those three things have in common.
- Ask participants for the connections they made, writing them on the flip chart as they announce them.
- Note: If this is used as a presession activity, some will do this; some will wait until the session itself. That's natural and okay.
- Continue brainstorming new commonalities and associations for another five minutes.

Individual:
- If you are doing this on your own, give yourself a time limit of three minutes to list as many connections as you can.

Common Threads Examples:
Lightbulb, cucumber, stopwatch

Gravity, speed, chaos

Nelson Mandela, the White Rabbit (from *Alice in Wonderland*), Celine Dion

Operations, marketing, finance

NOTE: I usually use the topic for the idea-generating session as one of the words in a threesome. For example, on generating new cereal ideas I asked what the following three things have in common: Cereal name, keychain, and feather. It was amazing what new ideas for cereals followed from that!

TOOL #3 Creative Heroes

Special Materials
- Flip chart, markers

Benefits and Considerations:
- Gives participants a chance to contribute to building the creative environment
- Creates a group tool to use later
- Asks people to imagine, reflect, connect with, and value someone for his or her creativity; shifts their day-to-day thinking to focus on what they value in others' creativity.

How It's Done:

Group:
- Ask each person who his or her creative hero is for the day. It could be someone real or fictional, alive or from the past, famous or everyday. Top-of-mind responses are welcome.
- Then, tell them you will ask each to name their hero along with one prime heroic characteristic.
- As they report out, write both the name and the prime heroic characteristic on the flip chart.
- When you are finished, tell the group that this is your "creative board of directors" and when the time is appropriate you will ask the board of directors for suggestions and input to your process. Make sure the flip chart sheet is hung in an easy-to-see spot on the wall.

Individual:
- Ask yourself who your creative heroes are for your session. List two or three names. Then next to each name, write two or three characteristics you admire—from a creativity perspective. Later, you can call on these individuals, in your imagination, to help you with your idea generating.

TOOL #4 Expert Game

This exercise was outlined in a story format on pages 95–96. These are the basics.

Special Materials:
- Timer, attention-getting device

Benefits and Considerations:
- Works to break the ice and to level the political playing field somewhat
- Promotes you as the person to trust to lead the session
- Demonstrates that everyone uses imagination and has unique things to say
- Allow fifteen minutes

How It's Done:
- Ask people to group into trios. (Sometimes the number of people in the group is not divisible by three. In that case, ask people to pair or ask for trios and pairs. You can still do the exercise three times. Those in the pairs will have an opportunity for one partner to be an interviewer twice.)
- Tell them to select who will go first, second, third. After a minute, check to make sure all have done this.
- Ask for a round of applause for those going first, the true risk takers.
- Tell the group you will be leading an experience called the Expert Game. Everyone will act as an expert and also as an interviewer, and you will tell people what their area of expertise is.
- Outline the procedure. The expert will be told the area of expertise. The other two in the group will act as interviewers to find out as much as they can about that area of expertise. After two minutes the interviewing will end. The next area of expertise will then be announced and the second person in each group will respond to questions from the other two for two minutes. Then the third expert area will be announced, and again two minutes of interviewing will follow. Everyone will act as the expert and everyone will act as interviewers in three separate rounds. Ask for any questions. Clarify that they will stay in their groupings of three for the next six minutes. Ask if the first expert is ready.
- Announce the first area of expertise. Say something like, "Expert number one, you are an expert in fitting silkworms with dentures. Interviewers, find out as much as you can about this area of expertise for the next two minutes, starting now."
- Start the timer and observe the dynamics.
- After two minutes, using the same format as above, announce the second area of expertise. And then in another two minutes, tell the third expert his or her domain of expertise.

Sample Areas of Expertise:

Fitting silkworms with dentures
Teaching elephants to skydive
Being a psychologist for bees
Being an electrician for fireflies
Being a tailor for fish
Forecasting the weather for clouds
Switching lights on for lawyers
Make up your own!

Processing the Experience:
- Once all have had their turns, ask what they have learned about the areas of expertise, making sure to touch base briefly with all the groups for the content of their conversations.
- Point out the differences in their learnings and ask why they think this is so. Note that although the topics are the same, the questions are different and the people playing the experts and interviewees are different, so different information is asked for and given.
- Make a relationship between this experience and the group of people for the idea-generating session. Point out that each person is unique. Therefore, you expect different kinds of ideas will be generated and that here, all ideas are welcome.
- Ask, "Why do you think we did this exercise?" Record their responses on a flip chart.
- Ask, "What did you like about the exercise itself? What was challenging?" Highlight that what is challenging for some is easy for others—such is the nature of humanness.
- Ask for key observations and learnings and also ask what it was like to be the expert and what it was like being the interviewer. Relate this to the group, incorporating what everyone said and announcing that it is natural for some to have an inclination toward asking questions and others to be more motivated to give answers.
- Point out what you observed from their body language and the levels of laughter.
- Ask, "As the interviewer, did you pay attention to the responses of the expert?" (Usually they say yes and that these responses triggered more questions for them to ask.)
- Follow with, "As the expert, did you pay close attention to the questions being asked?" (Again, the responses generally are yes.)

| **TOOL #4** Expert Game continued | **TOOL #5** Wouldn't It Be Nice If...? |

TOOL #4 Expert Game continued

The key point is that we all are experts in the room because each person sitting at the table brings a unique perspective. Each has different experiences, outlooks, and function areas. Each also has a different family situation, educational background, and hobbies. So in the idea-generating session, it is important to listen intently to what the experts around the table are saying and pay attention to and give value to the different ideational offerings.

- Summarize the comments so far. Point out the boundary breaking and fresh thinking that took place. The levels of laughter signal that true boundary-breaking thinking is going on. We laugh when we encounter the unexpected, the novel, or a shift in perspective. Mention that laughter is encouraged because there is a direct link between laughter (the "ha ha") and the insight (the "aha"). Also mention that it is important to have fresh thinking before starting an idea-generating session.

Defining the Challenge

Identifying the challenge prepares you for generating the kinds of ideas you want. And, as Aristotle is known to have said, "Well begun is half done."

Sometimes groups are brought together before idea-generating sessions to brainstorm challenges and to define the problem. Actually, it is a smart facilitator who leads definition sessions before the actual idea-generating activity.

The benefits are enormous: a definition session builds and strengthens team ownership, gets many perspectives and orientations of the situation "on the table," and lets people know that this is not a one-shot experience, that it is one stage in the creative process.

In essence, by defining the challenge accurately, a purposeful direction for generating ideas emerges. The approach can be targeted to a specific situation or can be open-ended to capture the thinking, concerns, and stirrings around the table.

Any special worksheets or tools you need to conduct the experiences are listed in instructions for each exercise.

TOOL #5 Wouldn't It Be Nice If...?

Benefits and Considerations:

- Helps you or a group to generate options to decide on a challenge to embrace.
- Allow a minimum of twenty minutes.

How It's Done:

- One way to find some challenges is to begin to use divergent thinking to collect "wouldn't it be nice if..." statements.
- For yourself or in a group, using the best divergent thinking you can muster, list as many "wouldn't it be nice if" statements. This will provide a wealth of options from which to choose the best challenge to engage. Feel free to use individual sticky notes for each statement and then to post them on a wall or flip chart. Alternating between using this method and a more interactive one, such as brainstorming, attends to both introverting and extraverting energies.
- Be sure to focus on at least three statements for each of the cognitive processes. Feel free to generate more—go with your energy. And remember, generate at least one more in each category than you think you need. Remember too to write the statements down. Feel free to amend these cognitive process triggers to suit your specific needs.

  Se—current situation: home, school, work, hobbies, and so on. Wouldn't it be nice if...?

  Si—past performance. Wouldn't it be nice if...?

  Ne—potentials. Wouldn't it be nice if...?

  Ni—insights. Wouldn't it be nice if...?

  Te—measurable standards. Wouldn't it be nice if...?

  Ti—your frameworks for understanding. Wouldn't it be nice if...?

  Fe—meeting others' needs. Wouldn't it be nice if...?

  Fi—personal or organizational values. Wouldn't it be nice if...?

- With your collection in tow, isolate the recurring themes if that appeals to you.
- Alternatively, look over the list and see which is the most involving, compelling, and exciting challenge. Also consider what absolutely needs to be addressed from a timing perspective.
- Most important, choose one statement that warrants using imagination, one that can be assuredly influenced. Winning the lottery may engage your imagination, though the control factor for winning it is minimal.

With the diverging done and the initial converging completed, it's time to delve a bit deeper if you like. See Ladder of Abstraction (Tool #6) for a possible next step.

TOOL #6 Ladder of Abstraction

Benefits and Considerations:

- Helps you to understand the breadth and depth of the challenge you have selected to work on to offer more choices and for a better overall definition.
- Sometimes when we isolate a challenge to work on, we bolt ahead and do our best to solve it, only to find that the answers we come up with don't really address the issue. By using the Ladder of Abstraction you have a greater capability of "hitting the nail on the head," finding the true challenge.
- Allow at least twenty minutes.

How It's Done:

- Use it after the first-stage final or best statement of the opportunity/challenge is given. If the statement is specific (S), use the "Why" questioning list. If it's a broad (N) statement, ask, "What's stopping you?"

Why?

Ask, "Why do you want to do that?" or "Why is that important?" The client will respond.

Turn the client's response into a how-to statement.

Ask, "Why do you want to do that?" or "Why is that important?" The client will respond.

Turn the client's response into a how-to statement.

Continue this process for at least five levels.

Example:

1. How to lose weight.
   Q: Why do you want to lose weight?
   A: To look better.

2. How to look better.
   Q: Why do you want to look better?
   A: To feel better.

3. How to feel better.
   Q: Why do you want to feel better?
   A: To enjoy my life more.

4. How to enjoy life more.
   Q: Why do you want to enjoy life more?
   A: To have more fun.

5. How to have more fun.
   Q: Why do you want to have more fun?
   A: To have a richer and fuller life.

What's stopping you?

Ask, "What's stopping you from doing that?" The client will respond.

Turn the client's response into a how-to statement.

Ask, "What's stopping you?" The client will respond.

Turn the client's response into a how-to statement.

Continue this process for at least five levels.

Example:

1. How to live a richer and fuller life.
   Q: What's stopping you?
   A: My kids, my partner, all the demands from other people.

2. How to respect the demands of other people.
   Q: What's stopping you?
   A: Sometimes their demands cut into what I want to do.

3. How to do what I want to do more often.
   Q: What's stopping you?
   A: I'm not sure what it is I really want because I'm so busy meeting other people's demands.

4. How to find out what I really want.
   Q: What's stopping you?
   A: Making the time to do it.

5. How to get some personal quiet time.

Ask the client to review the list and select the how-to statement that best represents the issue at hand. Then begin generating ideas to meet that challenge. Different kinds of ideas emerge depending on which of the statements is chosen, so tell the client to consider his or her choice of challenges thoughtfully.

Notice that in the "why" list, the options became broader as the questioning continued. In the "what's stopping you" list, the options became more manageable and narrower in scope. It's like traveling from Sensing to iNtuiting in the first example and from iNtuiting to Sensing in the second. A great film showing this concept is Powers of 10 (Eames and Eames 1989). I've used it successfully many times in idea-generating sessions to help people recognize different levels of thinking.

Do yourself a favor and experiment with this tool on yourself first. Then use it with someone with whom the threat level is minimal. Then, use it when the stakes are a little higher.

General Group Techniques for Diverging

You already know how to brainstorm. And you know the rules: Defer judgment. Quantity breeds quality. Seek connections. Use tools and techniques deliberately. All ideas are welcome. Write them down.

And you already know what a typical brainstorming session is like. Someone is at the flip chart, others seated, usually around a table, and ideas are flowing from the mouths of the participants through the ears of the facilitator. Magically, it seems, the words appear verbatim on the flip chart. Occasionally, the facilitator asks some probing questions and the ideas continue to flow. And occasionally there's a lull, when no one speaks and everyone feels uncomfortable.

Lulls are good. Lulls are a sign to the facilitator that it's time to use a tool or a new technique because the current way of thinking is exhausted.

Generally, people overlook the nonverbal ways to contribute ideas. Included in this section are two ways to access and support the introverting preferences: Brainwriting and Stick-on Brainstorming.

Special Materials:
- Two Brainwriting sheets per person
- Flat surface for writing
- Pens/pencils

Benefits and Considerations:
- Divergent technique
- Facilitates linking of and triggering from ideas
- Used to alter group energy direction; good quieting technique
- Allows time to reflect and incubate
- Works well in small groups of five to eight people
- Allow fifteen to twenty minutes

How It's Done:

To Diverge:
- Each person receives a Brainwriting sheet (have extras within reach of each person).
- Each writes the topic on the top line of his or her sheet.
- Tell each person to generate and write down three ideas for the topic using the top row of the grid—one idea per box.
- Tell participants once they have finished their row to put the sheet in a common area for others to reach.
- Tell them to trade their sheet for another and to complete another row either by triggering off of the ideas already there or by generating new ones.
- If only one person is finished, tell him or her to take an empty sheet to continue.
- Continue until all the started sheets are completed.

To Converge:
- Ask each person to choose three of the best ideas or "hits," from the sheet in front of him or her. The ideas may be the person's own or ideas of others. Another benefit of this technique is no one knows whose ideas are being brought forward.
- Ask people to announce the ideas they selected. (Note: This can also be done in small groups where the groups share their collected "hits" and summarize them for presentation.)
- Write or have someone else write them on the flip chart.
- You may continue to do verbal brainstorming from there.

Brainwriting

Summary of Challenge _____

_____

_____

_____

ROW 1			
ROW 2			
ROW 3			
ROW 4			

TOOL #8 Stick-on Brainstorming

Special Materials:

- 3" x 5" or larger sticky notes—one pad per person
- Medium-tip marker—one per person
- Flip chart/wall space

Benefits and Considerations:

- Divergent technique
- Used to affirm individual processes
- Used to involve each participant
- Used to relieve facilitator from having to write all ideas
- Facilitates building on and triggering from others' ideas
- Enables movement of ideas into clusters for highlighting (see Highlight, Cluster, Theme on p. 118)
- Allow fifteen to twenty minutes

How It's Done:

- Announce the topic for the idea-generating session and post it in large letters for all to see.
- Have each person write his or her ideas, one per sticky note, using a medium-tip marker. Allow about three to five minutes.
- Ask each person to post his or her ideas on the flip chart, and say each aloud as it is posted.
- New connections are made with the posting of ideas. Encourage participants to capture these on sticky notes as well. Continue posting the ideas as they emerge. Remember to remind people to record their ideas before they announce them.

General Group Techniques for Converging

Converging means coming to closure—deciding, evaluating, analyzing, valuing. And we all do it successfully and differently.

Decision making in a group can be nerve-racking. Unlike diverging, where there is a give and take in a free-flow exchange of perceiving information (impressions, insights, innovations, impacts, connections, and considerations), in converging we put on the brakes using our judging processes (the ones that work for us). And, as you recall from the section on Jung's theory, pages 65–68, there are four different ways to decide.

Some believe the greatest challenge in creativity sessions is to generate new ideas. The real challenge is to make new decisions. If we continue to use the same criteria to evaluate, then we continue to get the same kinds of solutions we always do. With creativity we want new decisions, new solutions, and new directions. Ergo, we need to shift our energies here as well as in the generation of ideas.

So, what's a facilitator to do with all the different energies in the room fighting for turf and at the same time wanting to challenge well-respected decision-making processes? Take a look at the two different techniques included here: Highlight, Cluster, Theme, and PPH2. When you use these, you'll get a head start on turning the tensions into a well-choreographed dance.

Tools for Inspiring the Many Voices of Creativity

TOOL #9 Highlight, Cluster, Theme

Special Materials
- Sticky dots (three to five per person), markers or highlighter pens

Benefits and Considerations:
- Convergent technique, follows idea generating
- Used to screen, select, and sort options
- Good to use for large number of ideas
- Enables encapsulation of many ideas into manageable categories
- Best done after using Stick-on Brainstorming (see p. 117)
- Allow twenty to thirty minutes

How It's Done:
- Review all the ideas generated.
- Have each person select three to five ideas that are appealing—the hits and highlights—using sticky dots, markers, or highlighter pens.

  Option for selecting highlights: Instead of limiting the choices to three to five per person, tell participants they can vote for whichever ones they want. The ideas with the highest votes are used for the clustering step.
- Ask one person to group the appealing ideas together into meaningful clusters.
- Ask the same person to give a name or theme to the clusters.
- Ask the group to rank the clusters.
  Some ranking options: (feel free to add your own)
    Order of importance, immediacy, and influence (To what degree does this group have influence over making this cluster happen?)
    Short term, medium term, long term
    Nice to do, need to do
    Do now, do later, and do never
    Exciting, boring
    Levels of risk involved
    How each measures up to achieving the objective
- Flesh out and add to the ideas of top-ranking clusters for depth and direction.

TOOL #10 PPH2 (Pluses, Potentials, How-To's)

Special Materials:
- Optional: PPH2 sheets

Benefits and Considerations:
- Convergent exploration technique
- Helps overcome quick judgments of new ideas—engages new ways
- Creates interest and movement by generating ways to solve objections
- Used on one option at a time
- Engages different mental processes
- Supports using the "Angel's Advocate" (see section 1, p. 20)
- Allow twenty to thirty minutes

How It's Done:
- After initial converging is done and you have three or four options to consider as solutions, ask the following set of questions to evaluate each one. Complete one set of questions before moving on to the next idea, recording all responses.
  - What are three pluses about the idea? What is good about it now?
  - What are three potentials, spin-offs, and possible future gains that might result from implementing this idea? It might…
  - What concerns do you have about the idea? Phrase these concerns in the form of a statement or question starting with "How to...?" or "How might we...?"
- When the questions have been answered for each idea, select one of the options to move forward on.
- Generate ideas regarding the concerns listed for the selected option.
- Choose from those ideas and write up your newly-arrived-at solution, including its plan for action.

Notes:
- This tool can be used by the total group; it can also be assigned to small groups as a tool to help their thinking and to prepare a report back to the total group.
- Presentations made using this tool generally include
  1. The solution
  2. Its pluses
  3. Its potentials
  4. Some how-tos regarding obstacles
  5. Some ways to overcome selected obstacles
  6. A plan to implement the solution
- Integrating the cognitive process or temperament frameworks into the questioning helps to broaden the scope for generating ideas to overcome the obstacles.

PPH2

Idea 1

Pluses
Potentials
How Tos

Idea 2

Pluses
Potentials
How Tos

Idea 3

Pluses
Potentials
How Tos

Diverging Tools that Actualize the Temperament Energies

Chances are you have favorite tools to use in idea generating. You respond well to them, enjoy them, and effortlessly lead them. You may also be disappointed if your "brand" of tools is not used in a session and may feel like something is missing. You are not alone.

As you peruse the following temperament pattern idea-generating techniques, you will likely be drawn more to some than to others. Some will naturally appeal to you while others will test your patience. It's natural.

You are the facilitator, the mentor, the coach. You need to be responsive and proactive—responsive to the desires for new ideas by encouraging the energies in the room and proactive, being ready for any of these energies to emerge to create breakthroughs. So look at the eight tools for diverging with a thoughtful eye. Expand your repertoire. You deserve the best options available and so do the people with whom you work. And note that even though the tools are positioned within the different temperament pattern energies, when you build trust between you and the group, each of these tools can be used by all.

If you know the temperament patterns in your group, then you can target them specifically to immediately establish a comfort base. If you are unaware of their temperament energies, use the "Segal fallback plan." Start with Guardian techniques first. Make sure you explain the imagination (see page 103) before beginning, as part of the setup to the session as a whole. Once your participants have experienced success using a tool to get new ideas, they are more likely to follow your instructions and to allow themselves to stretch into uncharted waters.

Risking produces anxieties and raises the emotional temperature, so it's best to build on small successes. Start with the familiar; build to the strange.

Tools for Self-Expression—Honoring Idealist Energies

TOOL #11 Collage

Special Materials:
- A variety of picture/photograph-laden magazines from a diversity of interest areas: sports, computers, business, fashion, home design, photography, travel, and so on.
- Glue sticks
- Paper for gluing pictures onto (flip chart sheets work well)
- Wall space
- Sticky notes
- Soft, flowing instrumental music (CD and CD player)

Benefits and Considerations:
- Divergent meaning-making technique
- Helps people access and act on their imagination
- Involving—engages hands, eyes, mind
- Gives a break from traditional methods
- Supports individuals and group working together
- Allow twenty to thirty minutes

How It's Done:
- Randomly distribute magazines throughout the group beforehand. They can be placed in a messy stack on the table or floor, for example.
- Play soft instrumental music.
- Conduct a guided imagery experience for the group to imagine a situation in the past, present, or future related to the topic. (An example follows.)
- After the guided imagery experience, ask participants to randomly select magazines, skim through them and pull any images, editorials, or advertising that connects to their visualization. Instruct them to do this without talking to each other. Continue playing the music.
- After five to seven minutes, tell the participants to create a collage using their collection of images, words, and so on. This is also done without talking. Continue to play the music.
- When the collages are complete, tell the participants to post them on a wall to create a "gallery."
- Stop the music. Conduct a gallery tour of the collages. As each is viewed, ask participants to respond to these questions individually on sticky notes, again without sharing their ideas with each other:
    - What I see is…
    - The people/images in this collage are…
    - What I feel is…
    - Key words, meanings, or phrases that come to mind are…
- Bring the group together. Share everyone's responses using the Stick-on Brainstorming method.
- Cluster the offerings, name the clusters, and then build on the clusters to generate more ideas about your topic.

TOOL #11 Collage continued

Guided Imagery Example

Topic for idea generating: how to position toothpaste differently

Instructions:

Begin by playing soft, flowing instrumental music—something new age. In the following script, "Pause" means to halt the script for thirty seconds; "long pause," for a minute.

Sample script:

"To begin this part of our process, we are going to experience something called 'guided imagery.' For the next few minutes I am going to ask you to relax and to let your imagination take over. Rational thinking will come later. Right now it's important to tap into other ways of suggesting ideas. People tell me that they really enjoy doing this. Are you ready?"

"To help you to tap your imaginative powers, and yes, you all have them, we will begin to relax by breathing. First, put your feet flat on the floor. Close your eyes. Now, relax your jaw; let it hang. We carry tension in our jaw area, and this is a great way to begin to release that tension."

"Now, take a deep breath right down into your stomach. Let your stomach fill up like a beach ball. Hold that breath to the count of three. When you exhale, do it through your mouth and make sure you empty all the air you were holding. Good. We'll do that twice more. And we'll introduce only one change. The next time you exhale, imagine that all the tensions in your body are leaving with the breath. Ready? Inhale, beach ball, hold, 2, 3, release. Once more. Inhale, beach ball, hold, and release."

"Feeling a little more relaxed? Good. Now our journey begins."

"In your imagination, travel to a time sixty years in the future. Imagine it's you now, as you are, living sixty years from now. What do you see around you? (pause) How are you dressed? (pause) How are the people around you dressed?" (pause)

"What does your work environment look like? (long pause) Your home environment? (long pause)

"How do you get exercise? (pause) What do you eat on a regular basis? (pause) How do you wake up in the morning?" (pause)

"What surprises you about living in this time period?" (long pause)

"What are you doing differently now?" (pause)

"What is the mood of the culture?" (pause) What colors are prominent? (pause)

"What is one thing, memory, message, value that you wish to bring back to the present?" (pause)

"Now, let's come back to this time. See the years turning back from sixty years ahead, to fifty years ahead (pause) to forty years ahead (pause) to thirty years (pause) to twenty years (pause) to ten years (pause) to today."

"Wiggle your toes, move your fingers, and come back to the room we are in now."

"Open your eyes. Randomly choose a number of magazines. In them are images, editorials, and advertising. Pull pictures from the magazines that remind you of or connect with the images in your visualization. Let's hold off on talking for another few minutes."

TOOL #12 Relay Race Drawing

Special Materials:
- Flip chart pads, unlined
- Colored markers—one set for each small group
- Masking tape
- Timer
- Lots of empty, obstruction-free, floor space

Benefits and Considerations:
- Divergent meaning-making technique
- Helps people access and act on their imagination
- Involving and energizing—engages hands, eyes, mind, legs
- Supporting metaphoric thinking
- Gives a refreshing break from traditional methods
- Supports groups working together
- Allow fifteen to twenty-five minutes

How It's Done:
- First, place chart pads on easels (or paper on walls) one for each cluster of five to eight people. (If we use the word "team" here, it implies competition, and there isn't any in this experience. This exercise involves collaboration, an Idealist concept.)
- Then use the masking tape to make a line on the floor, like a starting line, about ten feet (three meters) from each chart pad.
- Tell each of the clusters which chart pad it will use.
- Ask each cluster to line up at the starting line.
- Give the first person in each cluster a set of colored markers.
- Tell each participant to make one mark on the chart pad using one marker, like a relay race. They have one and a half minutes to get as many people up to the chart pad as they can.
- When you give the signal, the first person approaches the pad, makes a mark, rushes back to the line, and hands the markers to the next person. The next person then goes to the chart pad, makes a mark, rushes back to the line, and hands the set of markers to the next person. This continues for a minute and a half.
- When time is up, tell the clusters that they need to make meaning out of their "artwork." What message is being delivered by their markings? What "whole" can they make out of the pieces? Ask them to relate their meaning to the topic at hand.

Tools for Incremental Change—Honoring Guardian Energies

TOOL #13 SCAMPER (Substitute, Combine, Adapt, Modify, Put, Eliminate, Rearrange)

Special Materials:
- Optional: SCAMPER sheet

Benefits and Considerations:
- Divergent technique
- Facilitates linking of and triggering from tangible ideas
- Used during lulls when using other idea-generating tools
- Highly adaptable to suit your needs
- Great when used in conjunction with Attribute Listing (see page 124)
- For small groups work allow fifteen to twenty minutes (see notes)

How It's Done:
- Ask trigger questions, based on the framework of SCAMPER.
- Substitute: What else can you use instead? Who else? What other group can be involved? What other process? What other material?
- Combine: How might there be a blend of parts? Persons? Processes? Purposes? Materials?
- Adapt: What does this suggest? What from the past can be adapted to suit the current need? How might this be changed to suit the present/future?
- Modify: How can you change the shape? Size? Color? Sound? Height? Frequency? Weight?
- Put to other uses: What else can it be used for as it is? What other markets can we approach? What other uses might be made?
- Eliminate: What might be eliminated? What can we do without? What can be sacrificed?
- Rearrange: What other patterns or arrangements might work? What can be transposed? What can be reversed? Be turned upside down? Do the opposite?

Notes:
- Facilitator asks questions as needed. Great for using as triggers during both individual and group brainstorming. Pick and choose questions at random.
- See the following worksheet for one idea for implementation.
- Can adapt these triggers to suit your purpose.
- For small group use: Give each group a SCAMPER sheet (see next page) and instruct the participants to use one of the categories as a trigger when they experience a lull. Please make sure to tell them that if they get no ideas from one of the triggers, move on to another category.

SCAMPER*

How to...

Triggers	Idea-spurring questions	Ideas
Substitute	Swap Change Replace	_____ _____ _____
Combine	Mix Blend Associate	_____ _____ _____
Adapt	Copy Fit Fashion	_____ _____ _____
Minify **M**odify **M**agnify	Smaller, fewer Change one part Larger, more often	_____ _____ _____
Put to other uses	Make it do something it usually does not	_____ _____ _____

Eliminate	Remove a: part
	      function
	      use
		_____
		 _____
		 _____

Rearrange	Reorder Reverse Invert	_____ _____ _____

* Adapted from Eberle, (1971).

TOOL #14 Attribute Listing

Benefits and Considerations:
- Divergent fact-finding technique
- Facilitates focus on individual parts, characteristics, and functions of any topic
- Can be used during lulls
- Great lead-in to using SCAMPER (see page 122) and also for Forced Relationships (see page 125)
- Allow twenty minutes, longer for a greater depth and breadth of ideas

How It's Done:
- Ask specific trigger questions, based on the topic. Responses can be given in a group setting or individually using sticky notes. (An example follows.)
- What are the parts of…?
- What are the characteristics of…?
- What are the functions of…?
- Once the list is generated (and remember to keep asking "What else?") then look at each idea mentioned and challenge individuals, small clusters, or the total group to find ways to modify each to generate new ideas. SCAMPER can be used here to trigger the new ideas. Then select from the modifications a new idea/possible idea to work with, perhaps by using PPH2 (see page 118).

Simple Example: (Feel free to generate some responses)

How can we position toothpaste differently?

What are the parts of toothpaste?	New modifications/ideas
Cap	
Tube	
Toothpaste	
Teeth	

What are the characteristics of toothpaste?	New modifications/ideas
Mint flavor	
Decorations on tube	
Gel	

What are the functions of toothpaste?	New modifications/ideas
Cleans teeth	
Promotes use of toothbrush	
Responsibility putting the cap back on	
Freshens mouth	

New positioning options:

Tools for Boundary Breaking— Honoring Artisan Energies

TOOL #15 Forced Relationships

Special Materials

- Flip chart, markers, sticky notes
- Optional: Word Dance sheet (see p. 126), newspaper, dictionary, photos, magazine pictures, a keen eye (for objects around the room)

Benefits and Considerations:

- Divergent technique
- Facilitates linking of and triggering from ideas
- Associative technique
- Changes mind-set to see new perspectives
- Can be used with Brainwriting and Stick-on Brainstorming
- Allow fifteen to twenty minutes

How It's Done:

- Show or point to a word, object, or picture.
- Ask, "What ideas for this challenge can you get by looking at this?"
- Tell the participants to force a connection in their mind to generate new and different kinds of ideas.
- Ask each person to contribute his or her new connections.
- Make sure all ideas are recorded.

Notes: (The variations on this technique are exciting!)

- Word Dance (see p. 126): Ask each person to randomly choose one word and then associate implications of that word to the topic. If nothing comes to mind, then tell the person to choose another word.
- Fine Art: Go to an art museum and ask participants to jot their connections on sticky notes as they view the artwork.
- Fine Art comes to Corporate Land: Post photographs, pictures, postcards, and/or other visual images on a wall in a pleasing arrangement. Have participants view the gallery in-house and make connections using sticky notes.
- Nature Hike: Ask participants before the session to bring something with them from nature. When in the room, ask them to force connections between their item and the topic.
- Attribute Listing Step 2: Ask participants to create an attribute list of something not related to the topic. Apply the attributes from the unrelated item to the topic at hand. For example, create an attribute list for a horse, then apply those attributes to the positioning of toothpaste.

Word Dance

crown	curb	fingerprint	guerrilla	iodine	jam	silver	microscope
nail	piston	priest	doctor	salt	mouth	horizon	griddle	candle
banjo	anteater	tent	funeral	gear	carpet	windsurfer	champagne
salmon	underwear	diaper	lug nut	microphone	paperweight	griddle
rifle	paper clip	EKG	copier	desk	vibrator	earrings	shower
podium	Scotch	hat	jet	stoplight	confession	roulette	spaceship
judge	explorer	dice	electrical outlet	nose	drain	bookmark	torch
tomb	can	gold	spear	beans	spark plug	bat	lawn mower
pothole	bookends	fly	cufflinks	belt	tie	piano	skyline	creek
snow	biology	cow	cowboy	bandage	calendar	calculator	cake
fence	toothbrush	rainbow	apartment	wagon	magnifying glass	wire
dock	rock	top	cursor	tire	drawer	sock	taxi	zebra
elevator	stairs	branch	ladder	bus	toy	hair	rubber band	pond
dream	pencil	steak	template	compass	tattoo	insulation	wheat
legs	bread	paper	soda	insurance	pennant	chess	stew	waiter
goose	sandwich	sneakers	chair	gutters	zipper	want ads	vest
crab	lottery	soldier	disk	necklace	flashlight	monument	dam
teacher	bank	China	fan	steering wheel	silk	earthquake	supermarket
leash	tea bag	noodles	theatre	mast	cabin	bone	buffalo
disk	chopsticks	allegory	globe	computer	brainwash	ladle	clock
desk	comforter	lamp	subway	ivy	oceanfront	parsley	minnow
sex	intersection	seed	egg	glasses	fork	radio	noose	jeans
mailbox	match	sugar	aerial	shelf	aspirin	Rolex	Jeep	fetus
cell	baton	journey	blood	poem	blueprint	angel	safari	brook	stone
tree	coffee	clouds	sin	suicide	Genesis	parachute	comb	maid
hubcap	snail	iceberg	photocopier	carton	secretary	eyebrow	salesman
wallpaper	costs	chapter	kitchen	locker	bed	thumb	basket
purse	arch	seam	bonnet	orange	remote control	myth	syrup
mosquito	umbrella	fender	flag	eggs	ballet

TOOL #16 Morphological Analysis (a.k.a. Idea Grid)

Special Materials:
- Flip chart, markers, sticky notes

Benefits and Considerations:
- Divergent technique
- Facilitates linking of and triggering from ideas
- Associative technique
- Changes mind-set to see and create new perspectives
- A variation of Forced Relationships that you can use with your children on a rainy day (appears below)
- Allow twenty to twenty-five minutes

How It's Done:
- Isolate five to seven major aspects of your topic: e.g., function, store placement, shape, texture, taste, how used, pet peeves
- Make each of these a heading on a grid with ten spaces below each. (An example follows.)
- Under each heading, generate both real and imaginary ideas for your topic. All ideas are welcome, even unusual ones.
- When the grid is full, use your phone number to select one idea per column.
- Force a relationship among these variables to create new ideas.

How to use this with your children on a rainy day:
- Use story-line headings across the top of the grid: Hero/Heroine, Enemy/Villain, Location, Allies/Friends, Weapons, Quest
- Generate ten options in each category.
- Use birthdates, dice, names translated into numbers, or another method to pick one option from each of the columns.
- Ask the children to make up a story using their selections. Consider asking them to make a video of the story, complete with costumes, backdrop, and so on.

Idea Grid for Positioning Toothpaste Differently

	Functions	Store placement	Texture	Taste	Pet peeves
1	Clean teeth	Dental aisle	Liquid	Mint	Cap on/off
2	Freshen breath	Pharmacy	Gel	Cinnamon	Storage
3	Sex appeal	Candy aisle	Powder	Lemon	End of tube use
4	Keeps dentist visits friendly	Internet shopping	Chewing gum	Thyme	Price point
5	Keeps us using toothbrushes	Condom rack	Plastic	Chocolate	Trusting good ingredients
6	Stimulate gums	Ice cream freezer	Paper	Vanilla	Still get cavities
7	Gives good grades	Produce refrigerator	Cellophane	Musk	Not available at video shops
8	Promises computer literacy	Cosmetics aisle	Sticky	Strawberry	No toothpaste aimed at teens
9	Makes us happy	Checkout counters	Ice cream	Mango	Branding is ubiquitous
10	Generates loving energy	Pharmacist needs to distribute	Yogurt	Eucalyptus	Commercials are all the same

Phone number: 487-1379. Using the last five digits, the options chosen are these:
Gives good grades, dental aisle, powder, musk, branding is ubiquitous.
Differentiate this toothpaste by giving it a name that makes other brands take a powder. Something strong and masculine that oozes the successes of testosterone. Still available in the dental aisle, it will stand out because its shape will be manly and musky. Getting good grades in work—succeeding because of its hygienic superiority. Support the claim by adding an ingredient that raises the feeling of well-being as well as maintaining good mental health.

Remember, this is an example of the thinking. Others in the group will also have their own combinations. These are shared, and elements are combined from each to achieve the best options.
Experience the Idea Grid for yourself using your phone number. See what combination you get and the way you work with the elements. If you can't seem to force a relationship, then use another phone number.

Tools for Vision—
Honoring Rational Energies

TOOL #17 Word Webbing

Special Materials:
- For group process: flip chart sheets (taped together to form very large working area), markers
- For individual process: paper and pens

Benefits and Considerations:
- Divergent technique
- Helps get people away from the specific target to generate and consider alternative concepts
- Allow fifteen to twenty minutes

How It's Done:
- Begin with one word, a key concept, consideration, obstacle, or component of your idea-generating session. Write this on the top of the page.
- Draw two lines, one going southeast from the word, the other going southwest (assuming north is at the top of the page). Ask for two words that connect with the main word. Write these down at the end of each line. (An example follows.) Remember, we are deferring judgment here. What's important is to follow through on the process to capture thinking. Unusual connections are welcome.
- Draw two lines from each of those words in the same fashion. Ask for two connecting words for each. Continue for a total of four levels.
- At level four, reverse the procedure by delimiting the thinking. Draw one line from the second word and one from the third, and ask, "What do these two concepts have in common?" Continue through the rest of the web until you have one final word or phrase. Note: on level four, join together the two outer words. This is shown in the example as a + b.
- Ask participants to use any of the concepts brought forward to apply to the idea generation.

Word Webbing Example: how to position toothpaste differently?

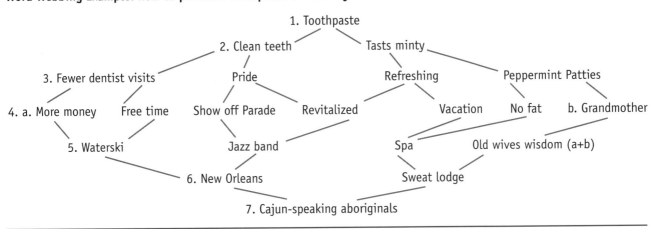

New ideas for positioning toothpaste from concepts chosen at random:

Heritage, pulling from the ancient cleansing rituals. This toothpaste contains ancient revitalizing ingredients. Support: An occasion-based tooth cleaner that lifts your spirits and connects you to all the wisdom collected through the ages.

What connections did you make? How else might you use the above word web? What if you were to complete one for yourself? What concepts and associations might you make? Feel free to give it a try.

The point to remember is that we are using concepts and connecting them for deeper insight and strategic considerations.

TOOL #18 Creating System Leaps

Special Materials

- Newspapers or TV/radio/Internet news, trade journals relevant and also not associated to your industry or association—one for each participant
- Sticky notes, markers, flip charts
- Prompting scripts
- Lettersized envelopes

Benefits and Considerations:

- Divergent technique
- Uses active imagination
- Concept-based to access future knowing
- A lengthy, involving process requiring prework
- Approximate session timing for twelve people is five hours, without breaks

How It's Done:

Part One: Prework

- Ask participants to review a news source for system shifts, new ideas, trends, and business/industry threats and opportunities, compared to the ways things are being done now. Alternatively, people can mention their own trends, opportunities, challenges, and threats without using the news sources.
- In clusters, before the meeting, ask them to prepare "How to" statements in relation to the threats and opportunities for the entrepreneurial and strategic exploration.

Part Two: In the Meeting

- Ask participants to present their findings in the form of "How to" statements. They may also provide brief (no longer than five minutes) background information. Have each "How to" transcribed onto a sticky note and placed on the flip chart.
- Cluster the "How to" statements according to like themes.
- Title each of the clusters.
- Choose the most intriguing one to work through. If more than one theme is intriguing, then work with that energy and have different clusters working on the different titles, one topic per cluster of people.

Part Three: Future Leap Setup

- Pair the participants, or ask them to work in trios. You may ask people from different clusters to work together.
- Have the pairs/trios work together for five minutes to generate and then select a "How to" statement based on their topic.

- Tell them that one person is the prompter, one the responder, one the recorder. The prompter asks the responder questions based on the topic. Each response is recorded. These roles shift over time so eventually each person acts in each role. If working in pairs, then one is the responder, the other the prompter and recorder.
- Please make special mention that the responder is considered the expert and when he or she is speaking, no one else may add to his or her comments. Adding to the comments takes place at the end of each questioning period.
- Help the groups to relax a little. Tell them they are going into the future, to imagine this trend/challenge/opportunity/threat worked through to competently successful perfection.
- Tell the prompters their role is to trigger, listen to, and record (if in pairs) the responses of the experts.
- Distribute scripts in envelopes. Tell participants to open their envelopes when asked to do so. (See example below.)

Part Four: Prompting Script (person 1)

- Ask the first prompter to open the envelope and to lead a ten-minute session based on the questions on the sheet. The prompter may ask additional questions as they come up.
  - Imagine a future where this issue is integrated and working successfully in the system. What's it like? (pause)
  - How are other systems affected by the shift? (pause)
  - Talk about the ideal and the implications on our business with that ideal in place? (pause)
  - What is different from today? (pause)
  - What are some ways to get there? (pause)
- Discuss the responses within the trio and record any new ideas and considerations. Allow ten minutes for this conversation.

Part Five: Prompting Script (person 2)

- Ask the second prompter to open the envelope and to lead a ten-minute session based on the questions on the sheet. The prompter may ask additional questions as they come up.
  - Imagine a future fifty years beyond where this concept/insight has formed a new educational institution. What might be taught there? (pause)
  - How might the people learn? (pause)

TOOL #18 **Creating System Leaps continued**

- How might this be represented in the fine arts? (pause)
- What other systems are affected? (pause)
- What is different from today? (pause)
- What are some things we need to be cautious about? (pause)
• Conversation about the responses is held in the trio. New ideas and considerations are recorded. Allow ten minutes for this conversation.

Part Six: Prompting Script (person 3)
• Ask the third prompter to open the envelope and to lead a ten-minute session based on the questions on the sheet. The prompter may ask additional questions as they come up. If working in pairs, then both people can respond in conversation, making sure their responses are recorded.
- Bringing it back to today, what do we need to initiate to open our system to embrace the changes? (pause)
- What do we need to be cautious about? (pause)
- What model best represents our thinking? (pause)
- Where is our energy best used? (pause)
• Conversation about the responses is held in the trio. New ideas and considerations are recorded. Allow ten minutes for this conversation.

Part Seven: Bringing It Together
• Ask the trios, or pairs, to prepare a presentation based on their shared visioning model, including:
- Ideal future concerning the trend/threat/ opportunity/challenge
- Implications for the business in the future
- Future learning
- Impacts on other systems
- Things to be cautious of
- Some ways to get to the ideal
- Best use of our energies today to achieve the ideal
  Allow twenty minutes for this.

Part Eight: Sharing the Wealth
• Form three groups, containing one person from each cluster. If working in pairs, then form two groups.
• Have each person in these smaller groups present their model, allowing no longer than seven minutes per model.
• Have the small groups integrate, synthesize, prioritize, and prepare a collectively shared model to present to the total group. Allow twenty to thirty minutes for this synthesis.
• Ask that the two (or three) merged models be presented to the total group.
• Ask for comparisons between the two (or three). Overlaps and similarities should be brought forward as well as their unique aspects. Ask for suggestions for merging the two (or three).
• Have the entire group decide where it is best to focus energy today in light of the shared vision, then generate "How to" statements. Make fact-finding recommendations as well as developing a list of idea-generating tasks, responsibilities, and commitments.

Converging Tools that Access Different Voices

It can't be said enough: No matter how much effort you put into idea generating, if you continue to use the same decision-making processes, then you may lose out on some of the gems and opportunities for breakthrough—both professionally and personally.

It's challenging to shift from your accustomed decision-making criteria. Your organization, for example, may insist on one certain formula to use. That's fine. Feel free to do some alternative decision-making before you engage the corporate process.

Personally, you are quite good at using the processes you've been using for a while. For a breath of fresh air, and to shift your energy, use alternative criteria as well.

For example, you may already quite naturally use the Feeling process to come to decisions. Your knee-jerk experience to new ideas may be to consider, How is this a good decision for the people involved? To shift your energy, use a thinking process too.

In the corporate world, the focus is mainly on Thinking criteria and Extraverted Thinking in particular. True breakthroughs and new directions can be accessed when some of the Feeling considerations are integrated into the decision-making process.

What follows are some different converging, or decision-making, tools to use, all based on accessing the cognitive processes for decision making.

Tools for Decision Making

TOOL #19 I.C.E. Introverted Feeling (Fi)

Special Materials:
- Sticky dots

Benefits and Considerations:
- Convergent technique
- Helps people access their passions
- Encourages people to pay attention to what they want
- Allow fifteen to twenty minutes

How It's Done:
- After a list of ideas has been generated, ask participants to narrow down the list, to "cull the wheat from the chaff," so to speak.
- Invite participants to consider using a different set of evaluation processes. Instead of looking at what is doable and what fits the measurement criteria, suggest a new method based on personal likes.
- Ask participants to put a sticky dot next to those ideas they find

> I—Involving
> C—Compelling
> E—Exciting

- Those ideas with the most sticky dots are the most motivationally inspiring.
- To finish the process, continue by asking participants to complete a PPH2 on the top three ideas:
    - What's good about the idea now? (Pluses)
    - What are the future potentials for this idea? (Potentials)
    - What are some How tos—what obstacles must be overcome to make this happen? (H2)
- After completing the PPH2, ask, "Which of the three ideas is the one that captures the best use of our energy?" Sometimes, rather than one being selected as the idea, the three are ranked in order of approach. Which is the easiest to get going? Which is the easiest to commit to? Which is the easiest to get buy-in on? Which best supports the work of our people? Which best answers our immediate needs, customer needs, and so on.
- Caution: sometimes good motivational ideas are overlooked because they don't fit the criterion of being doable. The wise facilitator uses this point as leverage and responds by saying, "So, how do we make this idea doable?"
- It is critical that motivational ideas are honored and worked with if you want commitment and breakthrough. Excitement levels prevail and commitments are honored throughout the implementation stages toward success with a natural "can do" attitude.

TOOL #20 Politics 101
Extraverted Feeling (Fe)

Special Materials:
- Flip chart pad and markers

Benefits and Considerations:
- Converging technique
- Helps people focus on the people involved in making an idea a success
- Best used as a second-level converging tool after initial converging is done, that is, after the pool of ideas have been narrowed down
- Varies the dynamic—involves role-playing
- Allow at least two hours for the entire process

How It's Done:

Part One: Identifying Key Idea Receivers
- Once the initial converging has been done, ask participants to list who will be affected by the implementation of the idea.
- Sometimes it is safer to mention the individuals involved by descriptive titles rather than by names, such as merry marketing, hard-to-please VP, honor-bound finance, frantic customer, tumultuous teen, and so on.
- Diverge. Generate as full a list of these stakeholders as possible. Then converge and identify the key individuals who both influence and impact the successful execution of the idea.

Part Two: Role-Play
- Now, step inside the head and heart of each of these individuals in a role-play scenario.
- Consider having each key individual role-played by one person in the group, so that as many different participants as possible have the opportunity to portray a stakeholder. Another of the group acts as the idea presenter.
- An idea is presented to the stakeholder. The stakeholder responds by saying
  - what he/she stands to gain by its implementation
  - what he/she stands to lose
  - what he/she needs from this group to buy in to the idea
- Additional questions from other group members may be entertained.
- Capture all responses on the flip chart pad. Make sure each stakeholder's comments are kept intact. Use a different page for each new stakeholder.

TOOL #21 Consistency Check
Introverted Thinking (Ti)

Special Materials:
- Flip chart pad and markers
- Completed sticky note ideas from other exercises

Benefits and Considerations:
- Converging technique
- Helps people focus categorical breakthrough shifts
- Allow twenty to twenty-five minutes

How It's Done:
- Ask participants to review the ideas generated and to cluster them into three categories:
  - Those that are consistent and improve on what we are doing now
  - Those that are consistent with and move us forward on what we are aiming for
  - Those that are inconsistent with the status quo and provide interest
- Once the clustering is done, ask participants which of the three clusters represents the best use of energy.
- Then flesh out that cluster of ideas.

NOTE: Politics 101 is a good follow-on exercise for this converging technique.

TOOL #22 Measuring Innovation
Extraverted Thinking (Te)

Special Materials:
- Flip chart pad and markers
- Completed sticky note ideas

Benefits and Considerations:
- Converging technique
- Helps people focus on deliberate innovation
- Provides measures against which participants can weigh the ideas
- Best used as a second-stage converging technique where only a few ideas are to be considered
- Allow thirty to forty minutes

How It's Done:
Step One
- Tell participants the criteria for creative products (Besemer and O'Quin 1987), which are
    - Originality: How new the idea is to the context
    - Usefulness: How well the idea meets the needs of the situation
    - Elaboration: How well the idea is executed
    - Synthesis: How well the idea combines different parts into a whole
- Present the innovation scale (example below) by which to evaluate the "creativity" of the ideas under consideration.

Step Two
- Have each participant evaluate each idea using the Innovation Scale.
- Ask participants to share their results in pairs and merge their results on a third scale.
- Join two pairs to make groups of four who share their results. Have them merge their results on another scale.
- Bring together the entire group, sharing collective innovation scales. Discuss which idea to pursue. Ask the group to generate ways to modify an idea to help it meet the innovation criteria. SCAMPER or Attribute Listing can be used to help this process.

NOTES: If there is a disagreement on any of the ratings of the idea, these disagreements must be noted. This is a good tool to use following I.C.E.

Innovation Scale

On a scale of 1–5, where 5 is the highest ranking and 1 is the lowest, rate the selected idea on these scales of innovation measures.

Originality: How unique is this idea to our brand/team/office/unit/division?

    1   2   3   4   5

Originality: How unique is this idea to our organization/industry?

    1   2   3   4   5

Usefulness: How well does this idea, as is, meet the required needs?

    1   2   3   4   5

Elaboration: How easily can this idea be well executed?

    1   2   3   4   5

Synthesis: How well does this idea combine different parts into a whole?

    1   2   3   4   5

Some ways to improve upon this idea for innovation are: _____

_____

_____

_____

_____

_____

_____

Diverge/Converge Together— A Simple Tool for Creative Problem-Solving

What follows is a very simple tool for you to use. It easily choreographs the dance between divergent and convergent thinking. And it helps you to progress to generating meaningful ideas from a sea of options. Have you ever felt that there are so many things going on that it's almost overwhelming? The Opportunity Grid℠ is a great tool to use during those times.

TOOL #23 Opportunity Grid℠

Special Materials:
- Optional: Opportunity Grid (see following)

Benefits and Considerations:
- Divergent and convergent technique
- Used to explore general challenges to achieve confident problem definition
- Good to use with client prior to designing the session or when you or a team needs to focus on one topic amid a sea of options
- Enables clear understanding and communication with you and your client
- Allow thirty to thirty-five minutes

How It's Done:
- Write the initial statement of the pet peeve/wish/opportunity/challenge in the first left-hand column, "Opportunity." You may change the name of this column to suit your needs.
- Diverge. Generate other opportunities. These may be triggered by the first or they may stand alone. Asking, "In what ways might we...?" and "I wish that..." sometimes helps to generate more opportunity statements. Write each addition and restatement.
- Converge. Ask the client (and this may be you if you are doing it on your own) which opportunity best identifies the objective for the session.
- Diverge. Ask the client to restate the key issue in a "how to" format. Record this in the "How Tos" section of the grid. Begin to generate other "how to" statements surrounding the key objective.
- Converge. Ask the client to select the "how to" statement that best articulates the objective of the idea-generating session.
- Diverge. You and the client both begin to generate ideas for the objective chosen from the "Ideas" section. Feel free to use any of the diverging tools to help you when you experience a lull. Remember, you are looking for new ideas.
- Converge. Ask the client to select a few ideas that are appealing.
- Check with the client for agreement and clear understanding of the initial issue, objective, and preliminary ideas.
- Set a plan to actualize the results.

Opportunity Grid^{SM}

Opportunity	How Tos
	Ideas

Opportunity Grid is a service mark of Creative Problem Solving, Toronto, Canada

Notes

SECTION

6

Appendices

Essential Qualities of the Personality Patterns
by Linda V. Berens

The 16 Personality Types

(For a complete explanation of the sixteen personality types, see the References for *The 16 Personality Types: Descriptions for Self-Discovery*.)

Sixteen personality patterns have been observed over time from various perspectives and theoretical bases. Each of these patterns has a theme of its own.

The 16 Personality Types			
Foreseer Developer	Harmonizer Clarifier	Planner Inspector	Protector Supporter
Envisioner Mentor	Discoverer Advocate	Implementor Supervisor	Facilitator Caretaker
Conceptualizer Director	Designer Theorizer	Analyzer Operator	Composer Producer
Strategist Mobilizer	Explorer Inventor	Promoter Executor	Motivator Presenter

We use three lenses to look at the sixteen types—Temperament, Interaction Styles, and Cognitive Dynamics. Each lens provides different information about personality. Sometimes it is useful to explore each lens on its own. Other times two lenses are used together for a more complete picture. The three lenses taken together give the fullest picture and provide the most information.

Temperament

(For a complete explanation of Temperament Theory, see the References for *Understanding Yourself and Others®: An Introduction to Temperament*.)

Temperament Theory is based in descriptions of behavior that go back over twenty-five centuries. It tells us the "why" of behavior, our motivators, and sources of deep psychological stress. Knowing our temperament patterns tells us our core needs and values as well as the talents we are more likely to be drawn to develop. Temperament gives us four broad themes in a pattern of core psychological needs, core values, talents, and behaviors—all of which are interrelated.

The four temperament patterns also have qualities in common with each other and can be described in those terms as well.

Abstract versus Concrete language—the way we tend to think about things and the way we use words. The Idealist and Rational patterns are characterized by abstract language with a focus on intangibles—concepts, ideas, implications, and meaning. People with these patterns as primary seek to know or explain the meaning of something that is not seen in order to access information that is not obvious. The Guardian and Artisan temperament patterns are characterized by concrete language with a focus on tangibles—experiences and observations. Those with these patterns seek to get or give useful concrete information to plan for the future of take action in the present.

Affiliative versus Pragmatic roles—the way we prefer to interact with others. The Idealist and Guardian patterns are more Affiliative in nature, with a focus on interdependence, human and group effectiveness, inclusion, agreement, and sanction. The Rational and Artisan patterns are more Pragmatic in nature with a focus on independence and operational effectiveness, self-determination, autonomous actions, and expedience.

The Four Temperament Patterns		
	ABSTRACT	CONCRETE
AFFILIATIVE	**IDEALIST** ABSTRACT/AFFILIATIVE — Meaning and Significance Unique Identity — DIPLOMATIC—Clarifying, Unifying, Individualizing, and Inspiring	**GUARDIAN** CONCRETE/AFFILIATIVE — Membership or Belonging Responsibility or Duty — LOGISTICAL—Organizing, Facilitating, Checking, and Supporting
PRAGMATIC	**RATIONAL** ABSTRACT/PRAGMATIC — Mastery and Self-Control Knowledge and Competence — STRATEGIC—Engineering, Conceptualizing, Theorizing, and Coordinating	**ARTISAN** CONCRETE/PRAGMATIC — Freedom to Act Ability to Make an Impact — TACTICAL—Actions, Composing, Producing, and Motivating

Another dimension not shown on the matrix is the focus on Structure versus Motive—where we focus our attention when interacting with others. The Rational and Guardian patterns are characterized by a focus on structure, order, and organization to gain a measure of control over life's problems and irregularities rather than be at the mercy of random forces. The Idealist and Artisan patterns are characterized by a focus on motives and why people do things in order to work with the people they are communicating with rather than trying to force them into a preconceived structure.

Of the three lenses, temperament is the broadest and each temperament pattern describes the driving force of four of the sixteen types.

Interaction Styles

(For a complete explanation of Interaction Styles theory, see *Understanding Yourself and Others®: An Introduction to Interaction Styles*, available summer 2001)

Interaction Styles is based on observable behavior patterns that are quite similar to the popular social styles models and DIS^C®. Interaction Styles tells us the "how" of our behavior. It refers to patterns of interaction that are both highly contextual and yet innate. Knowing our interaction style helps us locate interpersonal conflicts and situational energy drains. It gives us a map for greater flexibility in our interactions with others.

These four interaction style patterns are characterized by different interactional dynamics. Those dynamics are Directing/Informing and Initiating/Responding.

The *Directing* style has a time and task focus with a tendency to direct the actions of others to accomplish a task in accordance with deadlines, often by either telling or asking. Regarding motivations and process, the Directing style is explicit.

The opposite style is *Informing*, with a motivation and process focus. Using this style, people tend to give information in order to enroll others in the process. When a task needs to be accomplished, the Informing style engages others, describing outcomes and processes that can be used to complete the task.

Each style has its own best and appropriate use, and most people use both at different times but have more comfort with one.

Each of these patterns can also be further differentiated by another dimension—a preference for either *Initiating* interactions and a faster pace or for *Responding* to interactions and a slower pace. The four different interaction style patterns are shown in the matrix to the above right.

The Four Interaction Style Patterns

	DIRECTING	RESPONDING
RESPONDING	**CHART THE COURSE** DIRECTING/RESPONDING Push for a plan of action Keep the group on track Deliberate decisions Define the process focus	**BEHIND THE SCENES** INFORMING/RESPONDING Push for the best result Support the group's process Consultative decisions Understand the process focus
INITIATING	**IN CHARGE** DIRECTING/INITIATING Push for completion Lead the group to the goal Quick decisions Results focus	**GET THINGS GOING** INFORMING/INITIATING Push for involvement Facilitate the group's process Enthusiastic decisions Interaction focus

Cognitive Dynamics

(For a complete explanation of Cognitive Dynamics, see the reference for *Dynamics of Personality Type: Understanding and Applying Jung's Cognitive Processes*.)

Cognitive Dynamics is based in the Jungian theory from which the Myers-Briggs Type Indicator® (MBTI®) is derived. Each of the sixteen types has a theme based in a unique dynamic pattern of cognitive processes and their development. Knowing our innate tendencies to use these processes in certain ways can help us release blocks to our creativity and to effective communication. This model provides us the key to growth and development.

Carl Jung's Theory of Psychological Type

In examining individual differences, Swiss psychiatrist Carl Jung differentiated two fundamentally different orientations. He noticed some people seem primarily oriented to the world outside themselves. He called these people *extraverted*. He saw other people as primarily oriented to the world inside themselves. He called these people *introverted*. This extraverted-introverted difference is related to where you focus and recharge your energy. Then Jung noticed that people could be further distinguished by their preferred mental processes. Jung saw two kinds of mental processes used in everyday life: the process of *perception* (becoming aware of) and the process of *judgment* (organizing or deciding).

He then further differentiated two kinds of perception—*Sensation* and *Intuition*. *Sensing* is a process of becoming aware of sensory information. *Intuiting** is a

---

* We use *Sensing* and *Intuiting* to refer to mental processes rather than *Sensation* and *Intuition*, which refer to names of something. Our focus is on the activity, not the "type."

process of becoming aware of abstract pattern information and meanings. Both kinds of information are available to us, but we pay attention to only one kind at a time. Both are necessary and valuable in everyday life.

Likewise, he noted two kinds of judgment—*Thinking* and *Feeling*. Thinking judgments are based on objective criteria and are detached from personal values. Feeling judgments are based on subjective considerations and are attached to personal and universal values. Even the smallest act involves either Thinking or Feeling judgments, and both kinds of decisions are needed and valuable.

Each of these four mental processes can be used in either the external world of extraversion or the internal world of introversion, producing eight mental processes. Then Jung outlined eight psychological types, each characterized by the predominance of one of these eight mental processes (extraverted Sensing, introverted Sensing, extraverted iNtuiting, introverted iNtuiting, extraverted Thinking, introverted Thinking, extraverted Feeling, and introverted Feeling). In his writings he suggested that each of these eight dominant mental processes was supported by one of two opposing processes and that each of these eight types might vary according to which opposite mental process was used in support of the dominant. For example, the extraverted Sensing

type with Thinking would be somewhat different from the extraverted Sensing type with Feeling. Thus, his notions imply sixteen type patterns, each characterized by preferences for the use of two of the eight mental *processes,* as shown in the table to the left.

Enter Measurement and the Four-Letter Code

When Isabel Myers began developing the MBTI, she faced several challenges. One challenge was the beginning of the self-report movement. Prior to that time, psychologists doubted that a self-report format would work. Also, it was a time of "measurement," and the scientific thinking of the time was to understand the world by dividing it into parts. Myers faced the challenge of keeping the holistic quality of Jung's types in the forefront, while meeting the demands of the tests and measurement world. She chose to focus on the opposites in Jung's theory. Jung said that the orientations of extraversion and introversion were dynamically opposite. You can't be in two places at one time! He also said the mental processes were dynamically opposite. Thus, one would have a preference for either Sensing or iNtuiting and Thinking or Feeling in one's day-to-day interactions. The genius of Isabel Myers (and her mother, Katharine Briggs) was to develop questions about everyday actions and choices that reflected these underlying opposing preferences.

When the preferences for each of these pairs of opposites were indicated, then the type pattern could be inferred. However, a difficulty remained in how to determine which mental process was dominant in the personality and which was auxiliary. Myers reasoned that we can more readily observe what we do externally, so she decided to add questions to try to find which preferred mental process individuals used in the external world. If they used their preferred judging process to order the external world, they would be likely to make lists and structure their time in advance. If they used their preferred perceiving process to experience the external world, they would avoid such planning and structuring and prefer to keep things open-ended. Thus, the Judging-Perceiving scale of the MBTI was born. The resultant four-letter code is used around the world to give people insights about themselves.

The Four Sensing Types

extraverted **Sensing**	with introverted Thinking	(ESTP)
extraverted **Sensing**	with introverted Feeling	(ESFP)
introverted **Sensing**	with extraverted Thinking	(ISTJ)
introverted **Sensing**	with extraverted Feeling	(ISFJ)

The Four iNtuiting Types

extraverted **iNtuiting**	with introverted Thinking	(ENTP)
extraverted **iNtuiting**	with introverted Feeling	(ENFP)
introverted **iNtuiting**	with extraverted Thinking	(INTJ)
introverted **iNtuiting**	with extraverted Feeling	(INFJ)

The Four Thinking Types

introverted **Thinking**	with extraverted Sensing	(ISTP)
introverted **Thinking**	with extraverted iNtuiting	(INTP)
extraverted **Thinking**	with introverted Sensing	(ESTJ)
extraverted **Thinking**	with introverted iNtuiting	(ENTJ)

The Four Feeling Types

introverted **Feeling**	with extraverted Sensing	(ISFP)
introverted **Feeling**	with extraverted iNtuiting	(INFP)
extraverted **Feeling**	with introverted Sensing	(ESFJ)
extraverted **Feeling**	with introverted iNtuiting	(ENFJ)

Type Dynamics and Development

Type dynamics is based on the theories of Carl Jung and refers to a hierarchy of cognitive processes (Sensing, iNtuiting, Thinking, Feeling) and a preference for being either in the external world (extraversion) or the internal world (introversion). Type dynamics and type development refer to the unfolding of the personality pattern as expressed through the development of the mental processes of perception and judgment. Since the personality is a living system, it is self-organizing—self-maintaining, self-transcending, and self-renewing. Growth and development follow principles of organic development, and there is an order to the evolution of the personality.

The first cognitive process to develop and become more refined is often called the dominant. It is the favorite. The second is often called the auxiliary because it "helps" the first one. It develops second (usually between the ages of twelve to twenty). Development of the third process usually begins around age twenty and continues until age thirty-five or so. The fourth or least preferred process usually comes into play more between the ages of thirty-five to fifty. These developmental ages are general, not fixed. At these times, we find ourselves drawn to activities that engage and utilize the processes.

Thus we can say that development is dynamic and growing. Development in this sense is like readiness to learn to talk or to walk. We don't have to make children do these, we only need to provide models and opportunities and then stay out of the way. Development can be diverted due to environmental pressures and so is not always in this order as we develop some "proficiencies" using these cognitive processes. Still, the innate preference pattern will remain the same.

Using the MBTI®

In looking at how the models relate to the MBTI, it is important to remember that the results of any instrument are just an artificial snapshot in time. Also, an instrument is not the theory. The results of an instrument are neither the whole of a theory nor the whole of a personality. This is why ethical and competent users of the MBTI follow the person-to-person feedback standards of self-selection and validation by the client. One must not assume the results of the MBTI (or any other instrument) are 100 percent accurate. They must always be validated through an exploratory process such as we describe in this book.

How Do the Models Relate?

The temperament patterns (extended out to the four variations of each) meet Jung's theory at the level of the sixteen type patterns. The four-letter codes produced by the MBTI, when they are accurate and verified for individuals, match Keirsey's sixteen type patterns. While at first glance the matching process looks illogical, it occurs at a deep theoretical level when comparing Jung's and Kretschmer's original works. More importantly, it occurs on a descriptive, behavioral level. Following, is The Temperament Matrix™ with the sixteen themes, Interaction Styles, the four-letter MBTI codes, and the type dynamics patterns represented by the type code. (The dominant is listed first, auxiliary second, tertiary third, and inferior fourth.)

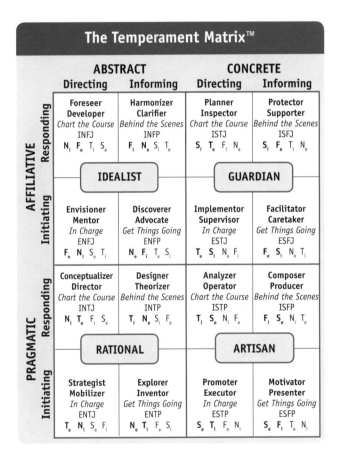

The Temperament Matrix™

		ABSTRACT		CONCRETE	
		Directing	Informing	Directing	Informing
AFFILIATIVE	Responding	Foreseer Developer *Chart the Course* INFJ N_i F_e T_i S_e	Harmonizer Clarifier *Behind the Scenes* INFP F_i N_e S_i T_e	Planner Inspector *Chart the Course* ISTJ S_i T_e F_i N_e	Protector Supporter *Behind the Scenes* ISFJ S_i F_e T_i N_e
		IDEALIST		**GUARDIAN**	
	Initiating	Envisioner Mentor *In Charge* ENFJ F_e N_i S_e T_i	Discoverer Advocate *Get Things Going* ENFP N_e F_i T_e S_i	Implementor Supervisor *In Charge* ESTJ T_e S_i N_e F_i	Facilitator Caretaker *Get Things Going* ESFJ F_e S_i N_e T_i
PRAGMATIC	Responding	Conceptualizer Director *Chart the Course* INTJ N_i T_e F_i S_e	Designer Theorizer *Behind the Scenes* INTP T_i N_e S_i F_e	Analyzer Operator *Chart the Course* ISTP T_i S_e N_i F_e	Composer Producer *Behind the Scenes* ISFP F_i S_e N_i T_e
		RATIONAL		**ARTISAN**	
	Initiating	Strategist Mobilizer *In Charge* ENTJ T_e N_i S_e F_i	Explorer Inventor *Get Things Going* ENTP N_e T_i F_e S_i	Promoter Executor *In Charge* ESTP S_e T_i F_e N_i	Motivator Presenter *Get Things Going* ESFP S_e F_i T_e N_i

Glossary for the Temperament Targets™
by Linda V. Berens

This glossary provides further explanation of the words on the Temperament Targets.™ We realize words can have many meanings and want you to know the meaning we were thinking of when we developed the targets. We also reference the names of Spränger's Value Types (see page 2, *Understanding Yourself and Others: An Introduction to Temperament 2.0,* [Huntington Beach, Calif.: Telos Publications, 2000]) to add to your understanding.

Artisan Temperament
Core Needs

Freedom to Act on Impulses: To understand Artisans, you really must grasp the nature of being impulse driven. This does not mean that they are totally impulsive and irresponsible. It does mean that well-functioning Artisans have managed to arrange their lives in such a way that they get to respond to impulses. These impulses are not just about fun or zany things; they often form the basis for exceptional problem solving. These impulses build inside them, and given that impulses do not last long, there is a tremendous urge to act on them. Artisans trust these impulses, and when all is going well, these impulses serve them well. When the impulses are no longer there, or when they have too many restrictions, Artisans suffer incredible stress and say they feel bored or empty.

Ability to Make an Impact: Many of us want to have an impact, but the need for the Artisan to elicit an immediate response from others is stronger and more concrete (here and now) than for the rest of us. This need for impact also shows in the drive to action to get a result.

Values

Spränger's Aesthetic Value Type is revealed in the Artisan. An appreciation of **Aesthetics**, the sensuous beauty of the immediate experience, captures an essential aspect of this temperament. Artisans value **Variety**, which is the essential aspect of art. The influence of their core needs shows in their drive to **Action** and love of **Excitement** and **Stimulation** and **Immediate Adventure**. Whatever they do, they want to **Perform** with **Skill** and appreciate skill in the performance of others as well. The relationships they seek are **Fraternal**—camaraderie with equals.

Talents—Roles

Operator or Maneuverer: Artisans are often found in these roles in relation to people or machines; with people there is an element of persuasion. These roles require that they define the relationship and be more directive. In these roles, they might run a business, troubleshoot problems, train others, maneuver bills through Congress, operate equipment, and so on.

Player or Performer: These roles are more informative and allow for the tremendous talent of the Artisan in creating variations on a theme. Take the meanings in a general sense and notice how Artisans, especially Informing Artisans, make a performance out of anything.

Troubleshooter/Negotiator: To troubleshoot means to "read" a situation and see an opportunity or a solution to a problem. It requires a here-and-now focus and an ability to improvise. Negotiation requires reading very slight nonverbal cues to know just what someone is willing to give and then getting the two sides to agree.

Crisis Manager: Artisans are usually quite adept at managing a crisis, even though some don't like crises. A crisis provides the opportunity to use their talents. It meets their needs and values of responding to impulses, excitement, and stimulation and making an impact.

Talents—Skills

Tactics: This means skillful management for a desired result. Tactics are an immediate action to achieve a desired end. It requires reading the immediate situation and making instant decisions in line with an objective. (Note that many people do not think of Artisans as decisive, but they can be very decisive.)

Variation: This is the ability to vary something while keeping its essence the same. Artisans are masters of the free variable. It is nearly impossible for them to not vary things.

Contextual Thinking: Artisans tend to reference everything to the present context. This tendency allows them to see the relevance of things, how they fit, and to notice when something is awry. Artisans prefer to learn in the applied context and tend not to like learning in the abstract.

Promote: This refers to the ability to see what someone's interest is in something or what someone's self-serving interest might be. Artisans do this especially well as they "read" very slight nonverbal cues.

Adapt: This is to make small adjustments to make something fit. Artisans do this themselves as well as with objects and situations.

Perform: This means to do, to get things done. Given their core need to have impact, Artisans are skilled at making even the most mundane act a performance.

Behaviors

Impact Centered: Much of the behavior of Artisans is centered around creating an immediate impact, to see people's eyes light up or get a result from their actions.

Seizing Opportunities: Constantly reading behaviors and situations, Artisans often see opportunities others are not aware of.

Epicurean: This refers to a love of pleasures of the senses. Artisans want things to taste good, smell good, feel good, sound good, and look good. Sometimes neatness is about this aesthetic sense. This attribute relates to Spränger's Aesthetic Value Type.

Spontaneous: Artisans are responsive to immediate situations and needs or even the impulse of the moment.

Restless: When there is a drive for action but waiting is called for, restlessness results. This may take the form of some kind of movement.

Entertaining: Very often Artisans love to entertain with their performances from flamboyance to a quiet remark that makes people laugh.

Impulsive: Artisans are so quick to read the needs of a situation, their behavior looks more impulsive than it may be.

Present Orientation: Artisans are oriented to the here and now. This orientation is clearly related to the need for freedom to act on impulses as impulses only occur in the present.

Fast Reacting: Artisans frequently react instantly to stimuli or circumstances.

Risk Taking: Where else would you find excitement and stimulation? Also, when you trust your impulses, you may not perceive situations as full of risk. The perception of risk may be in the eye of the beholder.

Improvising: Artisans tend to compose or perform on the spur of the moment, without any preparation. This also means making do with what is at hand and making up or creating an adaptation.

Cynical: The basic stance of the Artisan is cynicism. This is an astute ability to recognize that people do things for their own benefit and therefore to automatically question the altruism or goodness of their motives.

Stories: Artisans communicate best with stories since stories entertain, have impact, are concrete and contextual. Anecdotes bring abstract material to life and instill it with action.

Colloquial Language: Artisans tend to be on the cutting edge with their language. It, too, is contextual. They are such masters at variation that they vary language in such a way that they create the current buzzword of the day.

Guardian Temperament
Core Needs

Membership or Belonging: This is related to Spränger's Economic Value Type, for whom the major concern is that the world go on. There is a strong need for connectedness and affiliation among Guardians.

Responsibility or Duty: Guardians need to be and feel responsible. They hunger for responsibility. This need is so strong that they will take on too many responsibilities at times, and if they do not feel that they have done the responsible thing, they will experience stress.

Values

Guardians' values are closely related to their core needs and the value put on maintaining life as in Spränger's Economic Value Type. The relationships Guardians foster are based on bonds within a group. **Hierarchical Procedures** let them know the structure of the relationships, and that in turn provides **Stability** and **Security**. **Rules and Regulations** and **Conformity** serve to **Preserve Social Groups**.

Talents—Roles

Monitor or Overseer: It suits the Guardian temperament well to make sure that things are done right, and more directive Guardians frequently find themselves in monitoring and overseeing roles. In these roles, they are often given the authority required to regulate and standardize to keep production quality consistent.

Conservator or Provider: More informative Guardians are drawn to these roles. In this way they contribute to maintaining life by saving and providing. They facilitate and accommodate, making life easier and more comfortable for those in their charge.

Stabilizer/Traditionalist: In a group, Guardians are likely to be the ones who focus on traditional ways of doing things. This provides the stability to ensure that life goes

Be aware that traditions vary according to the group. The membership group is what is important, not tradition in the absolute sense.

Rule Maker/Enforcer: Given their core need for responsibility and duty, Guardians often find themselves making rules and enforcing them. Rules make things predictable and stable, as well as facilitate accountability.

Talents—Skills

Logistics: Guardians are skilled in getting the right things and the right information in the right place, at the right time, in the right quantity, in the right quality, to the right people, and not to the wrong people. All manners of things are logistical.

Measurement: Measurement is an important aspect of logistics. Guardians are most interested in accurate measurement.

Sequential Thinking: Guardians naturally look at things in sequence and are very interested in putting first things first and getting them in order.

Supervise: They take very seriously the responsibility of making sure things are done right.

Protect: Protecting is one important way of preserving the world.

Provide: Guardians take pride in their ability to provide for others, either for their comfort or their material well-being.

Behaviors

Authority Centered: Guardians are quite concerned with authority. They want to have the necessary authority to do what they are supposed to do, and they want those giving orders to be duly authorized to do so.

Stabilizing Organizations: In organizations, Guardians often work toward making the organization stable. They put great stock in the procedures, rules, and regulations that make the organization last.

Economical: The drive to preserve life often translates into conserving resources—money, time, energy, and so on. This relates to Spränger's Economic Value Type. Guardians hate to waste resources and may focus on money-saving efforts.

Structured: They want structure in what they do—sequence, schedule, a beginning, and an end.

Dependable: Guardians usually can be counted on to follow through on commitments. They often are so dependable that they are taken for granted. This does not mean they are the only ones who are dependable. It is just that they must be dependable or they feel shame.

Appraising: One of their talents is to notice when something is missing or not done right. Thus, they are prone to be critical of things that are out place or not done according to accepted standards or social norms.

Meticulous: Guardians are very careful of small details that others may not notice. These are usually logistical.

Past Orientation: Guardians look to the past to know what to trust for the future. Their point of reference is what has gone before and the tangible sense of their experiences.

Cautious/Careful: Wanting to protect and preserve, Guardians are alert to danger and the possible things that could go wrong. They frequently give cautions and warnings about these negative possibilities. They recognize Murphy's Law—if anything can go wrong, it will—and prepare so things don't go wrong.

Responsible: They generally are very responsible, but that does not mean they never break rules or do irresponsible things. It does mean that they are likely to feel ashamed if they have not behaved responsibly.

Standardizing: Logistics become much easier when things are standardized and uniform.

Fatalistic: This refers to the willingness to accept situations the way they are and not expecting them to change. This does not mean Guardians are not willing to change, they just don't waste resources on change for change's sake. Not expecting things to change allows them to conserve resources.

Comparisons: Given their sequential thinking style, Guardians frequently compare one thing to another. It is by making a connection to what they already know that they understand, explain, and trust.

Customary Language: In keeping with their traditional bent, Guardians tend to use the language of the group to which they belong. They are not prone to be on the cutting edge of word use but will use words as they become more accepted among their peers.

Rational Temperament
Core Needs

Mastery and Self-Control: Rationals want to master whatever they set their minds to, while being able to predict courses of events. They must feel as if they have will power and control over themselves.

Knowledge and Competence: Their worst fear is to be incompetent. They want to know and understand the operating principles of the universe. Developing new knowledge, solving abstract problems, conducting scientific research, and being an expert all meet these needs.

Values

Very closely related to their core needs, Rationals' values are related to Spränger's Theoretic Value Type, studying and seeking objective knowledge and **Truth**, **Concepts**, and **Ideas**. Rationals promote **Progress** and **Scientific Inquiry**. They frequently find themselves in **Expert Relationships** where their friendships revolve around shared expertise and talking about knowledge. And of course, these all relate to **Intelligence**, as it is traditionally defined. It isn't just logic that appeals to Rationals, but **Logical Consistency**. This means that they want arguments and persuasions to be logical throughout. They are most likely to look at the whole system and value the logic of it.

Talents—Roles

Organizer or Director: More directive and structured Rationals find themselves drawn to the roles of organizer and director. These roles involve defining relationships, which Directing Rationals are quite comfortable doing. The organizing is usually of a strategic, rather than a logistical, nature.

Engineer or Inventor: More informative and process-oriented Rationals find themselves in design roles that require keeping the information flowing to make sure that every contingency is covered. Think of engineering and inventing in a very broad sense. These roles are design roles and require analysis, usually of complex systems.

Visionary: This role comes naturally to most Rationals. They find it almost impossible to *not* think ahead, often way ahead of their time.

Perpetual Learner: This role relates to the core needs of knowledge and competence. Other temperaments like to learn, but for Rationals, learning is sustenance.

Talents—Skills

Strategy: Rationals tend to think of all the possible contingencies and develop multiple plans for handling all of them. In strategy, there is a level of abstraction required that is missing from the more logistical planning of the Guardian. To be strategic, one has to abstractly analyze a situation and consider heretofore unthought-of possibilities.

Analysis: Rationals have a talent for being at least one step removed from something, considering it in abstractness. Distinguishing components and their interrelationships involves the use of reasoning.

Differential Thinking: Talent for seeing differences. This penchant is so inherent in the intelligence of Rationals that they can hardly stop themselves from seeing differences.

Marshal: Marshaling is the tendency to lead or guide or array personnel in order, which is tied to strategy. Taken in this sense, it is the ability to see what skills are needed and to find people of the necessary expertise to get the job done and then mobilize them to do it.

Design: This is design in the sense of thinking of all the components necessary to make a system or an object work. The focus is not on variation as with the Artisan's design work. Rationals usually design a whole system, considering all the relevant aspects.

Categorize: Categories are naturally created from Rationals' differential thinking. This categorization process is integral to the mental functioning of Rationals. Some engage in it so much that they won't file things until the proper categories are set up!

Behaviors

Knowledge Centered: Nearly everything Rationals do is centered around the acquisition and sharing of knowledge. If they had their way, everyone would pursue knowledge (which they define differently than just information).

Forming Hypotheses: Rationals approach nearly everything as a hypothesis. This is closely related to the need for knowledge and valuing scientific inquiry.

Theoretical: This relates to Spränger's Theoretic Value Type with a focus on theories or assumptions about everything. Rationals seem to have a capacity to look at situations from many different perspectives and to engage in "as if" thinking.

Cold-Logical: When one's favorite skills are to objectively analyze and when one's values center around concepts and knowledge, it can appear that one is cold in one's use of logic. This does not mean that Rationals are without feeling; rather, to be objectively logical, they believe one must separate from emotion. The frequent use of "one" instead of personal pronouns is an example of this objectivity.

Oblivious: Rationals can be so much "in their heads" (deep in thought) that they notice little else. They have the capacity to become so absorbed in thought as to not notice people or events around them, even if they are truly sensitive to these much of the time.

Critiquing: Analysis is not limited to objective events or data. It also gets applied to oneself, especially when one has not lived up to a level of competence expected of oneself.

Perfectionistic: Actually, all types can be perfectionistic in some ways about some things. For Rationals, this perfec tionism usually applies to theories and concepts as well as the accurate expression of them.

Infinite Time Orientation: While they are future oriented in their strategic orientation, they often do not think of time. Rather, they are in pursuit of the ultimate truths or theories that transcend time—past, present, future. (This does not mean they are always late!)

Problem Solving: So great is the hunger for solving problems that they may seek out problems to solve. This is the application of analysis.

Analytical: Given that analysis is one of their favorite skills, they tend to analyze a situation before they do anything else so they can take a strategic approach.

Inventing: Rationals enjoy devising new and better ways of doing things. They rarely can stand to do something the same way twice.

Skeptical: In keeping with their theoretical and analytical stance, Rationals question everything. They realize there is always another way to view things, so they accept very little on faith.

Conditionals: Their language reflects their theoretical approach to life and is full of phrases like, "if...then," "tends to," "hypothetically speaking," and so on.

Precise Language: They want the words chosen to express precisely what is intended and may nitpick over the tiniest nuance of meaning. They are offended by imprecise and vague language. Sometimes the "if" is unspoken or often unheard and others assume a definiteness that is not there.

Idealist Temperament

Core Needs

Meaning and Significance: These are especially related to Spränger's Religious Value Type and center around a high value on the "greater good," something beyond the material and more toward the ideal.

Unique Identity: Idealists are forever in search of the answer to the question, "Who am I?"

Values

The values are closely related to the core needs. An integral part of Idealists' need for meaning and significance and unique identity is their search for wholeness and **Unity**, thus their high value on **Cooperative Interaction** and **Empathic Relationships**. If they do not have empathic, very personal

relationships, they feel a sense of loss and emptiness. They will devote a great deal of time and energy to fostering and maintaining these relationships. Not only must these relationships be empathic, but they must also be **Authentic**. Idealists place a high value on being authentic and genuine themselves and want nothing fake or phony in their relationships. Again, we see the theme of Spränger's Religious Value Type in their high value on **Ethics and Morality** and an **Idealized and Meaningful World**.

Talents—Roles

Mentor or Foreseer: While most Idealists find themselves drawn to these roles, Directing Idealists are most likely to fall easily into these roles. They are naturally tuned in to information about others and desire to help them develop their potential (self-actualization). These roles usually involve giving directives to others to achieve a helping effect.

Advocate or Proponent: Most Idealists advocate and spread the word. Informing Idealists find these roles particularly satisfying since these are information-giving roles.

Catalyst and **Romantic Idealist** roles are directly related to the core needs and values. In any relationship, Idealists are often catalysts for bringing out the best in others. People often report being more productive and creative in their presence. This makes Idealists' actual "job" difficult to see and describe in tangible ways.

As romantic idealists, they are not only romantic in the sense of love and romance, they tend toward the fanciful and imaginative.

Talents—Skills

Diplomacy: Idealists tend to build bridges between people and help them resolve deep issues behind conflict. This still is related to the core values of empathic relationships and unity.

Interpretation: Idealists have a talent for explaining to others what people mean or intend, to transform the communication while maintaining the meaning.

Integrative Thinking: Idealists have a talent for seeing similarities across sometimes disparate categories. It is related to the core value of unity.

Counsel: Idealists seem to know what to say to help others help themselves.

Reveal: They seem to have an antenna that allows them to know others' deeper motivations and a talent for expressing that knowledge so others also know it.

Facilitate: This term is used in the sense of easing relationships between people, of drawing out issues that need to be addressed.

Behaviors

Relationship Centered: Idealists' lives revolve around relationships, deep empathic ones. When push comes to shove, relationships will win out over tasks. They are willing to expend a great deal of energy to preserve relationships.

Creating Harmony: They will go to great lengths to create harmony in relationships. This does not mean they are totally averse to addressing conflict, and they will in fact brave conflict for the greater good of future harmony and integrity.

Spiritual: This word relates to Spränger's Religious Value Type with a focus on some greater good. Often Idealists engage in spiritual practices.

Warm-Hearted: Idealists' tendency to instantly empathize with others makes them appear caring or warm-hearted.

Involved: They can be very involved and committed to relationships and causes. They tend to be intense. This is related to the values of empathic relationships and an idealized and meaningful world.

Praising: Idealists are natural givers of sincere compliments. It is almost as if they are often capable of seeing positive aspects that others miss. They believe that you bring out the best in people through praise. They are sometimes blind to faults and certainly are not prone to focus on them.

Impressionistic: They often have vague global impressions that are very meaningful and significant to them, which they trust. This is the opposite of the demand for precision of the Rational.

Future Time Orientation: Idealists are pulled by their vision of the ideal world in the future. Their focus is on "how it can to be," not on "how it is."

Inspiring: When they have a cause, they inspire others to action. This behavior springs from their strongly held beliefs.

Empathic: To be empathic is to feel what others feel. There seem to be two kinds of empathy. One is feeling what others feel when in their presence. The other is more predictive, knowing how others will feel in a given situation.

Imagining: Reflecting their idealistic, future orientation, Idealists tend to be imaginative, dreaming up all kinds of possible scenarios.

Credulous: Idealists tend to believe. They want to believe in the goodness in everyone and start with a position of faith first, skepticism second.

Metaphors: Metaphors build bridges between people by giving a common experience they can relate to, thereby increasing understanding. Idealists tend to develop metaphors easily, and their language is often rich with them. These metaphors are often deeply symbolic.

Global Language: Their language tends to mirror their impressions and they often speak in broad, general terms. Thus others can see their own personal meanings in what the Idealist has said and thus have their own unique identity. While this global language usually has a positive effect, it can sometimes lead to misunderstanding.

Appendix C: Bibliography

Amabile, T. M. 1983. *The Social Psychology of Creativity.* New York: Springer-Verlag.

Amabile, T. M. 1995. Assessing the Work Environment for Creativity: Promises and Pitfalls. Keynote address at the International Conference on Organizational Climates for Creativity and Change: Research and Applications, hosted by the Center for Studies in Creativity, Buffalo, N.Y., October.

Arieti, S. 1976. *Creativity, the Magic Synthesis.* New York: Basic Books, Inc.

Barron, F. 1990. *Creativity and Psychological Health: Origins of Personal Vitality and Creative Freedom.* Buffalo, N.Y: CEF Press.

Basadur, M. and Thompson, R. 1986. Usefulness of the Ideation Principle of Extended Effort in Real World Professional and Managerial Creative Problem Solving. *Journal of Creative Behavior* 20, no 1: 23~34.

Benetti, P. 1997. Private conversation with author.

Berens, L. V. 1999. *Dynamics of Personality Type: Understanding and Applying Jung's Cognitive Processes.* Huntington Beach, Calif.: Telos Publications.

Berens, L. V. 2000. *Understanding Yourself and Others: An Introduction to Temperament—2.0.* Huntington Beach, Calif.: Telos Publications.

Besemer, S., and K. O'Quin. 1987. Creative Product Analysis: Testing a Model by Developing a Judging Instrument. In *Frontiers of Creativity Research*, ed. S. G. Isaksen. Buffalo, N.Y.: Bearly Limited, 341~357.

Bloch, D., and D. George. 1987. *Astrology for Yourself.* Berkeley, Calif.: Wingbow Press.

Bridges, W. 1980. *Transitions.* Reading, Mass.: Addison-Wesley.

Bridges, W. 1990. *Surviving Corporate Transitions.* Mill Valley, Calif.: William Bridges and Associates.

Bridges, W. 1991. *Managing Transitions.* Reading, Mass.: Addison-Wesley.

Briggs, H. 1990. *Fire in the Crucible: The Self-Creation of Creativity and Genius.* Los Angeles: Jeremy P. Tarcher, Inc.

Burnside, R. M., T. M. Amabile, and S. S. Gryskiewicz. 1988. Assessing Organizational Climates for Creativity and Innovation: Methodological Review of Large Company Audits. In *New Directions in Creative and Innovative Management: Bridging Theory and Practice*, ed. Y. Ijiri and R. L. Kuhn. Cambridge, Mass.: Ballinger, 169~185.

Center for Studies in Creativity: www.buffalostate.edu/~creatcnt.

Creative Education Foundation: www.cef-cpsi.org.

Cziksentmihalyi, M. 1990. *Flow: The Psychology of Optimal Experience.* Harper Collins.

Dierckins, T. 1999. *Creative Voices: 366 Quotes on Creativity.* Kansas City, Mo.: Andrews McMeel Publishing.

Eames, C., and R. Eames. 1989. *The Films of Charles & Ray Eames, Volume 1: Powers of Ten.* Santa Monica, Calif.: Pyramid Film & Video.

Eberle, B. 1971. *SCAMPER.* Buffalo, N.Y.: DOK.

Estes, C. P. 1991. *The Creative Fire.* Boulder, Colo.: Sounds True Recording. Audiotape.

Ekvall, G. 1983. *Structure, Climate and Innovativeness of Organizations. A Theoretical Framework and an Experiment.* Stockholm, Sweden: The Swedish Council for Management and Organizational Behavior, Report Number 1.

Ekvall, G. 1987. The Climate Metaphor in Organizational Theory. In *Advances in Organizational Psychology,* ed. B. M. Bass and P. J. D. Drenth. Newbury Park, Calif.: SAGE Publications, 177~190.

Ekvall, G. 1991. The Organizational Culture of Idea Management: A Creative Climate for the Management of Ideas. In *Managing Innovation,* ed. J. Henry and D. Walker. Newbury Park, Calif.: SAGE Publications, 73~79.

Ekvall, G. 1995. Assessing the Climate for Creativity and Change. Keynote address at the International Conference on Organizational Climates for Creativity and Change: Research and Applications, hosted by the Center for Studies in Creativity, Buffalo, N.Y. October.

Goleman, D., P. Kaufman, and M. Ray. 1992. *The Creative Spirit.* Toronto, Canada: Dutton, Penguin Publications.

Gordon, W. J. J. 1961. *Synectics.* London: Collier Books.

Gryskiewicz, S. S. 1981. Targeted Innovation: A Situational Approach. In *Creativity Week III Proceedings,* ed. S. S. Gryskiewicz. Greensboro, N.C.: Center for Creative Leadership, 77~103.

Gryskiewicz, S. S. 1987. Predictable Creativity. In *Frontiers of Creativity Research*, ed. S. G. Isaksen. Buffalo, N.Y.: Bearly Limited, 305~313.

Hamaker-Zondag, K. 1985. *Planetary Symbolism in the Horoscope.* Jungian Symbolism & Astrology, vol 2. York Beach, Maine: Samuel Weiser, Inc.

Harris, A. S. 1996. *Living with Paradox: An Introduction to Jungian Psychology.* Pacific Grove, Calif.: Brooks/Cole Publishing Company.

Here's an Idea. *Fast Company* (April 2000).

Hofstede, G. 1997. *Cultures and Organizations: Software of the Mind.* New York: McGraw-Hill.

Hopke, Robert H. 1999. *A Guided Tour of the Collected Works of C. G. Jung.* Boston: Shambhala Publications Inc.

http://www.ozemail.com.au/~caveman/Creative/Resources/crquote2.htm.

Isaksen, S. G. 1987. Introduction: An Orientation to the Frontiers of Creativity Research. In *Frontiers of Creativity Research*, ed. S. G. Isaksen. Buffalo, N.Y.: Bearly Limited, 1~26.

Isaksen, S. G., K. J. Lauer, M. C. Murdock, K. B. Dorval, and G. J. Puccio. 1995. *Situational Outlook Questionnaire: Understanding the Climate for Creativity and Change (SOQ)--A Technical Manual.* Buffalo, N.Y.: The Creative Problem Solving Group.

Isaksen, S. G., M. Murdock, K. J. Lauer, K. B. Dorval, and G. J.Puccio. 1995. Some Recent Developments on Assessing the Climate for Creativity and Change: Assessing the Situational Outlook for Creativity and Change. Keynote address at the International Conference on Organizational Climates for Creativity and Change: Research and Applications, hosted by the Center for Studies in Creativity, Buffalo, N.Y., October.

Isaksen, S. G., G. J. Puccio, and D. J. Treffinger. 1993. An ecological Approach to Creativity Research: Profiling for Creative Problem Solving. *Journal of Creative Behavior* 27, no. 3 (third quarter): 149~170.

Jung, C. G. 1921. *Psychological Types.* CW, vol. 6. Princeton, N.J.: Princeton Press, 1971.

Keirsey, D. 1998. *Please Understand Me II: Temperament, Character, Intelligence.* Del Mar, Calif.: Prometheus Nemesis Book Company.

Keirsey, D., and M. Bates. 1984. *Please Understand Me: Character & Temperament Types.* Del Mar, Calif.: Prometheus Nemesis Book Company.

Kirton, M. J. 1976. Adaptors and Innovators: A Description and Measure. *Journal of Applied Psychology* 61: 622~629.

Kirton, M. J. 1999. *Manual: Kirton Adaption-Innovation Inventory,* 3d ed. Berkhamsted, U.K.: Occupational Research Centre.

Kirton, M. J., ed. 1989. *Adaptors and Innovators: Styles of Creativity and Problem Solving.* London: Routledge.

Land, G. A. 1973. *Grow or Die: The Unifying Principle of Transformation.* New York: John Wiley & Sons.

Land, G., and B. Jarmon. 1992. *Breakpoint and Beyond: Mastering the Future--Today.* New York: Harper Business.

Lavie, S., K. Narayan, and R. Rosaldo, eds. 1993. *Creativity/Anthropology.* Ithica, N.Y., and London, U.K.: Cornell University Press.

Lewin, K., R. Lippett, and R. K. White. 1939. Patterns of Aggressive Behavior in Experimentally Created "Social Climates." *Journal of Social Psychology* 10: 271~299.

Loomis, Mary E. 1991. *Dancing the Wheel of Psychological Types.* Wilmette, Ill.: Chiron Publications.

MacKinnon, D. W. 1978. *In Search of Human Effectiveness: Identifying and Developing Creativity.* Buffalo, N.Y.: Bearly Limited.

Malsin, P. 1991. *The Eyes of the Sun: Astrology in Light of Psychology.* Tempe, Ariz.: New Falcon Publications.

Mayer, R. E. 1999. Fifty Years of Creativity Research. In *Handbook of Creativity,* ed. R. J. Stienberg. Cambridge, U.K.: Cambridge University Press, 449~460.

Merriman, R. A. (1991). *Evolutionary Astrology. The Journey of the Soul through States of Consciousness.* W. Bloomfield, Mich.: Seek-it Publications.

Michalko, M. 1991. *Thinkertoys: A Handbook of Business Creativity for the 90s.* Berkeley, Calif.: Ten Speed Press.

Myers, I. B., and M. H. McCaulley. 1985. MBTI *Manual: A Guide to the Development and Use of the Myers-Briggs Type Indicator.* Palo Alto, Calif.: Consulting PsA.L. 1998 *MBTI Manual: A Guide to the Development and Use of the Myers-Briggs Type Indicator,* 3d ed. Palo Alto, Calif.: Consulting Psychologists Press, Inc.

Myers, I. B., with P. B. Myers. 1980. *Gifts Differing.* Palo Alto, Calif.: Consulting Psychologists Press, Inc.

Myers, K. D., and L. K. Kirby. 1994. *Introduction to Type & Type Dynamics: Exploring the Next Level of Type.* Palo Alto, Calif.: Consulting Psychologists Press, Inc.

Newman, J. 1991. The Human Brain: A Frontier of Psychological Type. Gainseville, Fla.: Center for the Applications of Psychological Type. Audiocassette tape.

Northrup, C. 1998. *Women's Bodies, Women's Wisdom.* New York: Bantam Books.

Noller, R. B., S. J. Parnes, and A. M. Biondi. 1976. *Creative Actionbook.* New York: Scribners.

Osborn, A. 1953. *Applied Imagination.* 3d rev. ed. 1963. New York: Charles Scribners Sons.

Osborn, A. 1991. *Your Creative Power,* special edition reprint. Motorola University Press.

Parnes, S. J. 1988. *Visionizing.* East Aurora, N.Y.: D.O.K.

Publishers.

Parnes, S. J., ed. 1992. *Sourcebook for Creative Problem Solving.* Buffalo, N.Y.: Creative Education Foundation.

Parnes, S. J., and A. Meadow. 1959. Effects of Brainstorming Instruction on Creative Problem Solving by Trained and Untrained Subjects. *Journal of Educational Psychology* 50: 15~36.

Parnes, S. J., and R. B. Noller. 1973. Applied Creativity: The Creative Studies Project: Part IV--Personality Findings and Conclusions. *Journal of Creative Behavior* 7: 15~36.

Parnes, S. J., R. B. Noller, and A. M. Biondi. 1977. *Guide to Creative Action.* New York: Charles Scribners Sons.

Pearman, R. R., and S. C. Albritton. 1997. *I'm Not Crazy, I'm Just Not You.* Palo Alto, Calif.: Davies Black Publishing.

Prince. G. M. 1970. *The Practice of Creativity.* New York: Macmillan Publishing.

Quenk, N. L. 1993. *Besides Ourselves: Our Hidden Personalities in Everyday Life.* Palo Alto, Calif.: Consulting Psychologists Press, Inc.

Reinhold, B. B. 1997. *Toxic Work: How to Overcome Stress, Overload, and Burnout and Revitalize Your Career.* New York: Plume.

Rhodes, M. 1961. An Analysis of Creativity. *Phi Delta Kappa,* 42: 305~310.

Rothenberg, A., and C. R. Hausman, eds. 1976. *The Creativity Question.* Durham, N.C.: Duke University Press.

Segal, M. 1992. MBTI® Type and Creativity. In *Tell-A-Type,* a newsletter of the Ontario Association for the Application of Personality Type, Toronto, October 4~5.

Segal, M. 1997. Type & Creativity: Personal Assistors and Resisters to Creativity Using the MBTI. In Proceedings from Association for Psychological Type 12th International Conference, Boston, Massachusetts, July 7~12.

Segal, M. 1999. How Type Helps People to Achieve Breakthroughs. *Bulletin of Psychological Type* 22, no. 8 (year end): 41~43.

Sternberg, R. J. 1999. *Handbook of Creativity.* Cambridge, Mass.: Cambridge University Press.

Sternberg, R. J., ed. 1988. *The Nature of Creativity: Contemporary Psychological Perspectives.* Cambridge, Mass.: Cambridge University Press.

Stein, M. I. 1974 *Stimulating Creativity, Volume 1: Individual Procedures.* New York: Academic Press.

Stein, M. I. 1975. *Stimulating Creativity, Volume 2: Group Procedures.* New York: Academic Press.

Torrance, E. P. 1979. *The Search for Satori and Creativity.* Buffalo, N.Y.: Creative Education Foundation & Creative Synergetic Associates.

Truman, K. K. 1991. *Feelings Buried Alive Never Die* Las Vegas, Nev.: Olympus Distributing.

Wallas, G. 1926. *The Art of Thought.* New York: Harcourt Brace and Company.

Weisberg, R. W. 1986. *Creativity: Genius and Other Myths.* New York: W.H. Freeman and Company.

Why Man Creates. Santa Monica, Calif.: Pyramid Film & Video. Video.

Foundations of Temperament

Kretschmer, Ernst. *Physique and Character*. London: Harcourt Brace, 1925.

Roback, A. A. *The Psychology of Character*. 1927. Reprint, New York: Arno Press, 1973.

Spränger, E. *Types of Men*. 1928. Reprint, New York: Johnson Reprint Company, 1966.

More about Temperament

Berens, Linda V., *Understanding Yourself and Others: An Introduction to Temperament*. Huntington Beach, Calif.: Telos Publications, 2000.

Choiniere, Ray, and David Keirsey. *Presidential Temperament*. Del Mar, Calif.: Prometheus Nemesis Books, 1992.

Delunas, Eve. *Survival Games Personalities Play*. Carmel, Calif.: SunInk Publications, 1992.

Keirsey, David. *Portraits of Temperament*. Del Mar, Calif.: Prometheus Nemesis Books, 1987.

Keirsey, David, and Marilyn Bates. *Please Understand Me*. 3d ed. Del Mar, Calif.: Prometheus Nemesis Books, 1978.

Keirsey, David. *Please Understand Me II*. Del Mar, Calif.: Prometheus Nemesis Books, 1998.

The Sixteen Personality Types

Baron, Renee. *What Type Am I?* New York: Penguin Putnam, 1998.

Berens, Linda V., and Dario Nardi. *The 16 Personality Types: Descriptions for Self-Discovery*. Huntington Beach, Calif.: Telos Publications, 1999.

Fairhurst, Alice M., and Lisa L. Fairhurst. *Effective Teaching, Effective Learning*. Palo Alto, Calif.: Consulting Psychologists Press, Inc., 1995.

Isachsen, Olaf, and Linda V. Berens. *Working Together: A Personality Centered Approach to Management*. 3d edition. San Juan Capistrano, Calif.: Institute for Management Development, 1991.

Nardi, Dario. *Character and Personality Type: Discovering Your Uniqueness for Career and Relationship Success*. Huntington Beach, Calif.: Telos Publications, 1999.

Tieger, Paul D., and Barbara Barron-Tieger. *Do What You Are*. Boston, Mass.: Little, Brown and Company, 1995.

Tieger, Paul D., and Barbara Barron-Tieger. *Just Your Type*. Boston, Mass.: Little, Brown and Company, 2000.

Tieger, Paul D., and Barbara Barron-Tieger. *Nurture by Nature*. Boston, Mass.: Little, Brown and Company, 1997.

Jung/Myers Model

Berens, Linda V. *Dynamics of Personality Type: Understanding and Applying Jung's Cognitive Processes*. Huntington Beach, Calif.: Telos Publications, 1999.

Brownsword, Alan W. *Psychological Type: An Introduction*. Nicasio, Calif.: HRM Press, 1989.

Harris, Anne Singer. *Living with Paradox*. Pacific Grove, Calif.: Brooks/Cole Publishing, 1996.

Jung, Carl G. *Psychological Types*. Princeton, N.J.: Princeton University Press, 1971.

Myers, Katharine, and Linda Kirby. *Introduction to Type: Dynamics and Development*. Palo Alto, Calif.: Consulting Psychologists Press, 1995.

Myers, Isabel Briggs, with Peter B. Myers. *Gifts Differing*. 1980. Reprint Palo Alto, Calif.: Consulting Psychologists Press, 1995.

Myers, Isabel Briggs, Mary H. McCaulley and Naomi L. Quenk. *MBTI Manual: A Guide to the Development and Use of the Myers-Briggs Type Indicator*. Palo Alto, Calif.: Consulting Psychologists Press, 1998.

Quenk, Naomi. *In the Grip*. Palo Alto, Calif.: Consulting Psychologists Press, 1985.

Sharp, Daryl. *Personality Type: Jung's Model of Typology*. Toronto, Canada: Inner City Books, 1987.

Systems Thinking

Bateson, Gregory. *Mind and Nature: A Necessary Unity*. New York: Bantam Books, 1979.

Bateson, Gregory. *Steps to an Ecology of Mind*. New York: Ballantine Books, 1972.

Capra, Fritjof. *The Web of Life*. New York: Anchor Books, Doubleday, 1996.

Oshry, Barry. *Seeing Systems: Unlocking the Mysteries of Organizational Life*. San Francisco, Calif.: Berrett-Koehler Publishers, 1996.

Wheatley, Margaret J. *Leadership and the New Science*. San Francisco, Calif.: Berrett-Koehler Publishers, 1992.

Wheatley, Margaret J., and Myron Kellner-Rogers. *A Simpler Way*. San Francisco, Calif.: Berrett-Koehler Publishers, 1996.

On the Internet

Marci Segal: www.marcisegal.com

Temperament Research Institute: www.tri-network.com

Center for Studies in Creativity: www.buffalostate.edu/ ~creatcnt

Creative Education Foundation: www.cef-cpsi.org

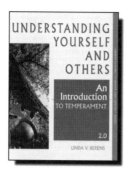
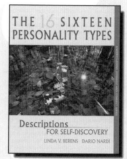
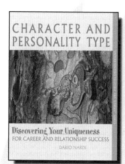